THE CONFESSIONS OF
ST AUGUSTINE

D1369226

Religious Books in the Fontana Series

The Confessions of St Augustine

In the translation of
SIR TOBIE MATTHEW, KT.

Revised by
DOM ROGER HUDLESTON

with an introduction by
DOM ROGER HUDLESTON

COLLINS
fontana books

First Printed 1923
First issued in Fontana Books 1957
Second Impression in Fontana Books 1959
Third Impression in Fontana Books May, 1960

NIHIL OBSTAT: INNOCENTIVS APAP, O.P., S.T.M.

CENSOR DEPVTATVS

IMPRIMATVR: EDM. CAN. SVRMONT

VICARIVS GENERALIS

WESTMONASTERII: DIE XXV JVLII MCMXXIII

PRINTED IN GREAT BRITAIN
COLLINS CLEAR-TYPE PRESS: LONDON AND GLASGOW

PREFACE

I. THE TEXT

In the Prologue to his *Retractations* St Augustine gives
a list of his writings, in which the *Confessions* appear
as the sixth work written by him after he became
a Bishop, i.e., after A.D. 395. This would place its
composition somewhere about A.D. 400, or thirteen
years after his baptism, at which date he would be forty-six
years old. The work circulated widely during the Saint's
lifetime, it soon acquired the place it still holds as the most
famous of Christian spiritual writings outside the New
Testament, and MS. copies of it were multiplied and
are still numerous.

The *editio princeps* was printed at Milan in 1475, but this
and other early editions were based on inferior MSS., and
their text is incorrect and unsatisfactory. In 1679 appeared
the first critical edition of the *Confessions,* in Vol. I of the
Opera S. Augustini, edited by the Benedictines of the Con-
gregation of St Maur, which held the field until 1896, when
its text was superseded by that of P. Knöll, which appeared
in Vol. XXXIII of the *Corpus Scriptorum Ecclesiasticorum
Latinorum,* published by the Vienna Academy. Knöll's
text, of which an *editio minor,* with some alterations,
appeared at Leipzig in 1898, is accepted as the best that
is now available, or is likely to be. It is based upon
fourteen MSS. of the seventh to the eleventh centuries—
of which the best is the *Codex Sessorianus,* now No. 2099
in the Bibliotheca Vittorio Emmanuele at Rome—all of
which Knöll holds to be derived from a single archetype,
an uncial MS. of the fifth or sixth century. In preparing
the present translation, this text has been used throughout.
Besides the two editions of it named above, there is one

with valuable English Notes by J. Gibb and W. Montgomery, issued by the Cambridge University Press in 1908; my indebtedness to these I gratefully acknowledge.

II. ENGLISH TRANSLATIONS

The honour of producing the first English translation of the *Confessions* belongs to Sir Tobie Matthew, Knight and Priest, 1577-1655, whose Life, by the Rev. Alban Butler, edited by Charles Butler, was published by Coghlan, London, 1795; a good account of him appears in Gillow's *Biographical Dictionary of English Catholics,* Vol. IV, and another in the *Dictionary of National Biography,* Vol. XXXVII.

Matthew's translation of the *Confessions* appeared in 1620. It was published anonymously and *sine loco,* but the place of publication seems to be in London, and the authorship was well known from the first. A second edition appeared at Paris in 1638. It was dedicated "To the most Glorious Perpetuall and All-Immaculate Virgin MARY, the Most Blessed Mother of GOD," with eight pages of "Epistle Dedicatory," no less than ninety-nine pages of "Preface to the Pious and Courteous Reader," eight of "Advertisement to the Reader," four of *Errata,* and 800 of Text. The long Preface is a controversial treatise in the style of the period, and this, coupled with the fact that Matthew, himself a son of the Archbishop of York, was a convert to Rome, produced from Matthew Sutcliffe, Dean of Exeter, a violent attack entitled, *The Unmasking of a Masse-monger,* London, 1626, "in which coarse allusion is made to the alleged libertinism of Sir Tobie's youth" (Gillow).

In point of accuracy the translation is very faulty, and although a number of its errors are clearly due to the corrupt state of the text[1] which Sir Tobie had to work

[1] For an example of this, see the last paragraph of Note 4, *infra,* p. 451.

upon, most of them cannot be excused in this way, while in some cases his zeal as a controversialist leads him to strain the meaning of the original badly.

From a literary point of view, however, Matthew's work must be ranked very high. Published within ten years of the Authorised Version, it has much the same splendid resonance and easy flow; and the flavour of old-world formality, which its periods retain, is a real advantage in a spiritual work of this character, where the author not only writes in the presence of God, but constantly addresses him directly.

The popularity of Matthew's translation led to the preparation of a second, by William Watts, Chaplain to Prince Rupert, and Rector of St Alban's, Wood Street, which was published in 1631. Watts's version is based upon Matthew's, especially in the first two books, which are simply the earlier translation revised; and even in the later books a large part of Matthew's work still remains. This point deserves to be noted, as Watts is constantly falling foul of Matthew, whom he calls "the Papist"; but his edition, though more correct, is far less distinguished in point of style, such grace as it possesses being due for the most part to the much-abused original. Watts's version, revised by Dr W. H. D. Rouse, has recently been re-issued in the Loeb Classical Library.

In 1679 appeared a third version, by Abraham Woodhead, Fellow of University College, Oxford, and a well-known controversialist. This edition, which contains Books I-X only, also owes much to Matthew's translation; but it is more diffuse, and much of the beauty of the original has evaporated in the process of revision. For want of a better, however, it became popular, and was several times reprinted.

In 1838 appeared Dr Pusey's well-known translation, which forms Vol. I of the Oxford "Library of the Fathers." Dr Pusey used Watts's version as a basis, but he modified it so much that, as he himself says, "the work has, in fact, been re-translated." It is interesting to find that he frequently restores the wording of Matthew's original version, where Watts had departed from it unnecessarily.

Of later editions only one need be mentioned, viz. that of Dr C. Bigg, of Christ Church, Oxford, published in 1897. This, which contains Books I-IX only, really is a new translation, the only one known to me which is not based on Matthew. It is a fine piece of work and has achieved great popularity, and the omission of the last four books, which make up nearly half the original work, is to be noted, but it must be owned that the version is at times so free as to be more a paraphrase than a translation.

From all this it is, I think, clear that Matthew has received far less credit than is due to him for his share in making St Augustine's masterpiece known to English readers. Of the translations named, all except Dr Bigg's contain a very large percentage of his work; and his fine style has supplied the model to which later versions owe most of their literary merit. In the present edition my aim has been to retain Matthew's work so far as possible, and to preserve his style while amending his translation; but the task of bringing it into line with the critical Latin text has forced me to modify it so much more than I had anticipated, that I could not issue it without qualification as Sir Tobie Matthew's translation, which was my first intention.

Dr Rouse, in the Preface to his re-issue of Watts's version, quotes a passage from that writer's Introduction, which describes the work of translation as "incomparably the hardest task that ever I undertook"; and he adds, "the present editor is inclined to echo this remark." Sir Tobie, whose powers as a linguist were regarded with wonder by his contemporaries, speaks at considerable length in the same strain; and the task of checking his version sentence by sentence with the original Latin has brought home to me the truth of his words. For the fact is that passages

are by no means rare in which it is impossible to decide
what precise shade of meaning St Augustine intended;
while in places, too, despite all the skill of critical editors,
the Latin text remains obscure.

The constant use of Scripture quotations is one of the
great characteristics of St Augustine's style, and to indicate
this I have printed the direct quotations in italics, but without giving any references. This method seemed to me
preferable to interrupting the reader with countless
footnotes, but it fails to bring out the Saint's use of
what may be called " quotations in solution," i.e. passages
which reflect the original Scripture closely enough to
preserve the flavour or even to identify the source, but
which are given in too free a form to be printed as actual
quotations.

The spelling and punctuation have been modernised
through the volume, and a few Notes are added at
the end to elucidate particular points. These have been
kept as few as possible to avoid undue interference between
the author and the reader, anything necessary to explain
the purpose an origin of the work being included in the
Introduction.

G. ROGER HUDLESTON, O.S.B.

Downside Abbey,
Bath.

CONTENTS

CONTENTS

NOTE

This edition of *The Confessions of St. Augustine* consists of books 1-9. The last four books are here omitted since they do not form an integral part of the biography but are rather in the nature of a treatise on the Scriptures.

TABLE OF DATES

INTRODUCTION

WHEN, at the request of his friends, St Augustine put into writing those recollections of his past life to which he often referred in conversation, he performed a literary achievement such as no one before him had ever undertaken. For the *Confessions* are above all things a human document, a piece of self-revelation, and in them we have a first-hand presentment of the greatest figure in Christianity since the Apostolic age. This no doubt is the reason why the work won its immediate and universal popularity, why it retained it throughout the ages of faith and of doubt, and why it does so still in this age of ours, which has been called an age that longs to be religious.

Taking religion in a wide sense as the bond between the human soul and God, it may be regarded under three principal aspects: the institutional, the doctrinal, and the personal; according as we study it in its organised systems, in its body of dogmatic teaching, or in the private relations which exist between the individual soul and God. Most of us find in our actual experience that one or other of these aspects is pre-eminent for us in interest and importance; but we must never allow the other two to pass out of our religious life, if that life is to reach its fullest and truest development. And here precisely it is that St Augustine stands out so wonderfully, for he combined in himself, in a supreme degree, all three of these great aspects of religion: and his *Confessions* are consequently a document of the highest value, alike from an institutional point of view, as showing the necessity of union with Christ's mystical body, the Church, which is the only authorised way of life for a Christian; from a doctrinal point of view, as evidence of the power of that Church to meet by her teaching every

17

religious need of the human mind and heart; and from a personal point of view, as a guide-book or map to succeeding generations, who work out their salvation along the way of life, as he has shown himself to have done with such convincing truthfulness and wonderful psychological insight.

It is important to remember that these three aspects of religion are not mutually exclusive, like water-tight compartments, but on the contrary are intertwined like the strands of a rope; and that it is impossible for personal religion to exist without being more or less institutional and doctrinal, just as it is for a religious system or a code of doctrine to possess any real evidence without a body of followers who live by it, and who model their lives upon its teaching. So we must not expect to find in the *Confessions* three separate and distinct things; on the contrary, the work is true to life precisely because it reveals the progress of Augustine's mind and heart to God, as that progress was really made; the motive influences which drove him onward, now of one kind, now of another— intellectual, moral, emotional—apparently jostling one another in a hubbub, whose order and sequence could be seen when the goal was reached, but not before. For Augustine worked out his problems, as we all do, not by any *a priori* reasoning, but by actual contact with life and its difficulties. He tested his conclusions by the only satisfying criterion known to him; by seeing if they would work. In this way he tried in turn the teaching of the Manichees, of Academic philosophy, of Neo-Platonism, and found them wanting; and lastly he tried Christianity, and it stood the test. It stood the test, or rather both tests : the theoretical test of his intellectual struggle, the practical test of his moral struggle, for the two went on side by side. Augustine did not first attain to moral self-control and then to intellectual satisfaction, or *vice versa,* but his growth throughout was in both directions; for him, as for all men, the Truth proved also the Way and the Life.

St Augustine was born on 13 November, A.D. 354, at Tagaste, the modern Souk-Ahras, a little provincial city of Numidia, now Algeria. Of his father, Patricius—a small landowner and one of the *curiales* of the city, who remained a pagan until shortly before his death, *circa* 371—we know nothing beyond the few details given in the *Confessions* (esp. IX 9). Of his mother, Monica, we have fairly detailed knowledge, thanks to the many exquisite sketches of her character, etc., which are scattered throughout the *Confessions,* especially the chapters which expressly deal with her in Book IX. To her influence doubtless it was due, that Augustine was educated as a Christian, but in accordance with the custom of the time he was not baptised, although he begged for baptism in childhood during an illness (see Note 2, *infra,* p. 449).

A boy of brilliant promise, Augustine acquitted himself so well in the schools at Tagaste and Madaura that his father determined to send him to Carthage to be trained for a legal career, and, to save the money needed for this purpose, he kept the boy at home during his sixteenth year. This enforced idleness led Augustine into evil ways, and when he reached Carthage, towards the end of 370, he fell a prey to the seductions of the great city, forming a sinful liaison with a woman, which lasted for fifteen years. From this union was born, in 372, Adeodatus, " the fruit of his sin " (IX 6). Of this period in his life Augustine speaks with great severity, but there is no justification for the picture of him as a monster of sensuality, which some writers have drawn, for he was only in his nineteenth year when the reading of Cicero's *Hortensius,* a lost treatise in praise of philosophy, won him back to the " love of wisdom "; turning his heart from rhetoric to philosophy, and rekindling in him a spirit of devotion and the practice of prayer, which he had abandoned.

In his search for wisdom Augustine naturally turned to the Scriptures, but he turned in vain; for their style seemed to him far inferior to that of the great classical authors, and he was as yet unable to solve the difficulties which met him in the moral inconsistencies of some Old Testament figures. His view as to the style of the Bible was due partly to the clumsy renderings of the "Old Latin" version, which was all he had, partly to the fact that the literary standard of his day was so thoroughly decadent that it condemned the exquisite simplicity and sincerity of the Gospels, serenely unconscious that the fault lay in itself. The other question, that of moral inconsistency, is one of much greater difficulty —such things as the polygamy of the patriarchs, the deception of Isaac by Jacob, or the murder of Sisara by Jahel, are still subjects of discussion—how Augustine eventually solved it, by his arguments from the difference in "times and seasons," will be found in Book III, Chapters 8 and 9. But even if such a solution had occurred to him at this time, it is unlikely that he would have been satisfied with it, for it must be remembered that he was still a very young man, and young men—impatient of difficulties—are always liable to be captured by anyone who will cut the Gordian knot for them, with a slashing, uncompromising answer. Such an answer was forthcoming in the teaching of the Manichees, and precisely at this moment, when his upward progress was checked by disappointment with the Scriptures, Augustine came upon Manichæism.

This system, which is often referred to as a heresy, though it originated outside the Church, was an astonishing farrago of Oriental fancies, plus a whole series of dogmatic statements on matters which belong to the domain of scientific fact. It will be sufficient here to say that it was an extreme form of Dualism, which taught that, from the beginning, there had been two rival principles, Light and Darkness, Good and Evil; and which built up on this basis a structure wildly fantastic, and so far as it

dealt with natural phenomena, demonstrably false. But—
and this is the point which fascinated Augustine and probably most of its more intelligent followers—it answered
his two conundrums for him; and in particular it solved
the question of moral responsibility in precisely the way
which appealed most to human vanity. To his question
as to the Hebrew Scriptures, Manichæism answered that
they had been tampered with, and that the moral inconsistencies of the patriarchs, etc., were due to these
interpolations. To the other question, the existence of evil,
and how far he himself was responsible for his sins, it
answered in effect: "You are not responsible at all. Sin
is all due to the interference of the Power of Darkness,
who has imprisoned the human soul, which came from
the Light Principle, in a body of darkness, so that it
cannot help acting and sinning as it does. But if you
will accept me as your guide and will obey me, I will
teach you how to free yourself from bondage." The offer
was a tempting one, and to the young enthusiast well
worth trying.

  Manichæism once adopted, Augustine became an ardent
proselytizer, drawing into error his pupil and admirer
Alipius—who was later baptised with him at Milan, and
eventually   became   Bishop   of   Tagaste—and   also
Romanianus, a wealthy friend of his family, who
was paying his expenses at Carthage; but his mother,
Monica, on his return to Tagaste, forbade him to eat at her
table or even to enter his old home, on account of his
pernicious opinions. After a year or so spent in teaching at
Tagaste, Augustine returned to Carthage, and opened a
school of Rhetoric there, when his brilliant talents soon
won him fame and public honours; there too he wrote
his first work, *de Pulchro et Apto,* a treatise on æsthetics,
which was already lost when he wrote the *Confessions*
(IV 13 and 14).

  The Manichæan sect was divided into two classes, the
Elect, and the Auditors. The former—who were strict

ascetics abstaining from wine, flesh-meat, and marriage, and living on vegetable food alone, which they were not allowed even to pluck for themselves—were supported by the Auditors, whom they repaid by giving them a share in their prayers. Augustine never advanced beyond the grade of Auditor, and before many years had passed, his acute intellect began to feel dissatisfaction with Manichæism. He explains at great length and very clearly how it failed him. First, there was the destructive character of Manichæan philosophy—"they destroy everything and build up nothing"; secondly, the immorality of the men themselves; thirdly, the feebleness of their arguments against the Catholics with regard to Scripture; fourthly, the obvious falsity of their so-called scientific teaching. This last point was one of special importance, for the Manichæan "science" was an integral part of its theological system. When, therefore, it contradicted natural facts, as it did, for example, in its theory of eclipses, the failure threw doubt upon all the rest, since all was based upon the authority of the founder, Mani. The teachers of the sect in Carthage could not answer Augustine's objections, but they put him off with promises. Let him wait for Faustus, their great Doctor; he was coming to Carthage and would explain everything. Augustine waited, and eventually Faustus came. But he proved a complete disappointment. A skilful rhetorician—as a speaker Augustine ranks him higher than St Ambrose—Faustus knew nothing of science, and at once acknowledged that he could not answer the difficulties raised. The spell was broken, Augustine rejected the teaching, and his mind was free again, though for want of anything better he still remained nominally a Manichæan.

In this state of unrest, Augustine for a time drifted towards the sceptic philosophy of the New Academy, the Agnosticism of his day. But his optimistic character rebelled against the teaching that Truth, which he regarded as the *Summum Bonum,* could never be attained by human reason;

and his was not the type of mind that could rank the search for Truth above the possession of it. Possibly this state of intellectual unrest had its share in urging him to leave Carthage for Rome, whither he went, apparently towards the end of 383 (V 8), and on his arrival there was taken seriously ill. When his health returned he opened a school of Rhetoric at Rome but, disgusted by the behaviour of his pupils, who defrauded him of his tuition fees, he applied for and obtained the post of Rhetoric Professor at Milan. Thither he went in 384, and there he was joined by Monica, who had now followed him from Africa.

At Milan he met St Ambrose, and though he seems never to have reached any intimacy with the great Bishop, he became a regular attendant at his sermons, which rapidly broke down the prejudice against Christianity that his ignorance of its real teaching had bred. But he was destined to approach the Church by a path which changed his whole philosophical outlook, and coloured his teaching to some extent even to the end of his life. This was the system known as Neo-Platonism.

Augustine's knowledge of Greek appears to have been slight, but soon after reaching Milan he fell in with some Latin translations of Platonic books—almost certainly the *Enneads* of Plotinus, translated by Victorinus Afer—and was completely captivated by their teaching. From this writer—a heathen, born in Egypt about A.D. 204, in whose writings Christianity is not once named—Augustine received the impulse which brought him ultimately to the feet of Christ. From him he learned that "God is Spirit," eternal, unchangeable, immaterial; and this was a vital matter to him, since hitherto he had been unable to conceive of any spiritual substance, and so had thought of God as some vast, luminous, all-containing body, much like the ether of space. Now, for the first time, he saw God presented as the One Reality, the Soul of souls and Life of lives. Now first he heard that evil is nothing but separation from God; that the whole purpose of man's

life is to mount up to him and be united to him; that he
can do this only by self-discipline and self-restraint, rising
from lower to higher levels by contemplation of God;
and that at length he may even reach the highest degree
of union possible in this life, that ecstasy wherein, for a
moment, the soul is lost to space and time in the all-
absorbing embrace of God. Indeed Augustine seems to
have become an adept, and to have achieved the summit
of Platonic vision; for the famous description of ecstasy,
wherein, for one brief moment, his intellect arrived at THAT
WHICH IS (VII 17), occurs at this period, when he was still
far from being a Christian.

All this, no doubt, Augustine might have learned from
Christianity, and at first sight it seems strange that, with a
mother like Monica, he should have remained ignorant of
such things, until he read of them in Plotinus; but the
explanation is really simple. Augustine, although in
boyhood he regarded himself as a Christian, was worse
than ignorant of the Church's teaching, he was positively
misinformed about it. His education had been of a poor
standard, in philosophy he seems to have been almost
wholly self-taught, and Monica, albeit a saint, was not
an educated woman, and in matters such as these could
not understand her brilliant son, far less guide him in
his difficulties. As a rhetorician Augustine was well
trained, according to the standards of his day, but his
studies in that line would give no help towards elucidating
the problems of life and conduct, for whose solution he
had gone to the Manichees. Even now, though Neo-
Platonism could satisfy his intellect, the craving of heart
and conscience remained. In that system God is regarded
as a Trinity—the Good, the Mind, and the World-Soul—
but he is an object of reception and contemplation by the
intellect alone. Plotinus knows nothing of him as the
Father who loved his children, still less as the Good
Shepherd who gives his life for his sheep, or as the

source of grace, whereby man's natural powers are made capable of that which is beyond their unaided strength. The Neo-Platonic God might satisfy one who had never fallen a victim to passion, one in whom the emotions had never been deeply stirred; but not one, like Augustine, to whom the consciousness of his divided nature had been brought home by a long established habit of sin, which all his efforts could not break.

When, therefore, Neo-Platonism told him that moral evil could be got rid of by moral discipline alone, that the soul's unaided powers could effect all that was needed in the way of reformation, Augustine knew that it was speaking falsely, for his past life proved to him that this was not so. It was useless to tell him that sin was merely an accretion, without any effect upon his personality, and that, by means of ascetical practices, the soul could gradually be brought back to spiritual health and freed from sin; Augustine knew in advance that this was impossible, without help from outside himself, and such help Neo-Platonism did not pretend to offer.

So, once again, came disillusionment, once more the panacea failed to cure; but by this time the clue to the secret was drawing upon him, through the preaching of Ambrose, and his revived interest in the Scriptures and in Christ. If Plotinus had revealed to him a God who was worthy of all love and honour, it was St Paul who showed him how he might become capable of fellowship with God through Christ. With this phase of his development he deals in great detail, revealing with unerring psychological insight the reality of his struggle, and how in the end God's grace prevailed over habits ingrained by half a lifetime. There have not been wanting critics who complain that, at the crowning moment, Augustine surrendered to emotion, and vitiated the whole process of his development by throwing his heart into the scales. But such a criticism may fairly be ignored nowadays, for modern psychology at least has this to its credit, that it recognizes the emotions as a part of man's nature, and condemns any theory of life which refuses to take them into account. Indeed the story of Augustine's progress is itself the best answer to his critics. He went on from one generalisation upon life to another, rejecting each in turn precisely because it proved too narrow, when tested by the facts of life. At the final stage he applied the same test to Christianity, and Christianity stood it : would he have acted more reasonably by refusing to accept it?

Resigning his professorship in the late summer of 386 Augustine retired with Monica, Adeodatus, and his most intimate friends and pupils to Cassiciacum, a country house lent to him by his friend Verecundus, there to prepare himself for baptism by prayer and by the study of Scripture and philosophy. Besides the account of this period given in the *Confessions* (IX), we have the philosophical *Dialogues* which were written by him at this time, with the aid of a secretary who took down a report of the discussions as they took place. On these contemporary writings certain modern critics have based a theory, that the account of his conversion, given in Book VIII of the *Confessions,* must be false, or at least that it cannot have occurred at the date there given. This too ingenious argument will not stand examination. The fact of his baptism at Easter, 387, is admitted, and the paucity of references to Christianity in the *Dialogues* is due to the fact that they report purely philosophical discussions, in which reliance on revelation would be out of place. Nevertheless, as Abbé Portalié puts it, the *Dialogues* "contain the entire history of his Christian formation. As early as 386, the first work written at Cassiciacum reveals to us the great, underlying motive of his researches. The object of his philosophy is to give to authority the support of reason, and 'for him the great authority, that which dominates all others and from which he never wished to deviate, is the authority of Christ.' If he loves the Platonists, it is because he counts on finding among them interpretations always in harmony with his faith. To be sure such confidence was excessive, but it remains evident that, in these *Dialogues,* it is a Christian and not a Platonist that speaks."[1]

With the death of Monica in Book IX, the *Confessions* cease to be reminiscences. Book X is a masterly psychological study, dealing with Augustine as he saw himself to be when, as Bishop of Hippo, he wrote the *Confessions,* that is some thirteen years after his baptism. The last three books contain a commentary on the account of Creation, given in the first chapter of Genesis. The custom of omitting these books from translations of the work was inaugurated by Abraham Woodhead, on the ground that they " have no relation to the life of Saint Augustine," and his example has been followed in many later editions. They are here restored for two reasons. First, because the modern view, which disapproves of truncated works, seems to the editor to be abundantly justified. Secondly, because they have a very definite " relation to the life of Saint Augustine," being in effect an exposition of his attitude towards the question of Scriptural exegesis, which was one of the great questions of the day. Since, therefore, the first ten books of the *Confessions* are a history of Augustine's intellectual life, even more than of his outer life, these concluding books are quite in place as an account of his intellectual interests at the date when he wrote. It is true that for us the whole question of exegesis has shifted, and that no one to-day would take up the position which Augustine and the allegorical school adopted, unless in a very modified degree. But there are still plenty of minds of the type against which he tilts, who will not admit that there can be anything good in any position other than their own, and

[1] *Cath. Encyc.,* s. v. " Augustine of Hippo ".

such a class may still benefit by the example of his width of mind and charity of heart.

Towards the end of his life, *circa* 426-8, Augustine wrote his *Retractations*, a revision of his works in chronological order, explaining the occasion and dominant idea of each: the passage therein which deals with the *Confessions* is given below. It seemed of interest to print this passage exactly as it stands in Sir Tobie Matthew's translation, both as a sample of his original work, and also as an *amende honorable* for the injustice done to him—no doubt unconsciously—by Dr C. Bigg, who gives this extract in his edition as a sample of Wm. Watts's style, being unaware that Watts took it bodily from Matthew, without altering so much as one word!

The thirteene books of my Confeſsions, both of my ſinnes, and my good deedes; do prayſe God, who is both juſt, and good; and do excite, both the affection, and vnderſtanding of man towardes him. In the meane tyme, for as much as concerneth me, they wrought this effect, when I wrote them; and ſo they yet do, when now, I read them. VVhat others find therby, let themſelves obſerue; but this I know; That they have much pleaſed, and do much pleaſe many of my brethren. From the firſt, through the whole tenth Booke, they are written of my ſelfe; in the three books following, of the holy Scripture; from that place where it is ſayd, In the beginning God made heauen and earth, *till he ſpeaks of the* Rest of the Sabbaoth. *In the fourth booke, when I confeſſed the miſery of my mind; upon occasion of my friends death, ſaying,* That my ſoule was, as it were made one, of both our ſoules; & that therfore it was perhaps, that I feared to dye, leaſt ſo he might wholy dye, whome I extremely loued; *this ſeemeth rather, a light kind of* Declamation, *than a ſerious* Confeſſion. *Though yet howſoever, that impertinency be ſomewhat moderated, by the addition of this word,* perhaps, *which then I vſed. And that alſo, when I ſayd in the thirteenth booke;* The firmament was made, betweene those superiour spirituall waters, and these inferiour corporeall waters, *was not confideratiuely inough expreſſed. But the truth heereof, is extremely hard to be diſcouered. This worke beginneth thus.* Great art thou, O Lord, & highly worthy to be prayſed.

BOOK ONE

He is kindled with the desire of praising God

Great art thou, O Lord, and greatly worthy to be praised:
great is thy power, and of thy wisdom there is no end.
And man, who is a part of what thou hast created, desireth
to praise thee; yea, man, who carryeth his mortality about
him, the proof of his sin and the testimony of this, that
thou, O God, *dost resist the proud,* even man desires to
praise thee. For thou hast stirred him up that he may take
pleasure in praising thee; because thou has created us for
thyself, and our heart knows no rest, until it may repose
in thee. Grant then, O God, that I may know and understand whether of these two things be first, to call upon
thee or to praise thee, and whether it be first, to know thee
or to call upon thee?

But yet, who calleth upon thee, if he know thee not?
For he that doth not know thee may call upon somewhat
else instead of thee. Or art thou rather to be called upon to
the end that thou mayest be known? But *how shall*
they call upon him in whom they have not believed, or
how shall they believe without a preacher? And they shall
praise the Lord that seek him. For they that seek him
shall find him, and they that find him shall praise him. I
will seek thee, O Lord, calling upon thee, and I will call
upon thee, believing in thee, for thou hast been preached
unto us. My faith, O God, which thou has given me,
and with which thou hast inspired me by the humanity
of thy Son and by the ministry of him, thy Preacher,
doth call upon thee.

He invoketh and beseecheth God to come into him

AND how shall I invoke my God; my Lord and my God?
Because when I invoke him, I call him into myself;
and what place is there in me that so my God may come
into me; God, who made heaven and earth? Is it so, O
Lord my God, that there is anything in me which
containeth thee? Or rather, do the heaven and earth
which thou hast made, and in which thou hast made me,
contain thee? Or is it therefore true that whatsoever is
containeth thee, because without thee it could not be?
Since therefore I also am somewhat, why do I desire that
thou mayest come into me, who should not be at all, unless
thou wert already in me? For I am not now in hell,
and yet thou art even there, for *though I should descend
into hell, there thou art present.* I should not therefore be,
O God, I, who could have no being at all unless thou wert
in me; or rather, I should not be at all unless I were in
thee, *of whom are all things, by whom all things, in
whom all things.* Even so it is, O Lord, even so. Why then
do I invoke thee, since I am in thee, or whence canst thou
come into me? For whither shall I go out of heaven
and earth, that my God may come thence into me, who
hath said, *Heaven and earth do I fill.*

*God is all everywhere, and is not contained by parts by
  his creatures*

Do therefore heaven and earth contain thee, because thou
fillest them; or dost thou fill them so that there is still an
overplus of thee, because they are not able to comprehend
thee? And into what dost thou pour whatsoever of thee
doth remain, after heaven and earth are filled? Or hast
thou no need to be contained by somewhat, thou who

containest all things, because those things which thou fillest, thou fillest by containing them? For those vessels which are full of thee do not give any stability to thee, nor, if they be broken, art thou poured out. When thou art poured out upon us, thou art not abased, but *thou dost raise us*. Neither art thou scattered, but thou dost gather us up. And thou, who fillest all things, dost fill them all with all thy very self. Or, because all things cannot contain all of thee do they contain a part? And do all things contain the same part together, or several things, several parts; great things, greater, and less, lesser? Is therefore any part of thee greater, and any other lesser? Or else art thou all everywhere, and so nothing doth contain thee all?

He admireth the unspeakable attributes of God

WHAT art thou therefore, O my God? What art thou, but the Lord God? For *who is Lord besides our Lord, or who is God besides our God?* O thou supreme, most powerful, most merciful, most just, most secret, most present, most beautiful, most mighty; most constant and incomprehensible; immutable, yet changing all things; never new and never old, yet renewing all things, and drawing such as are proud into decay, although they mark it not. Ever in action, and ever quiet; heaping up, yet needing nothing; upholding, filling and protecting, creating, nourishing and perfecting all things.

Thou lovest, yet thou art not transported; thou art jealous, yet thou art void of fear; thou dost repent, yet thou art free from sorrow. Thou art angry without being unquiet; thou dost change thy works without changing thy decree; thou takest what thou findest, yet didst thou never lose anything. Thou art never poor, yet thou art glad of gain; never covetous, yet thou exactest usury at our hands. If we give thee more than thou dost claim, thou becomest our debtor; yet who hath anything but of thy gift? Thou payest debts, yet owest nothing; thou forgivest debts, yet losest nothing. And what shall we say, O my God, my life, my holy, dear delight, or what can any man say when he speaketh of thee? And woe be to them that are silent in thy praise, when even they who speak most thereof may be accounted to be but dumb.

He aspireth to be united to God

Who, O Lord, will grant that I may repose in thee? Who will grant that thou mayest enter into my heart and inebriate it, that I may forget all my wicked ways and embrace thee, my only good? What art thou unto me, O Lord? Have mercy on me that I may speak to thee. Or what am I to thee, that thou shouldst command me to love thee; yea, and be angry and threaten to lay huge miseries upon me if I love thee not? Is it perhaps of itself no great misery, if I do not love thee? Woe be unto me. Tell me, even for thy mercy's sake, O Lord my God, what thou art unto me. *Say unto my soul, " I am thy salvation,"* but say it so that I may hear thee. Behold the ears of my heart are set before thee, open thou them, O Lord, and *say unto my soul, " I am thy salvation."* I will run after the sound of that voice and thereby lay hold on thee. Hide not thou thy face from me; let me die, that I may see it, lest otherwise I die because I see it not.

The house of my soul is too strait for thee to enter, but let it, O Lord, be enlarged by thee. It is ruinous, but let it be repaired by thee. I know and confess that it hath many things which may offend thine eyes, but who shall be able to purify it and to whom but thee shall I cry out, *" Cleanse me, O Lord, from my hidden sins and forgive those offences to thy servant, which he hath caused in other folks." I believe in thee, and therefore it is that I speak,* O Lord, thou knowest it. For *have I not, O my God, declared my sins against myself, and thou hast forgiven*

*the impiety of my heart? I will not stand in judgment
with thee,* who art Truth, for I will not deceive myself,
nor shall my sin make me think I am not sinful. I do
not therefore seek to justify myself before thee, because *if
thou, O Lord, shall mark the sins that are committed,
O Lord, who shall be able to endure the trial?*

*That he hath received all blessing from God, and how
he was preserved by him*

YET suffer thou me to speak unto thy mercy, me who am
but dust and ashes. Let me speak, for behold it is thy mercy
to which I speak, and not to any man who may deride
me. Yea and perhaps thou dost yet laugh at me, but *being
turned toward me thou wilt have mercy.* For what is it
which I should say, O Lord my God, but that I know
not whence I came into this mortal life; a dying
life, shall I call it, or rather a living death? Even then did
the sweetness of thy mercy take me up, as I have been
told by the parents of this flesh and blood, of whom and
in whom thou once didst frame me: for myself I
cannot remember it. The comfort of a woman's milk
entertained me, yet neither did my mother nor my nurses
fill their breasts therewith. But thou, O Lord, by them
didst give nourishment to my infancy, according to thy
ordinance and the riches of thy goodness, which extendeth
even to the root of all things. Thou also gavest me to desire
no more milk than thou gavest unto them, and thou gavest
unto them to give as much as was fit for me, for they dispensed to me with proportion that which thou gavest them
in abundance. It was a blessing to them that I received this
blessing from them, or rather not from them but by their
means I received it, whilst yet, originally, it came from thee.
For from thee, O God, come all good things, and from my
God proceedeth the whole course of my salvation. This I
observed afterwards, when thou didst cry unto me by these

thy benedictions, which both inwardly and outwardly thou bestowedst. For then I did but know how to suck and to be content with that which pleased me, and to cry when anything offended me, and this was all. Afterwards I began to laugh, first sleeping, and then, shortly, waking. For this was told me of myself and this I believed, because so it passeth with other infants, but these things I remember not.

Then, by degrees, I began to find where I was, and I desired to declare my will to those by whom it might be executed. But I could not do it, for my desires were within and those persons were without me, nor were they able to enter into my soul by any of my senses. Therefore would I be tossing my arms, and sending out certain cries, and making such other few expressions of my desires, as best I could, but they carried no good proportion to that which I felt within. And when they obeyed me not, either because they did not understand me, or for that the thing which I demanded might do me hurt, I would fall into a rage, and that not against such as were my subjects or servants, but against my elders and my betters, and I would revenge myself upon them by crying. Such, so I understand, all infants are, as I have seen; and such was I, so I have been told by them who brought me up: though even they may rather be accounted not to know, than to know these things. Yet behold my infancy is dead long ago, whilst I am alive. But thou, O Lord, who ever livest in thyself and nothing dieth in thee—because thou art before all ages and before all that which can even be said to have been before, who art God and Lord of all thy creatures, in whose presence do stand the causes of all things that are unstable and even of all things that are changeable—the unchangeable roots remain with thee, and the eternal reasons of things which are temporal and irrational do live. Tell me, I say, who am thy suppliant, O God, thou who art merciful, tell me, who am miserable, whether or not did infancy succeed to any other age or state which was then departed, or was there only that which I had whilst I was in my mother's womb? For of that also I have had some relation, and myself have seen women with child. What also was there, before that, O my God and my delight, was I anywhere, or anybody? For I have none to inform me hereof, my father and my mother can say nothing of it, nor yet the experience of others, nor mine own memory.

Dost thou laugh at me for demanding these things of thee, who commandest me to praise thee, and to confess myself to thee for what I know? *I will confess to thee, O Lord of heaven and earth,* and sing praise to thee for those first beginnings and for that infancy, which I remember not. For thou hast given man power to conjecture these things about himself by comparison with other men, and to believe many things of himself, even upon the authority of weak women. For even then I had a Being and a Life, and ere the end of my infancy I sought for some means whereby I might express myself to others. For whence could such a living creature come, O Lord, except from thee? Is any man able to frame himself, or is any one of the veins, whereby our Being and Life runneth into us, drawn from any other root than this, that thou dost frame us? Thou to whom Being and Living are not several things, because supremely to Be and supremely to Live is the very thing itself, which thou art. For thou art supreme and art not changed. Neither is this present day spent in thee, and yet, after a sort, it is spent in thee; because even all these transitory things are in thee, nor could they have their ways of passing unless thou didst contain them. And, because *thy years do not fail,* thy years are the present day. And how many of our days and of our fathers' days have now passed by this one day of thine, and have taken their measure thence, and received a kind of being, as others also shall pass and receive their measure also and their kind of being? *But thou art still the same;* to-morrow, with all that is to follow, and yesterday, with all that is past, in this day of thine thou shalt make, and thou hast made. What doth it matter if any man understand not this? Let even such a one rejoice and say, " *What thing is this?*" Let him, I say, rejoice so, and be rather glad to find thee thus, by not finding thee; than, by finding thee otherwise, not to find thee.

That even his infancy was subject to sin

HEARKEN to me, O God. Woe be unto the sins of men. Man sayeth this and thou hast mercy on him, because thou madest him, and didst not make sin in him. Who will bring to my remembrance the sin of my infancy? For *there is none free from sin before thee, no, not an infant, who hath lived but a day upon the earth.* Who, I say, will put me in mind of it? Will any of those little infants do it, in whom now I may see that which I remember not of myself? Wherein then did I sin? Was it perhaps when I cried too earnestly that I might suck? For if now I should do so, I say not for my nurse's milk, but even for food which is agreeable to my present years, I should most justly be derided and reprehended. I therefore then did that which, in itself, was reprehensible; but, because I could not have understood them that might reprehend me, neither custom nor reason suffered me to be reprehended; for, as we grow older, we easily root out and cast away such things as these. Neither have I seen any man, knowing what he doth, to cast away good things, when he pretendeth to purge himself. Or did I sin perhaps, not so much by the inordinate demand of what was good, as by striving to have somewhat else that might be hurtful to me? And by falling into a rage against my nurses and parents and many other discreet persons, and by endeavouring to strike and hurt them as much as I could, whensoever they did not punctually obey me? Though he ought not to be said to be obeyed, who is but obeyed to his destruction. If so, it is the weakness of an infant's body which is innocent, whereas the mind is not innocent.

Myself have seen and observed some little child, who could not speak, yet was he all in an envious kind of wrath, looking pale, with a bitter countenance upon his foster-brother. And who is ignorant of this? They may say, the mothers and nurses, that they expiate these offences, but I know not by what remedies.[1] Unless, perhaps, this also be accounted innocency, that an infant cannot endure a companion to feed with him in a fountain of milk which is richly abounding and overflowing, although that companion be wholly destitute, and can take no other food but this? But these things are easily endured, not because they are either no faults or are but little ones; but because a short time will make an end of them. For, although one should then allow them, in an elder person they would not be tolerated. Thou therefore, O Lord my God, who hast given a life and a body to an infant, which we see to be so accommodated by thee with senses, compacted with members, and beautified with due proportion and complexion, and, towards the total preservation and complement thereof, hast applied the endeavour of all thy inferior creatures; thou, I say, commandest me to praise thee. And so *I sing unto thy name, O thou most high,* because thou art God omnipotent and good, even though thou hast made but these things only, which none can make but thou alone, from whom proceedeth all way and order, O thou most beautiful God, who framest and, by thy law, ordainest all things.

This part of mine age, O Lord, this infancy whereof I remember nothing, but have partly understood by the relation of others, and partly by my observation of other infants —although these make the matter sure enough—it grieves me to reckon as a part of that life which I lead in this world; for, by reason of the darkness of oblivion wherein I am, it is like that state which I had within my mother's womb.

[1] See Note 1.

Now, if I be *conceived in iniquity and my mother nourished me, even within her womb, in sin,* where I beseech thee, O my God, where, O my Lord, was I thy servant, or at what time was I ever innocent? But I will pass from this state to another, and indeed what have I to do with that, whereof I can call nothing to mind?

A description of his childhood

FROM the state of infancy came I not forward to that of childhood? Or rather, came it not upon me and succeeded my infancy? Yet it departed not away, for whither could it go? And yet it was no more, for I was now no infant that could not speak, but I was grown to be a speaking child; and this I well remember, and I afterwards considered how I had learned to speak. For my elders did not teach me this by delivering words with any certain order of instruction, as afterwards I learned other things; but, by that mind which thou gavest me, O my God, when by divers kinds of noise and complaints and motions I would procure to express the thoughts of my heart, that so I might be understood and obeyed, though as yet I was not able to declare either what, or to whom I would. I began, I say, to observe with my memory, when they called any thing by a certain name, and according thereunto would by gesture show what they were speaking of; and thereupon I inferred that word which they uttered to be the name of such thing as then they showed. Now it was evident to me by the said gestures that so they endeavoured to make things easy to my understanding, as if by natural words which are common to all nations and are expressed by the countenance, the cast of the eyes, the action of the members and the sound of the voice, which show the affection of the mind in desiring, enjoying, rejecting, or avoiding of things. And thus, certain words being put in due place, and I having often heard what things they were appointed to signify, they were by degrees laid up in me; and having tamed, and as it were, broken my mouth to the pronouncing of them, I expressed myself by these means. In this sort I communicated the desire I grew to have of calling things by their true names with such persons as I lived among, and so I began to launch out more deeply into the tempestuous traffic and society of mankind, depending upon the authority of my parents and my other elders.

Of the hatred he had to learning, and of the desire which children have to play

O GOD, my God, what miseries did I here find, and what mockeries, when it was propounded unto me, as towards the happiness of my life, that I, being a child, must obey my teachers, that so I might prosper in this world, and excel in certain talking arts, which serve for the procuring of wordly honour and false riches. Then was I put to school, and care was taken that I might learn things, of the use and profit whereof I, poor wretch, was ignorant. Yet, if I were slothful, they would beat me, for this custom was recommended by our elders; and many, who had passed through this life before us, had chalked out certain laborious ways, by which we also were constrained to follow them, with a multiplication of pain and grief to the sons of Adam.

We observed, O Lord, that there were men who prayed to thee, and we learned of them; and we found, after our poor fashion, that thou wert some great thing which could, though without sensibly appearing, both hear and help us. And so, being yet a child, I began to be thine aid and succour, and I did loosen the knots of my tongue in praying unto thee; and I begged, being yet a little one, with no little devotion that I might not be beaten at the school. And, when thou heardest me not—*which yet was never the worse for me*—my stripes, which were so grievous and offensive to me at that time, were laughed at by mine elders, yea and by my parents themselves, who yet were far from wishing me any harm. Is there, O Lord, any man of so great a mind, united to thee with fervent affection—for such a thing also may grow in other wise out of a kind of sullenness—is there, I say, any man who, by devoutly adhering to thee, is so affected to thy service that he can think slightly of those racks and hooks and other torments, for the avoiding whereof men pray unto thee with great fear from one end of the world to the other, so that he can make sport at such as do most sharply inflict those things upon him, as our parents laughed at the torments which we children sustained at our masters' hands? For neither did we fear our punishments less than those others, nor pray thee less for to escape them; and yet we sinned by writing and reading and studying less than was exacted of us.

There was not wanting to us, O Lord, either memory or wit, whereof thou gavest us enough for that age, but we took delight in playing; and this was revenged upon us, by them who did the like themselves. But the plays and toys of men are called Business, yet when children fall into them, the same men punish them, and no man pityeth either of them; or, if some may pity one, none pityeth them both. Unless perhaps some discreet judge of things will esteem me to have been justly beaten for playing at ball, when I was a boy, and for hindering myself thereby from learning those arts quickly, wherewith—being grown older—I might play more deformedly and more dangerously. Even so did he by whom I was beaten; who, if in any little question of learning he were worsted by some fellow teacher, would have been more fed upon by rage and envy than I, if, in a match at ball, I had been mastered by one of my play-fellows.

He neglecteth the commandment of his parents, through the desire he hath to play at ball

AND yet I sinned herein, O my Lord God, Creator and Ordainer of all things which are natural, but not the ordainer of sins. O Lord, my God, I sinned in doing contrary to the directions of my parents and masters, for I might afterwards have made good use of that learning which they inclined me to, whatsoever design they had therein. But I was not disobedient to them out of any desire I had of doing better, but out of the love I had to play; aspiring proudly to be victorious in the matches which I made, and loving to have my ear scratched with lying fables, that so they might itch the faster, the same dangerous curiosity flashing out also by mine eyes, more and more, at sight of the representations of plays which were composed by our elders. And yet they, who publish these things, are accounted to excel in such a kind of eminency as that all men wish the like to their children; while yet they willingly suffer them to be beaten if, by seeing of such spectacles, they be hindered from their studies, whereby they would have them to arrive at the ability of setting forth the like. Behold these things, O Lord, with mercy, and deliver us who are now calling upon thee. Deliver also them who do not yet call upon thee, that so they also may be delivered.

How as a boy he fell sick, and deferred to be baptized

FOR I had heard somewhat, even whilst yet a boy, of eternal life, which was promised unto us by the Humility of our Lord and God descending down to this pride of ours. And I was signed with the sign of his cross and seasoned with his salt as soon as I came from the womb of my mother, who had much hope in thee. Thou sawest, O Lord, how, when I was yet a boy, being one day oppressed with a pain of the stomach I fell suddenly into a fever and was like to die; thou sawest, O my God, because thou wast even then my keeper, with what inclination of mind and with what faith I desired the baptism of thy Christ, my Lord, at the pious hands of my mother and the mother of us all, thy Church. Now the mother of my flesh and blood was much afflicted, because her chaste heart did most dearly desire my everlasting salvation in thy faith; and she was taking care that, with all speed, I might begin to be washed by thy life-giving sacraments, confessing thee, O Lord Jesus, for the remission of my sins, if I had not suddenly recovered. So my cleansing was then deferred, as if, should I live, it were certain that I should be more defiled, and the guilt of my future sins would be both greater and more dangerous after baptism.[1] For even so did I then believe, and so did my mother with her whole house, excepting only my father; yet could he not conquer in me the power of my mother's devotion, so far as to make me not to believe in Christ, as he, at that time, believed not in him. For she endeavoured that thou, O my God, mightest rather be my father than he, and herein thou didst help her to overcome her husband whom she yet did serve—though she were much the better of the two—because, in so doing, she did also serve thee, who didst so command her.

Yet I would fain know, O my God, if it were pleasing to thee, to what effect was my baptism then deferred, and whether it was for my good that the reins of sin should be laid loose upon me, or were they not laid loose? If not, whence is it then that our ears are so filled on all sides with this discourse, "Let him alone, let him do what he will, for he is not baptized?" Yet, when there is any question of bodily health, we say not "Let him be wounded more, for he is not yet recovered." How much better, therefore,

[1] See Note 2.

had it been if I had been quickly cured; and by the diligence of myself and my friends so good effect might have followed as that my soul, its health assured, might have been safe in thy custody who didst create it. Yea, this had been much better. But how many and how mighty waves of temptations did seem to threaten me after that state of boyhood, wherein I yet was, my mother did foresee; wherefore did she prefer to risk them on the clay whereof I was to be framed, rather than on the image of God itself.

How he was forced to study, which Almighty God used to good purpose

YET in this very childhood of mine, which seemed to hold less ground of fears for me than did my youth, I loved not to study, nay, I hated to be urged to it, and yet they urged me. And in so doing they did well, but I did not well, for I would not then have studied but by constraint. No man doth that well which he doth unwillingly, although what he doth be good. Neither did they greatly do well that urged me, but it was thou, O my God, who wert good to me. For they considered not any other end in that which they made me learn, but only to satisfy the insatiable desires of a rich kind of poverty and a base kind of glory. But thou, before whom *the very hairs of my head are all numbered,* didst use to my profit all the errors of those who urged me to study, and so didst thou use my fault, when I would not learn, in making me to be punished, whereof I was not unworthy, being so little a boy and yet withal so great a sinner. So didst thou well with me, at their hands who did not well; and upon me, who was a sinner, thou didst justly lay a punishment. For thou hast commanded it, and so it is, that the inordinate affection of everyone shall be to him affliction.

With what studies he was most delighted

But what the reason was why I hated the Greek language, whilst I was taught it, being a child, I do not even yet understand. The Latin I loved. Not that which the first masters did teach—which was but to read—but that which was delivered by the Grammarians. For, as for the former, when reading and writing and the casting of accounts was taught in Latin, I held it not less painful or penal than the very Greek. Now, whence came even this, but from sin and the vanity of this life; because *I was made of flesh and had a spirit which went forward and returned not.* For that first learning, because there was more certainty in it, and because by it there was and is wrought in me that I can read what I find written and can write what I will, was better than that other, whereby I was constrained to learn by rote the wanderings of Æneas whilst I forgot mine own, and to bewail Dido, dead because she killed herself for love, whilst, in the meantime, I, most miserable creature, with dry eyes did behold myself to depart and die from thee, O my God and my Life. For what is more miserable than a wretch not pitying himself; lamenting Dido's death, which was caused by her loving of Æneas, and not lamenting his own death, which is caused by not loving thee, O Lord, the light of my heart, and hidden bread of my soul. O Virtue, thou that knittest into one the faculties and powers of my mind, I did not love thee, but I committed spiritual fornication against thee; and, whilst I was so doing, everyone gave me "Good speed." For *the friendship of this world is an unclean departure from thee,* and herein we are so encouraged and congratulated that we are ashamed to do otherwise. Yet these things I wept not for, but I wept for Dido's death, who made herself away with the sword; myself following thy inferior creatures and leaving thee, going on from earth to earth. And if, at any time, I were forbidden to read these things, I was sorry, because I could not then be made sorry with reading them. For such madness as this, such kind of learning, is counted more profitable and polite than that other, whereby I learned to write and read.

But now, O my God, let thy Truth cry unto my soul and say, "It is not so; the former knowledge is far better than the latter." For I had rather forget the wanderings of Æneas and all such like, than forget how to write and read. Truly there are hangings put up at the portals of our Grammar schools, but these serve not more for keeping a decent kind of privacy than for hiding the foolish faults that are committed within. Let not those, of whom I have now no fear, cry out upon me, whilst I confess to thee, O my God, in what things my soul taketh pleasure, and how I am delighted in the reproof of my own evil ways, that so I may love thy good ways. Let not, I say, these buyers and sellers of grammar rules exclaim against me. For, if I ask them whether or no it be true that Æneas came once to Carthage, as the poet sayeth, the unlearned will answer that they know not, and the learned will say, "It is not true." But if I ask with what letters this word "Æneas" must be written, all they that have learned to write will answer truly, according to that agreement and law whereby men have established these symbols among themselves.

Again, if I should ask which of these two things would be more incommodious to our life, either to forget how to write and read, or else to forget those poetical fictions, who sees not what any man that is in his wits would answer? I then, being a boy, did sin, whilst I preferred those vain things, before these other which are profitable; or rather whilst I hated these and loved those. Even so, to say "One and one make two, two and two make four," was an ungrateful thing to my ears; whereas the wooden horse full of armed men, the burning of Troy, and the very ghost of Creusa, these were to me a most delightful spectacle of vanity.

Of the Greek and Latin tongue

WHY then did I hate to learn the construction of the Greek tongue, which did sing of such things? For Homer also himself, though he be skilful in construing such fables as those, and though he be most delicately vain, yet to me, being yet a boy, he was of a bitter taste. I think that Virgil is so to them, to whom Greek is natural, when they first begin to learn Virgil, as Homer was to me. For to me the difficulty of studying a strange tongue did sprinkle, as with gall, all the delicacy of those fabulous narrations. For I understood not the words thereof, and they did urge me extremely, with cruel fears and pains, to understand them.

There was a time when, being an infant, I also understood not Latin. Yet, by observation I learned it, without any fear or torment, in the midst of the dandling which my nurses used, the dalliance of such as would applaud me, and the mirth of such as played with me. I did learn those things, therefore, without the cruel burden of such as constrained me, and by mine own heart I was urged to the expressing of my conceptions, which I could not do unless I learned some words. Yet I learned that of them, not as teachers of me, but as talkers with me, in whose hearing also I began to utter whatsoever I desired to express. Hereby it appears sufficiently that a free kind of curiosity doth contribute more to the learning of tongues than such a fear-driven kind of necessity. But thou, O Lord, dost restrain the free course of that kind of curiosity by thy laws; by thy laws, I say, which begin with the *ferula* that schoolmasters use, and go on even to the torment of martyrs. For those laws of thine can tell how to sprinkle our actions with wholesome bitterness, calling us back to thee thereby from that pestiferous delight whereby we departed from thee.

A prayer to God

O Lord, hear my prayer. Let not my soul faint under thy discipline, nor let me faint in confessing unto thee thy mercies, whereby thou has drawn me out of all my most wicked ways. That so thou mayest grow sweet to me beyond all those deceitful pleasures which I followed, and that I may love thee most fervently, and may embrace the hand of thy providence with all the roots of my heart, that so thou mayest finally draw me out of all temptation. For behold thou, O Lord, art my King and my God. To thy service let there be applied whatsoever good thing I learned as a child, and whatsoever I speak and write and read and number. For when I was learning vain things thou didst instruct me, and thou hast forgiven the sinfulness of my delight therein. In those studies I learned many words which might be profitable, but they also might have been learned in things which were not vain, and that is the safe way wherein children might walk.

Against immodest fables

But woe be unto thee, O thou torrent of human custom, who shall be able to resist thee? How long will it be ere thou be dry? How long wilt thou toss and roll those sons of Eve into the spacious and hideous sea, over which even they who are best shipped can hardly pass? Have I not read in thee of Jupiter, the thunderer and adulterer? These two things could not be true, but this was said that it might carry an authority to make men imitate that true adultery, to which that false thunder might play the broker. Yet which of our grave Masters would be able, with patient ear, to hear a man cry out in that same school and say, "This was but a fiction of Homer's. He hath ascribed the faults of men unto the gods: would rather he had drawn their virtues down to us?" But rather is it true to say he feigned them that, by attributing divine things to wicked men, they might not be thought sins; and to the end that whosoever should commit them might rather be esteemed to have imitated heavenly gods than wretched men.

And yet, O thou flood of hell, the sons of men are cast into thee, with promises of reward that they may be induced to learn these things. And is it no small matter when such things are done in the eye of the world, in sight of those laws which ordain stipends for the masters in addition to their scholars' fees? Thou dashest against thy rocks and cryest, "Here speech is learned, here eloquence may be acquired, most necessary by way of persuasion and for delivering oneself with advantage." But should we not come to understand those words, "the golden shower," "the lap," "the trick," "the temple of heaven," and the rest that are mentioned in that place, unless Terence did introduce a lewd young fellow holding up Jupiter to himself as an example, whilst he feasts his eyes upon a picture on the wall, wherein is expressed how "Jove rained a golden shower into the lap of Danae, by which the woman was deceived?" Now see, how he incites himself to lust, as if he were instructed therein from heaven; for what sayeth he? "Aye, what a God," he cries, "who shakes the whole vault of heaven with his sovereign voice. Shall not I, frail man, do that which he doth? For my part I confess I did, right willingly." Thus, whilst those words are not learned more easily by reason of that uncleanness, by means of those words is that filthiness more impudently committed. I blame not the words which, of themselves, are choice and precious vessels, but that wine of poison I blame, which was delivered to us by those drunken teachers. If we refused to drink, we were beaten; nor was it lawful for us to appeal to any sober judge. And yet, O thou my God, in whose sight I now recall these things with confidence, I gladly learned these things and, like a wretch, took pleasure in them, and for that I was accounted to be a towardly boy.

How he was exercised in writing

SUFFER me, O my God, to tell thee somewhat of my wit, which I had by thy gift, and upon what dreaming fancies it was spent. There was propounded to me a business, which I found troublesome enough, under a promise of praise or of punishment, either of shame or stripes, that I should declaim the words of Juno, who was both angry and sorrowful that she could not avert the Teucrian king from going to Italy. These words I had heard that Juno never said, but we were forced to follow the steps of those poetical fictions, and were enjoined to deliver in prose some such thing as the poet had expressed in verse. And he deserved most praise, in whose speech—according to the dignity of that person who was represented—there did appear a most natural affection of grief or rage, apparelled with fit words to express that sense. To what purpose was it for me, O thou my true Life and my God, to what purpose was it, that there should be a greater acclamation made in my favour than for many other of my school-fellows? Behold, are not all those things wind and smoke? Is it true that there was nothing else, wherein my wit and tongue might have been employed? Thy praise, O Lord, thy praises in the scriptures might have stayed up the climbing vine of my heart, so it should no more be carried away into those windy vanities, a prey to the foul creatures of the air. For there are more ways than one whereby men offer a kind of sacrifice to the rebellious angels.

*Men take more care to observe the precepts of grammar
  than the laws of God*

BUT what marvel was it, if I were carried thus towards
vanity and estranged-from thee, O my God, when such men
were proposed for models unto me as were confounded
with shame if they fell into any barbarism or solecism
of speech, when recounting some deed of theirs, albeit
harmless; whereas if they should have related the uncleanness of their own life, but in a style that had been copious,
elegant, and well ordered, they would have taken pride
in being praised. Thou seest these things, O Lord,
and thou holdest thy peace, *being longanimous and full
of mercy and truth.* But wilt thou hold thy peace for
ever? Even now thou dost draw out of this vast
and hideous pit the soul which seeketh thee and thirsteth
after thy delights; *whose heart sayeth to thee, " I have
sought thy countenance, O Lord; thy countenance will I
seek."* For I was gone far from thy face, through the dark
affections of my soul.

For it is not by motion or by measure of space that we
either go from thee or come to thee. Nor did that younger
son of thine seek horses or chariots or ships, nor did he
fly away with visible wings, nor make a journey with the
speedy motion of his feet that, living loosely, he might
dissipate in a remote country that which thou hadst given
him at his departure. A dear father thou wert, in giving
him that portion when he went; but yet more dear when he
returned so full of misery. For to be sunk in unclean
affections is to be in darkness, and to be in that darkness is
to be far from thee.

Behold, O Lord, and patiently behold, as thou dost
ever, how diligently the sons of men observe the order
which hath been delivered by their predecessor touching
letters and syllables, whilst yet they neglect the eternal

covenant of everlasting salvation which they have received from thee. And how he that teacheth words according to this old tradition, if, contrary to the order and use of grammar, he shall pronounce, without aspiration or H, this word *Hominem,* which signifieth a Man, he shall more displease man than if he hate a man contrary to thy law, being himself a man. As if any man could find himself more hurt by his enemy than he is by the hatred which he himself bears against the other; or that he could afflict another man more grievously by a persecution, than he doth waste his own heart by that uncharitable affection. Certainly there is no knowledge more intrinsically true than that which is written in our own consciences, of not doing to others that which we would not suffer in ourselves. How secret art thou, who dwellest in the highest heavens in silence, O thou only great God, sprinkling with an unwearied providence certain penal blindnesses upon such as have unbridled desires. When a man aspires to have the fame of eloquence, pleading before a judge environed with a great multitude of people, and prosecuting his enemy with implacable hatred, he takes extreme care not to speak the least word by any error of his tongue, in the hearing of men; but he takes no heed at all lest indeed he commit so great a sin as, through the malice of his heart, to destroy a man.

How he took more care to avoid barbarism of speech than corruption of manners

Thus miserable, being a boy, did I lie in the highway to such actions and customs as these, and my course of life was such that I was more afraid to use a barbarism of speech than I was careful—when I had used any such— not to envy another who used none. I declare and confess to thee, O my God, what things I was praised for by them to please whom was, at that time, the very rule of a good and pleasant life to me. For I saw not that deep pit of filth into which *I was cast, out of thy sight* But, before thine eyes, what was more ugly than myself, who displeased even such as those others were, whilst I deceived with innumerable lies both my tutor, my teachers, and my parents, through the desire of playing, and of beholding worthless sights, and affecting a sportful restlessness. I also committed certain thefts, out of the storeroom of my parents' house and from the table, either upon the instigation of gluttony, or that I might have somewhat to give to my play-fellows, who would be selling me their games, though they also took delight in them. In which games I, if I were conquered, would often aspire through desire of vain glory to gain a victory by cheating. Yet naught would I so impatiently endure, and against naught would I argue so desperately as this, when I took others in the act of doing that which I used to do myself. But if I, in such a case, were caught tripping, rather would I fall into a rage than admit it. Is this the innocency which should accompany the state of childhood? It is not, O Lord, it is not. I cry to thee for pardon, O my God. Yet, as there is trickery among boys, for nuts and balls and birds, which are proffered as rewards by their masters, so is there with respect of gold and farms and slaves, in our dealings with magistrates and princes. For even as the *ferula* yieldeth to greater punishments in process of time, so do these toys give place to those other things. Thou therefore, O our King, didst set up the emblem of humility in the person of a child, when thou saidest, " *Of such is the kingdom of heaven.*"

He giveth thanks to God for his benefits bestowed upon him

But yet, O Lord my God, our most excellent and perfect Creator, Ruler of the whole world, my thanks should still be given to thee, although thou hadst brought me no further than to this state of childhood. For even therein I had a Being, yea, I had Life and feeling. And I had care for the preservation of my personality, which is a kind of picture in little of the most secret unity of thine Essence, whence also I am derived. And I made sure of the accuracy of my outward senses by the help of that consciousness which was within, and I had delight in Truth, even in little things and in thinking upon little things. I liked not to be deceived. I had a vigorous memory and a ready speech. I was regaled by friendship. I fled from pain of body, from desolation of mind, and from ignorance. What is there in such a living creature that is not both admirable and delectable?

But all these things are the gift of my God, I did not bestow them upon myself. These things, I say, were good, and I had them all. Therefore he is good who made me, yea he is my God, and I rejoice unto him in all those benefits which he afforded me, even when I was a child. But herein I sinned, that not in him it was but in his creatures— in myself and the rest—that I sought for pleasures, honours, and truth; and by this means I rushed headlong upon sorrow, confusion, and error. Thanks be unto thee for all, O thou my Delight, my Glory, my Confidence, and my God. O Lord, I give thee thanks for all thy gifts; but, I beseech thee, keep them safe for me. For so shalt thou also preserve me, and those things which thou hast given me shall be increased and perfected in me. Yea, and I shall be with thee, for it is thou who hast given me being.

BOOK TWO

He entereth into the consideration of the sensuality of his
youth

I WILL call to mind the impurity of my life past and the
unclean corruptions of my soul; not for any love that I bear
to them, but for that which I owe to thee, O my God.
For love of thy love, O Lord, I do it, recording my most
wicked ways in the very bitterness of my soul, that
thou mayest grow sweet to me; thou who art no counterfeit,
but a happy and secure sweetness. Recovering me from
that division of myself, whereby I was all torn in pieces,
whilst, being averted from thee, the One, I vanished away
into the many. For in my youth I did sometimes burn with
a kind of hellish desire to be satisfied, and I dared to
run wild in many luxuriant pleasures. But in the meantime
the beauty of my soul was blasted, and in thine eyes,
O Lord, I was putrified, whilst yet I took contentment
in myself and had a care to please the eyes of men.

He accuseth his youth impurely spent

AND what was that wherein I took delight, but to love
and to be beloved? But I did not contain myself within
the enlightening bonds of friendship, wherein soul is
knit to soul. But there rose up certain foggy vapours
from my unclean desires and by the bubbling up of my
youth, which did obscure and benight my soul so far,
that it could not distinguish the beauty of chaste love from
the muddy darkness of lust. Both of them did confusedly
boil in me; and they carried me, in that unsettled age

of mine, over the precipices of unjust desires into the very whirlpool of sins, wherein they plunged me.

Thy wrath increased towards me, and I knew it not. I was already grown deaf by the continual noise of that chain which my sins had framed, in punishment for the pride of my soul. So I went yet further from thee, and thou sufferedst me. I was tossed up and down, and was poured out like water. I was scattered and did even seethe over in the midst of my fornications, and thou heldest thy peace. O thou, my late found Joy, thou heldest thy peace, and I still went yet farther off from thee, in pursuit of more and yet more fruitless seed-plots of sorrow, with a kind of proud dejection and a restless weariness.

Oh who would then have qualified that misery of mine, and have made me use the fading beauty of these inferior things with moderation, and so far cast a bridle upon these delights, as that the waves of my youth might have aspired no further than to break themselves upon the shore of a marriage bed; if I could not have contented myself without getting of children, as thy law, O Lord, ordains, who dost so frame this offspring of our mortality; being able to assuage, with thy soft hand, the pain of these thorns to them who are shut out of thy paradise. For thine omnipotency is not far from us, even then when we are far from thee.

But indeed I would that I had more carefully given ear to the sound of thy thunders, "*Nevertheless, such shall have tribulation of the flesh; but I spare you*"; and again, "*It is good for a man that he touch not a woman*"; and yet again, "*He that hath no wife fixeth his thoughts upon those things which are of God, to know how he may please him; but he that is married employeth himself upon the things of the world, to know how he may please his wife.*" Had I considered these words more attentively, had I become more entirely chaste *for the kingdom of heaven*, more happily might I have expected thine embracements.

But I, miserable wretch, having forsaken thee, did even

boil up again with the fervour of lust, following still the fury of my foul course and forsaking thee. I transgressed thy commandments, but I escaped not thy punishments, for who under heaven can do that? But thou wert ever present with me, being mercifully cruel, and sprinkling with extreme disgusts all my unlawful pleasures, that so I might be drawn to a desire of seeking pleasure without disgust. And where could this be found but in thee only, O Lord? In thee, *who feignest that there is pain in keeping thy law,* who dost wound us that thou mayest cure us, and who killest us, lest otherwise we should die in thy displeasure. Where was I, and how far off was I exiled from the dear delights of thy house, in that sixteenth year of my age, when the madness of unbridled lust took absolute dominion over me, unto which I wholly resigned myself? That lust which, by the shameless example of men, is made as if it were lawful, though it is prohibited by thy law. My friends took no care to deliver me by a course of marriage from the ruin that I was falling into; but the only care they took was that I might grow a famous orator, and be able by power of speech to persuade men.

Of a journey which he made in respect of his studies, and of the purpose which his parents had therein

For that year my studies were intermitted, when, being come back from Madaura, whither—as to a place near at hand—I had gone to get Rhetoric and other learning, the money was being saved, which might carry me further off, namely to Carthage. And this purpose grew rather from the courage and great affection which my father had than from his means, for he was an inhabitant of Tagaste, nothing rich. To whom do I relate these things? Not unto thee, O my God, do I relate them, but in thy presence to my fellows of flesh and blood, whereof some few may fall upon the sight of this book. And to what end do I this? That

I myself and whosoever reads it may consider from what profundity we are to call upon thee. Yet what is nearer thine ears than a heart which confesseth thee, and a life which is animated by faith?

Who then did not commend and extol my father because he, beyond the strength of his estate, accommodated his son with all things that were needful for the journey, that he might be able to study far from home; for many persons, richer by far than he, did no such thing as this for their children. Yet that same father never troubled himself with thinking how I might grow towards thee, or how chaste I might be, but only that I might be a man of culture; although withal the field of my heart were untilled and forsaken by thee, O Lord, who art the only lawful and good Lord thereof.

But when in my sixteenth year I grew idle at home with my parents, and through certain domestic needs was detained from going to the schools, the brambles of unclean desire grew up even over my head, and there was no hand to root them up. Nay, my father, observing my budding manhood, when I was at the baths, and finding youth to be lively stirring in me—as if thereby he had been put into a desire to have grandchildren of me—did gladly relate it to my mother: rejoicing in that intoxicating wine whereby the world is made to forget thee, the Creator thereof who art divine and invisible, and to love thy meanest creatures instead of thee, by an extreme perversion and abasement of the will. For at this time he was still a catechumen and that only recently. But my mother, in whose heart thou hadst already begun to build a temple and a holy habitation for thyself, did fall thereon into a pious fear and trembling, lest my ways—seeing I was as yet no faithful Christian—might prove crooked; as theirs are wont to be *who cast thee behind their back, instead of turning their faces towards thee*. Woe be unto me; and dare I say that thou, O my God, heldest thy peace when I was going further from thee? Is it true, indeed, that thou didst hold thy peace? Whose then but thine were those words which thou didst so often sing in my ears, by means of my mother, thy faithful servant? But yet did it never enter into my heart to do as she desired. For she advised me—and I remember well she did it with extreme solicitude—that I should keep myself pure from all women, and especially from any man's wife; which seemed to me to be but old wives' counsels, the which I should be ashamed to follow. But they indeed were thine, although I knew it not, thinking that thou heldest thy peace and it was only she who spoke, by whom thou wast not silent to me. Thus, in her person, thou wast contemned by me her son, *the son of thy handmaid and thy servant*.

Yet then I knew it not, but went on headlong with so great blindness amongst my companions, that I would be ashamed to be less vicious than, by their bragging of their wickedness, I understood that they were; for so much the more was their bragging as they were the more beastly. And we delighted in doing ill, not only for the pleasure of the act, but even for a desire of praise. What indeed is worthy of blame but only vice? Yet I, lest I should be ashamed, became more vicious; and, when I wanted means of growing as wicked as the rest, would falsely affirm myself to have done that which indeed I had not done, lest I might seem so much the more abject as I was more innocent, and so much the more poorly spirited, as I was more chaste.

Behold in what company I went up and down those streets of Babylon, and weltered in the mire thereof, as if I had been regaled in a bed of spices and precious odours. And, that I might be knit the more firmly to the very root of sin, my invisible enemy did tread upon me and seduced me as he listed, for I was then right willing to be seduced. Yea, and the mother of my flesh, although for her own part she *was fled out of the midst of Babylon,* yet was she still lingering in the outskirts thereof. Wherefore, on the one side she exhorted me to chastity, yet, on the other, she carried some respect of that which she had heard her husband say concerning me. And she inclined to remove present dangers and to keep my passions within bounds by procuring a wife for me, if these could not be cut off wholly to the quick. Yet she desired not even that so very much, lest the clog of a wife might have hindered her hopes of me, not those hopes of the other world, but the hope of fame through learning, which both my parents did extremely desire that I might attain. The one, because he thought little of thee at all; the other because she conceived that a course of regular studies would not only be of no prejudice to me, but of much profit towards my finding out and possessing of thee.

These, so far as I can remember and conjecture, were the dispositions of my parents towards me. In the meantime the reins were loosed to me without the curb of a due severity, which gave too loose a scope to my affections. And in all of them there was a mist, which conveyed itself between me and the beauty of thy truth, O my God, *and my iniquity stood out, as it were with fatness.*

How he took fruit out of another man's orchard

THY law indeed doth punish theft, O Lord, and this law is written in the hearts of men, which sin itself cannot blot out. For what thief will endure another man that is a thief? Nay, a rich thief will not excuse another man that steals, though he be urged by want. Yet I must needs commit a theft; and I performed it not constrained thereto by any misery or penury, but through a weariness of doing well and by an abundance of iniquity. For I stole that which I had at home both in greater plenty and much better. Neither cared I to enjoy that which I stole; but I took pleasure in the very theft and sin itself.

A pear-tree there was near our vineyard laden with fruit, which tempted not greatly either the sight or the taste. To the shaking and robbing thereof certain most wicked youths, of whom I was one, went at dead of night; for until then, according to our lewd custom, we had prolonged our horse-play in the open streets. We carried away thence huge burdens of fruit, not for our own eating but to be cast before the hogs; and, if we did taste thereof at all, it was not for any reason so much as because we would do that which was not lawful.

Behold my heart, O my God, behold my heart, whereon thou hadst mercy whilst yet it was even in the lowest depths. Behold now, let my heart confess to thee what it meant to seek in this theft; whilst I was wicked to no purpose, and there was no cause of this my malice but malice itself. It was deformed, and yet I loved it; I loved to perish. I loved the sin, not that which I obtained by the same; I loved the sin itself. And my deformed soul, springing away from the security that is in thee, was abandoned to a total ruin; not desiring any profit from my shame, but only thirsting after shame itself.

That no man sinneth but upon some clear motive

Now there is a beauty belonging to all things that be fair, to gold and silver and to all the works of thy hands. There is a kind of sympathy in the touch of flesh and blood, which is extremely agreeable; and every sense hath its proper object, wherein it is pleased. The honour of the world and the power of ruling and overcoming hath its own delight, from the frustrating whereof the desire of revenge proceedeth. But for the obtaining of these things, O Lord, we ought not to depart from thee nor decline from thy law. The life whereby we live hath in it a pleasure and delight, through the proportion and conveniency which it carrieth to all these other fair but inferior creatures. The friendship also of men is delightful for its ties and for the union which it maketh of many minds in one.

By occasion of these things and the like is sin committed, when things, which are only good in the lowest degree, are sought after with an extreme desire, and such as are good and excellent in the highest degree are forsaken; the which is thyself, O Lord our God, thy Truth and thy Law. For even these lower things carry a kind of inferior pleasure with them, though they are not like my God, who created all things. *In him is the just man delighted,* nay he is the total delight of such a one.

When, therefore, inquiry is made why any wickedness may have been committed, it is usually thought to have proceeded either from a desire of obtaining, or a fear of losing some of these things, which we have said to be of the lower rank. For even they have in them a kind of decency and beauty, although, if they be compared to those higher goods which make men truly blessed, they are altogether vile and base. One man hath murdered another, what moved him to it? Either he desired his wife, or his estate, or he would rob him of that whereby himself might live. Or he was afraid lest the other might put upon him some such injury. Or else, having been wronged, he thirsted for revenge. But would anyone murder a man without any other occasion than only for the delight he takes in murdering? It is not credible.

For as touching Catiline, that man of whom it is said that he was stupidly and strangely cruel, even for the very delight he had in wickedness and cruelty, there is a cause also assigned for that. Namely the wish to keep himself in practice, that so his hand or mind might not grow stiff in idleness. And why so? That, by the diligent exercise of himself in such crimes, when once he had subdued and sacked the city of Rome, he might obtain honour, dominion, and riches; being free from the danger of the Law, which indeed he feared through conscience of his own villainy, and from all possibility of want, wherewith he was threatened by wasting of his private fortune. So that not even Catiline himself did love the

very wickedness that he committed, but it was another thing
he loved, for the obtaining whereof he would be wicked.

*All those things which, under the show of good, invite
us to sin, are to be found true and perfect in God alone*

WHAT therefore did I, miserable creature, love in thee, O
thou theft of mine? Oh thou nocturnal sin, which I
committed in the sixteenth year of my age? Thou wert
not beautiful, since thou wast theft; or indeed art thou
anything, that I may thus talk to thee? That fruit which
we stole had a kind of beauty belonging to it, because it
was thy creature, O thou most beautiful Creator of all
things, thou God, my sovereign and my one true Good.
That fruit was beautiful, yet it was not that which my soul
desired, for I had better at home in abundance, and
I gathered this, only that I might steal. Yea, having
gathered it, I cast it away, and only fetched from it the sin
on which I feasted, finding therein my delight. For, if I
tasted any of the fruit, my sin was the sauce which made it
sweet.

See now, O Lord my God, I am seeking for that which
might delight me in this theft, and behold, there appears
nothing to me. I say not only that nothing appears whereby
in Justice or in Prudence I should be delighted, but neither
as I might take pleasure in the conversation or mind of a
man, or in the memory, or in the senses, or in vegetable life.
Nor is there aught that is fair, as in the beauty and order of
the stars; or as the earth or sea is fair, being full of fresh
offspring which supplies the place of what is spent. Nay,
there was not here even such counterfeit or lame show of
beauty as is wont to follow from those vicious actions which
deceive us. For Pride striveth towards advancement; whereas thou only, O God, art advanced above all. And
Ambition seeketh nothing but honour and glory; whereas
thou art honourable above all things and eternally glorious.

And Cruelty will have her power feared; yet who is to be feared but only God, from whose power what can be delivered or withdrawn, either by force or fraud, or when, or where, or whither, or by whom?

The dalliances of the amorous ask for return of love; yet neither is there anything more dearly sweet than Charity, nor aught to be delighted in more soundly than that Truth of thine, which is fair and bright above all. Curiosity seems to affect a desire of knowledge; whereas it is thou who dost supremely comprehend all things. Even Ignorance and Stupidity itself is cloaked by the name of Simplicity and Innocence; yet nothing can be found more simple than thou art, and what can be more innocent than thou, whose every work is all opposed to ill? Sloth too aspireth to a kind of quietness; yet where is true repose but in our Lord? Sensuality desires to be called but satiety or abundance; yet thou art indeed the fulness and the inexhausted plenty of incorruptible pleasure. Prodigality would fain seem to be liberality; but thou, most royally bountiful, art the sole giver of all good. Covetousness is eager to possess much; and thou possessest all things. Envy is ever wrangling about excellence; but what can pretend with thee for excellency? Anger seeks revenge; but who doth revenge more justly than thou? Fear is apprehensive of sudden and unusual things, such as are contrary to the things that are desired, and so is careful to be secure; but what can be sudden or unusual to thee, or *who can separate from thee anything which thou lovest,* or where, but with thee, can there be found any firm security? Sorrow is afflicted for the loss of those things which Desire found pleasant to enjoy; for she wisheth to be like unto thee, who canst not be deprived of anything.

Thus doth the soul commit fornication when it is estranged from thee, and seeketh, otherwhere than in thee, those things which it can never find sincere and pure unless and when it doth return to thee. Perversely do all they affect to be like thee, who depart far from thee and raise themselves against thee. Yet even so, by this kind of imitation, do they declare thee to be the Creator of all things; for that there is not any place whereto they can withdraw away from thee.

What, therefore, did I love in that theft of mine, and wherein did I affect to be like my Lord, though but in that perverse and vicious manner? Was I disposed to offend thy law by a kind of deceit, when I could not do it by a strong hand? That, whilst I was indeed no better than a kind of bondslave, I might yet counterfeit a false liberty, by doing that without punishment, which I could not do without sin, through a dark and misty resemblance of thine omnipotence. Behold, here is that servant of thine who fled from his Lord, and sought to hide himself in the shadow. O rottenness, O monster of life and profoundness of death. How could a man take pleasure in doing a thing which was not lawful, for no other reason but only because it was not lawful?

He giveth thanks to God for having forgiven his sins, and for preserving him from many others

What return shall I make unto the Lord, when now I call these things to mind, and yet my soul is not filled with fear thereby? I will love thee, O Lord, and will give thanks unto thee, and will confess unto thy name. For thou hast forgiven in me so great and so many wicked deeds, and hast dissolved my sins like ice. To thy grace and mercy also I ascribe it, that I have not sinned yet more grievously: for what sin could I not have committed, I who fell into this, for the mere affection I had unto the sin itself? All these sins I acknowledge to have been by thee forgiven; both those which, by my will, I have committed, and those which, by thy help, I have not committed.

What man is there who, considering his own frailty,

dares yet to attribute unto his own strength his chastity or his innocency? For then must he love thee the less, as if to him that mercy of thine had been less necessary, by which thou dost forgive their sins to them that return to thee after having fallen. He then that, being called by thee, hath followed thy voice and escaped those things which now he finds me to be remembering and confessing against myself, let him not laugh at me because I am recovered by the care of that Physician, to whom was due that he should not be sick at all, or else that he should be less sick. Therefore, let him love thee as much, nay, let him do so more, since he seeth me delivered from so many loathsome diseases of sin, by the same God through whom he seeth himself preserved from so great a burden.

What it was which he loved in that fault which he committed

What profit did I receive at any time, miserable me, *by those things which now I blush to relate;* and especially by that theft, wherein I loved nothing but the theft? And since there was nothing else to love, seeing that the thing itself was naught, I may account myself so much the more miserable. Alone I would never have committed it—for I can now recover the state of my mind as then it was—alone I should never have committed it. So then I did also love the company of them with whom I did it. There was then something else besides the theft that I loved? Nay indeed, there was nothing else; for that something, the company of which I spake, is nothing.

Who then can teach me what it is in truth, this act of mine? Who indeed but he who illuminates my heart and discerneth the very secrets of it? What is this thing which I have taken in hand to seek, to consider, and to discuss? For if I had loved that fruit which I stole and if I had desired to enjoy it, I might have done it alone. For I should thus have attained to gratify my lust for pleasure, without needing to inflame the itch of my own desire, by rubbing it on others of like mind to me. But, since I took no pleasure in the fruit, the pleasure lay only in the sin itself, to which the company of others, who jointly offended with me, did concur.

That company in evil is a contagious thing

WHAT kind of state or inclination of mind was that of mine? In truth it was too utterly deformed, and woe was unto me, who had it. But yet, what was it? *"Who is he that understandeth his sins?"* It was a delight and laughter, which tickled us even to the very heart, to think that we were deceiving them who feared no such thing of us; and who, if they had known of it, would forcibly have prevented us. Yet still, why was I delighted in this, that I did it not alone? Is it because no man when alone is readily moved to laughter? Ordinarily, indeed, a man doth not laugh alone. Yet sometimes such a one is even overcome with laughter, when anything which is extremely ridiculous doth occur, either to his mind or to his senses. But as for me, I should never have done it alone, infallibly I should not. Behold here, O Lord, the lively representation of my soul. Alone I should not have committed that theft, wherein the thing stolen pleased me not, but the theft itself; alone I should have taken no pleasure in it, and should have given over the purpose. O friendship, thou art too unfriendly, thou inscrutable seducer of our minds. Out of sport and play groweth the desire to hurt, and a coveting of another man's loss; yet with no appetite either to profit oneself, or to be revenged upon another. But whensoever it is said, "Let us go, let us do this or that," we are ashamed if we do not show ourselves to be past shame.

Of man's perverse nature and of his misery

WHO will open and discover to me this most intricate and crooked knot of my perverse nature? It is deformed, I cannot endure to behold or to reflect upon it. It is thou, whom I would fain behold; thou who art Justice and Innocence, most fair and beautiful to chaste eyes; who, to the insatiable, yieldest satiety. With thee is abundance and wealth of true repose, and a life that is subject to no degree of perturbation. He that enters into thee doth truly *enter into the joy of his Lord;* he shall have nothing to fear, but shall find himself most happy in thee, who art happiness itself. I fell from thee, O my God, and wandered far, too far from thy stability in that youth of mine; and I became unto myself thereby a land of want and misery.

BOOK THREE

How he carried himself when he first went to Carthage

I CAME to Carthage, where there was, as it were, a frying-pan full of flagitious loves, which crackled round about me on every side. I was not yet immersed in love, but I desired to be so; and, with a secret kind of poverty, I hated myself for not being poor enough. I was in search of somewhat that I might love, loving the mere thought of love, and I despised the way of safety wherein there were no pitfalls. For my soul was famished within me, for want of that spiritual food which is thyself, O my God. Yet I did not hunger after that food, nay, I was without all appetite for the incorruptible nourishment, not that I had been full fed therewith, but because, the more empty my stomach was thereof, the more queasy and fastidious was it. For this reason my soul fell sick, and broke forth, as it were, with ulcers, being miserably greedy to be eased by the solace of sensible creatures, which yet, if they had not life, could not deserve to be beloved. It was a dear thing to me to love and to be loved, and the more sweet if I arrived to enjoy the person whom I loved. I troubled therefore the water of friendship with the diet of unclean appetite, and I obscured the brightness thereof with hellish lust. Yet even when I was thus ugly and unclean I would needs be counted for a choice and polished person, with a superlative kind of vanity. So too I rushed headlong into love, whereby I desired to be enslaved. O my God, O thou who art my mercy, with how much gall didst thou sprinkle those delights of mine, and how good thou wert to me in doing so. For I was loved, I obtained my wished for bondage of enjoyment, in the midst of my jollity I was tied with heavy

chains, that so I might be beaten with the burning rods
of jealousy, suspicion, fears, angers, and brawls.

Of stage plays

THEN too I was enraptured by plays represented upon the
stage, which were full of images wherein my own miseries
were expressed, and these served as fuel to my fire. How
comes it to pass that a man is desirous to be made sorrowful
by beholding sad and tragical events, which he would not
willingly suffer in his own person? Yet, as a spectator, he
desireth to conceive thereby, and that very grief itself
is a pleasure to him. What is this but a wretched madness?
For they are the most affected by those things, who are the
least free from such passions as are there expressed. Howsoever, when a man suffers in himself, he is said to
have misery; but when he hath compassion or suffereth
with others, he is said to have pity. But indeed, what kind
of pity can be felt for those false things that are enacted
on the stage? For the hearer is not drawn thereby to help
the other, but only is he invited to be sorry with him; and
men do so much the more esteem the actors of these
imaginary shows; as they are made the more sorry by
them. And if these ancient or feigned tragedies of
men are so enacted that the onlooker be not made sad
thereby, he betaketh him away from thence, despising
and reprehending the thing; but if he grieveth, he
remaineth enraptured and weeps for joy.

Hereby it should seem that tears and grief are loved, yet
the truth is that all men desire joy. Or perhaps, though a
man love not to feel misery, he will yet be glad to feel pity;
and, since he cannot do this without some sorrow, for this
cause only we may say that grief is loved. And this proceeds
from a certain vein of friendship. But whither goes that
stream and whither flows it, but into that torrent of burning pitch, into those vast stoves of infernal lust, wherein the

soul, perverted of her own free will and cast down from the beauty and calm of heaven, is first distracted and then dejected?

Shall we therefore banish pity from us? Not so. Let us rather be content to love grief sometimes. But thou, O my soul, take heed of uncleanness; in the sight of my God and my Director, the God of my fathers, *who is praiseworthy and supremely exalted for all eternity;* take heed, I say, of uncleanness. For now I do not take myself to be without pity; but then, in those theatres, I had a sympathy of joy with such as played the part of lovers when wickedly they enjoyed one another, though it were only in the fiction of a stage play; and when they failed of their end I was sad, like one that pitied them, and yet I was delighted in both those contrary successes. But now I much more pity him that rejoiceth in his wickedness, than him who is afflicted, be it never so much, by the less of a pernicious pleasure and a miserable felicity. This is indeed a more true pity, but in it certainly a man takes no delight. For though he may be acknowledged to perform a work of charity who is sorry for a man in misery, yet such a one, if he be truly merciful, would rather there were no such cause for him to be sorry. For as it is impossible for one that loves another to hate him also, so it is impossible that he, who hath true and sincere pity for another man, should wish that he might still be miserable, to the end that he himself might still be pitiful.

There are, therefore, certain kinds of grief to be approved of, but none that is to be loved. For so dost thou proceed, O Lord my God, who lovest the souls of men with infinitely more purity than we do, even so dost thou have mercy on them far more divinely, because thou art wounded with no grief. *But what man is able to arrive at this?* Yet I, wretched man that I was, in those days did love to grieve, and sought for somewhat to grieve at; when, in the false and counterfeit stage-misery of others, that action of the player did please me better which struck the tears out of my eyes.

What marvel was it then that I, being a forlorn sheep all wandering from thy flock and not content to be under thy custody, was thus defiled with loathsome and infectious sores? And hence came the love I bore to that grief, whereby in truth I was not deeply pierced—for I loved not to suffer those things in myself, but only to behold them in others—that, by my hearing that which they devised, I might be wounded merely in the superficies and skin of my soul. Yet there did flow from this a burning swelling and a consuming kind of festering sore, as happens oft when the flesh is torn by nails. Such was the life I led, but, O my God, was it indeed to be called life?

Of his conversation among the young students of the law

AND thy faithful mercy did hover over me, round about, though afar off. Upon what great impieties did I waste my life! How did I follow a sacrilegious curiosity so that, after I had forsaken thee, it might carry me into the bottomless pit, to the service of those devils who were circumventing me and by whose means thou didst chastise me. I did presume also so far as to desire and plan a business, whereby I might gather the fruit of death, within the walls of thy church at the celebrating of thy divine mysteries. For the which thou didst scourge me with grievous pains, O my God, my infinite mercy, my refuge from those terrible dangers amid which I wandered with neck outstretched in the desire I had to be thereby so much the further off from thee; delighting in mine own ways and not in thine, and loving the liberty of a runaway.

Those studies of mine, which were esteemed liberal, had for their object the Tribunals of Justice, to the end that I might excel therein and be so much more worthy of praise as I should be more able to deceive. For such is the blindness of men that even their very blindness is the thing they brag of. And by that time I was grown to be a great man in the Rhetoric school, and I took pleasure in it with pride, and I did even swell with the puff of vanity. Yet was I much more modest than some others, as thou knowest, O Lord, and far off from the destructions which were wrought by the " Destroyers "—for that cruel and devilish name was adopted as the badge of their fine manners—amongst whom yet I lived with a kind of shameless bashfulness, because I was not of like humour to them. For I conversed with them and I was delighted sometimes with their familiarity, though I did ever abhor their actions, that is their " destructions," whereby they did wickedly offend the modesty of such as were but new-comers, scoffing at them upon no occasion and thereby feeding their own lewd mirth. For there is nothing more like the actions of devils than that fashion of theirs, and by no name can they be more fitly called than " Destroyers "; being themselves first utterly perverted and destroyed by those deceitful spirits, who secretly seduce and mock at them in this very matter, that they take delight to abuse and scoff at others.

How the book of Cicero, called Hortensius, *stirred him up to the search after true philosophy*

AMONGST these therefore, in my years of indiscretion, I attended to the study of Eloquence, for this it was wherein I desired to be eminent, out of a contemptible and ambitious end, to enjoy the delight of human glory. Thus, in the ordinary course of my study, I came upon a book by a certain Cicero, whose tongue almost all men do admire, but not his heart. This book of his containeth an exhortation to Philosophy, and it is called *Hortensius*. And this book altered my affection and made me address prayers to thee, O Lord, giving me other desires and purposes than I had before. All empty hopes did instantly grow base in mine eyes, and, with incredible heat of heart, did I aspire towards the immortality of wisdom, for now I had begun to rise that I might return to thee. That book indeed I applied not to the whetting of my tongue, which art I was buying, as appeared, at my mother's expense—seeing I was now attained to my nineteenth year and my father had died two years before—that book, I say, I applied not to the whetting of my tongue, but it persuaded me that not the manner but the matter of a discourse is to be cared for.

How was I kindled then, O my God, how was I kindled with a desire to fly from earthly things towards thee! And I knew not what thou wert then doing in me; for with thee is Wisdom, and that Greek term " Philosophy " signifieth but the love of Wisdom, to which I was inflamed by that book. Some there are who seduce men by colouring and painting over their errors with the smooth and noble and virtuous name of Philosophy; and almost all they who had been such, whether in its own or in former times, are noted and pointed out in that book. For a profitable admonition of thy spirit is given to men by thy devout and good servant, saying, " *Let no man deceive you by Philosophy and vain persuasions, which are according to the tradition of men and the principles of this world, and not according to Christ. For in him it is that all fulness of the divinity doth dwell corporally.*"

At that time, as thou knowest, O Light of my heart, I had not understood anything of the Apostle's writings; but in the exhortation of Cicero I was chiefly delighted in this, that it stirred up and kindled and inflamed me, not to this or that other sect, but to the loving, and seeking, and finding, and holding, and inseparably embracing of Wisdom itself, wheresoever it might be. In that so great delight this alone cooled me and took me off, that I found not the name of Christ therein; for this name, O Lord, through thy mercy, this name of my Saviour, thy Son, my infant heart had, even in the very milk of my mother, drunk in and carefully retained. And if any discourse whatsoever, though never so learned, so elegant, and so true, had wanted this name, it carried me not away entirely.

He contemned the Holy Scriptures, by reason of the simplicity of the style

I DID therefore resolve that I would study the holy Scripture, to see what kind of thing it was. And behold, I find a thing neither understood by such as are proud, nor yet open to such as are children, but humble in show, sublime in operation, and deeply overshadowed with mysteries. But I was not such a one as that I could have entrance into it, or bow my neck at its approach. When I met with the Scripture in those days, I thought not of it according to that which now I say, but I conceived that it was not worthy to be compared with Cicero's lofty style. For my vanity fled from the humility thereof, and the point of my sight could not pierce into the sense. In truth it is the nature thereof that it grow with the growth of the babe; but I disdained to be a little one and, being swollen big with pride, I took myself to be a grown man.

How he was deceived by the Manichees, and the misery to which they brought him

I FELL therefore upon certain men who, proudly doting, were too carnal and babbling, in whose mouth the snares of the devil were spread and a kind of bird-lime was made by putting together the syllables of thy name, yea and of the name also of Jesus Christ our Lord, and of the Paraclete, the Comforter, the Holy Ghost. All these were frequent in their mouths, forasmuch as concerned the sound and clatter of the tongue; but their heart was void of all Truth. "The Truth, the Truth," said they, and kept saying it often to me; *yet was it not to be found in them.* But they spake false things, not only of thee who art Truth itself, but even of the elements of this world, thy creature. Of which thing, even if the Philosophers themselves had spoken truth, yet ought I to have transcended them for love of thee, O my Father, my supreme good, the very beauty itself of all things that are beautiful. O Truth, Truth, how inwardly then did the very quintessence of my soul sigh after thee, when they did often and in many ways cry out thy name to me, but with the voice alone, or in their many ponderous books. These were the dishes wherein, when I was hungering, they served me up the sun and moon, goodly creatures of thine yet only creatures, not thee, nor yet thy first works. For thy spiritual creatures are before all these thy corporal works, be these latter never so celestial and bright.

Yet I did not hunger and thirst after those first works of thine but after thyself, who art Truth indeed, *wherein is no change nor shadow of alteration.* Yet still in those dishes they served me with glorious fictions; and it had been better to love the very sun, which we see with our eyes, than those fantastic things, the fictions of a mind deceived by the eyes. Yet, because I thought that it was thou, I fed upon it; not, I confess, with any greediness, because it did not savour in my mouth like unto thee. For thou wert not like unto those vain things, neither was I nourished but rather exhausted by them. For the meat which men dream that they eat in sleep, is very like the meat of waking men; yet by it such as sleep are not nourished, because they are but dreaming. But those other fancies were no whit like unto thee, as thou hast since manifested thyself unto me, because they were corporeal fancies and false bodies, the which are less truly bodies than those which we see with the eyes of the flesh, whether they be bodies celestial or bodies terrestrial. In common with the birds and the beasts we see these bodies, and

they are more real unto us than the things which we
do but imagine. And again, the things that we recall to
mind are far more real than the other greater and
even infinite things which we can conjure up with
our imagination; yet with such trash as this was I fed,
save indeed that it fed me not. But thou, O my Love, in
whom I languish that I may gather strength, art
neither these bodies, albeit celestial, which we see, nor yet
those others, which are also there although we see them not.
For them thou didst create and, when thou wilt, thou canst
make nobler ones than they. How far off then art thou from
being those fictions of mine, those fictions of bodies which
have no being at all. For the images that we frame of bodies
which have a being are more certain than these, and
the bodies themselves are again more certain than they, yet
thou art none of them; nay, thou art not the soul itself,
which is the life of the body. The life indeed of bodies is a
more noble and more stable substance than the body itself,
but thou art the life of souls, the life of lives, living of thine
own life, and thou art not subject to any mutation, O thou,
the Life of my soul.

Where, therefore, wert thou then to me, and how
far off? For far off did I wander and rove from thee, barred
even from being satisfied with the husks of the swine,
whom with like husks I was feeding. How much
better than these base traps of error are those paltry fables
of the Grammarians and Poets? For the verse and poem
of Medea's flight are of more use than the five elements
variously transformed through the five dens of darkness,
which have not material being and slay him that puts his
faith in them.[1] For verse and song may earn me a true
livelihood; and as for Medea flying, though I sang the
song I did not affirm it to be true, nor, if I heard it sung,
did I believe it; but those other things I believed. Woe, woe
be unto me, *by what steps was I carried down even to the
very depths of hell,* when, labouring and panting through

[1] See Note 3.

want of Truth, I sought thee, O my God? For to thee I confess myself, who didst pity me even when I did not confess, I sought thee not according to the understanding of the mind, whereby thou madest me to excel the beasts, but according to this fleshly sense of mine. But thou wast more interior to me than the innermost part of my soul, and superior to the highest part thereof. Thus did I stumble upon that bold woman, void of wisdom, the enigma that Solomon hangs out, sitting in the gate of her house and saying, "*Come, eat ye greedily this hidden bread and drink this sweet stolen water.*" This woman seduced me because she found me wandering abroad in the lust of my eye, and ruminating that food within myself which by that lust I had devoured.

On the doctrine of the Manichees, and its absurdity

FOR I was ignorant of something else, namely in what true Being consists, and I was persuaded in a somewhat subtle manner to conform myself to the belief of those foolish deceivers when they asked of me, Whence cometh Evil; and whether God is concluded within a corporeal form; whether he hath hair and nails; and whether they were to be accounted just who at one and the same time had many wives, or who slew men, or who sacrificed beasts. I, being ignorant, was troubled with these things; and, whilst I did indeed recede from Truth, I thought myself to be making towards it, because I knew not that Evil was no more than a mere privation of Good, and next indeed to that which is altogether nothing. And how should I come to see it, since mine eyes could reach to see nothing but Bodies and my mind could not go beyond ideas imagined of the brain? And I knew not that *God is a spirit* who hath no parts either of length or of breadth; and hath no bulk, because the part of a bulk must be less than the whole; for if that bulk be infinite, that part thereof which is limited within a certain space must needs be less than is the whole infinite; and then it will not be all everywhere, as a spirit and as God is.

And I was wholly ignorant what that might be in us in respect whereof we were like unto God, and wherefore we were termed in Scripture to be *made after the image of God*. Nor was I acquainted with that true interior justice, which judgeth not by custom but by the most righteous law of Almighty God, whereby times and places were governed according to the exigencies thereof, whereas itself is everywhere the same and not here after one manner and there after another; according to which Abraham and Isaac and Jacob and all those others were just, being praised as such by the mouth of God. For these indeed are held to be wicked by such as judge ignorantly, who measure *according to man's day,* judging the proceedings of all the generality of mankind by the small part thereof to which they are privy. As if one who, knowing not what belongs to every part of a man when arming him, should clap one of the greaves upon his head and a helmet upon his foot, and then should murmur because they do not fit. Or as if, when public justice should command the shops to be shut after noon upon some certain day, one should chafe for not being suffered to sell his wares, although the next day he might lawfully do it. Or as if a man, on seeing that in some house one servant will handle certain dishes, which it is not permitted to the cup-bearer to touch, or that somewhat is done in the stable which is forbidden in the dining-hall, should be aggrieved because each house or each family hath its several customs, and not all the same. Such are they that storm when they hear that it was lawful for holy men to do in one age that which is not lawful in this, or that God, for certain temporary reasons, commanded them one thing and these another, whereas both did observe the same rule of justice; or, when they observe that in one man, and in one day, and in one house, a thing agreeth to one part and not to another, and that the same thing, which before was lawful, within an hour after will not be so, and that somewhat is permitted or commanded in that corner, which is justly prohibited and punished in this other.

Shall the rule of Justice, therefore, be said to swerve and vary from itself? No; but the times, over which indeed it doth preside, are not all like to one another, because they are times. So men, whose life upon earth is short, because they are not able by means of their experience to knit the causes of former ages and nations, which they have never seen, to these others which are before their eyes—though in one person or day or house the same man can easily discern what is convenient for each part, ministry, person, and moment—because of this, I say, men are scandalized by the former things while they approve of the later.

These things I knew not or marked not then. Though they did even strike mine eyes on every side, yet I saw them not. I composed verses, in which it was not lawful for me to place every foot thereof where I listed, but in one kind of verse I must do it after one manner, and after another in another kind of verse. Nay, even in the selfsame verse I could not put every foot where I would. Yet the Art, whereby I made verses, taught me not merely to frame one sort in one place, but all sorts of verse everywhere. Yet I considered not that Justice, which those good and holy men obeyed, did contain all those things, which God commanded, in a much more excellent and sublime manner, and that it was not in the least degree variable; although, if we take the times in sunder, all those things were not disposed and commanded together, but each at its proper and particular season. So, being blind, I reprehended those holy fathers, not only for that they used their present day as God commanded and inspired them to do, but also because of their predictions of things future, according as God had revealed unto them.

*The variety and root of great sins, and how they are
    punished*

Is it at any time or in any case an unjust thing *to love God
with all the heart, with all the soul and with all the mind;
and our neighbour as ourselves?* No. Therefore those
crimes which are against nature are ever to be detested
and punished, such as were they of the Sodomites. For if all
nations were to commit the same through their wickedness,
they would thereby be obnoxious to the divine law, which
did not so make men that they might abuse one another.
For society itself, that fellowship which ought to exist
between man and God, is violated, when the Nature,
whereof he is the author, is defiled by the perversion of lust.

But those great crimes which are committed against the
customs of men are to be avoided, according to the diversity
of places and persons, for such customs vary. Yet no law
which is ratified by the constitution or the custom of any
city or nation must be transgressed at the fancy of any man,
be he native or foreigner. For it is not becoming that any
part shall rebel against the whole whereof it is a part. But
when God commandeth anything which is against the
custom or compact of any people, although it were
never done there before, it must then be done; and if it
were discontinued it must be restored, or if before it were
not instituted, it must be so then. For if it be lawful
for a King, in the state over which he hath dominion, to
command somewhat which, till then, neither he nor
any other had ever commanded, and it is not against the
common weal that he should be obeyed—nay it would
be against it if he were not obeyed, since it is a general
agreement of human society to obey them that rule—how
much more, without hesitation, must we obey God,
who, without any doubt at all, is to be obeyed in all things
whatsoever he commandeth. For as in the hierarchy of

human society the greater power receives obedience from the less, so God is to be preferred before all.

So is it likewise in respect of crimes, where there is a strong will to do hurt either by reproach or injury. For each of these may spring from the desire of revenge which one enemy hath towards another, or from hope of obtaining some profit, as the robber upon the highway from the traveller; or for the avoiding of some evil, as when another man is feared; or by envying, as the more miserable man doth envy him that is more happy; or as he that is in prosperity towards someone who, he fears, may grow equal to him, or who is already a cause of grief in that he has equalled him; or else for the very pleasure that he taketh in another man's hurt, as the spectators at a gladiatorial show, and all such as scorn and scoff at others. These are the chief heads of iniquity, which sprout forth from the inordinate appetite that men have either for command, or for curiosity, or for sensuality, or from one or two of these, or from all together. And men lead a wicked life against the three and the seven, which form that *instrument of ten strings,* thy Decalogue, O thou most high and most sweet God.

Yet what flagitious sins can be committed against thee, who canst not be dishonoured, or what crimes can be committed against thee, who canst not be hurt? But thou revengest that which men commit against themselves because, when they sin against thee, they do also wickedly against their own souls, and *their iniquity gives the lie to itself,* either by corrupting or perverting that nature which thou hast ordained, or by the immoderate use of things which thou hast permitted, or towards the use of things not permitted, by a *burning in lust which is contrary to nature;* or else when they are guilty of raging in mind and in words against thee, and so do they *kick against the pricks;* or when, by breaking open the hedges of human society, they do audaciously rejoice either in private bargains of pleasure or in wrong of rapine, according to their delight and convenience.

And these things are done when thou art forsaken, O thou fountain of life, who art the only true Creator and Ruler of all things; and when, by a foolish and particular pride, we grow to love that which is but a part of the whole, and which withal is false. But by humble devotion we return to thee again, and thou dost cleanse us from our evil custom, and art merciful to the sins of such as confess them, and dost *hear the groans of thy prisoners,* and dost loose the fetters which we have made for ourselves : but only if we do no more advance against thee the proud horns of liberty, through a covetous desire of enjoying more, which will prove unto us the loss of all, because we love our own private good more than thee, who art the common Good of all.

Of the difference there is between sins, and between the judgement made by God and by man

BUT, besides flagitious sins and heinous crimes and all the many iniquities there be in the world, there are also the faults of such as are making progress; the which are at the same time dispraised by those that judge strictly of them according to the rule of perfection, and yet withal are commended, as carrying in them some hope of good fruit, as a blade of corn does of the grain. Again there are some things like to flagitious sins and heinous crimes, which yet are not sins, because they neither offend thee, our Lord and God, nor human society; as when certain things are procured by a man, things well fitted to his needs and circumstances, but it is uncertain whether or no they were gotten by an inordinate desire of having; or again, when a man is punished by public authority, and it is uncertain whether or no that were done through a love of cruelty. Many things, therefore, are done, which seem disallowable to men and yet are approved by thy testimony; and many things again are commended by men, which by thy testimony are condemned. For the appearance of the act is often different from the intention of him that doth it; and the precise circumstances of the time, which are hidden from us, must often vary.

But when of a sudden thou commandest anything, how unlawful and unexpected soever—though thou hadst once forbidden it; though for some reason thou dost conceal the cause of thy commandment for a time; and though it prove to be against the custom of some particular commonwealth —yet who doubts but that it ought to be done; since that society of men doth truly observe the rule of Justice, which serveth thee? But happy are they who know that thou didst command, for all things are done by them that serve thee, either to perform that which is fit for the present or to foretell those things which are to come.

He speaks with scorn of the Manichees, and their doctrine

I THEN, being ignorant of these things, did scoff at those holy servants and prophets of thine. And what did I, whilst I was scoffing at them, but take order that thou shouldst make a mock of me? For by small and insensible degrees I was drawn to believe such trash as that, when a fig was gathered both it and the mother tree did shed tears of milk. Nevertheless, if any of our Manichean saints had eaten that fig—when forsooth it had first been gathered by the crime of some other man and not his own—he would digest in his bowels and breathe forth therefrom certain Angels, nay rather particles of God himself, while sighing and gasping in his prayers. The which particles of the supreme and true God would still have been tied to that fruit, if they had not been discharged and freed by the tooth and belly of an elected saint. And I, miserable wretch, did believe that more mercy was to be shewed to the fruits of the earth, than to men for whose use they were made. For if any man, who was not a Manichee, being hungry should demand a bit, I should have esteemed it to deserve the very sentence of death, should any be given him.

Of his mother's dream or vision

AND thou *didst send thy hand from on high,* and thou drewest my soul out of that profound darkness, when my mother, thy faithful servant, did weep for me in thy presence more bitterly than mothers are used to bewail the corporal death of their children. For she saw me as it were dead, by the faith and spirit which she had from thee, and thóu didst hearken to her, O Lord. Thou didst hearken to her and didst not despise her tears which, flowing down, did water the earth in all the places where she prayed. I say thou didst hearken to her, or whence came that dream whereby thou didst comfort her and madest her content to trust herself with me, and to let me be at the same table in the same house, which she had begun to refuse, detesting and abhorring the blasphemies of my error? She saw herself standing upon a certain rule of wood, and a glorious young man, all cheerful and well disposed, coming towards her, she herself being sad and even overwhelmed with grief. On his asking her the cause of her sorrow and continual tears— with intent rather to teach her somewhat than to be taught by her, as sometimes happens—and her answering that she lamented my destruction, he advised her for her comfort that she should observe and see that where she was, there was I also. And as soon as she looked, lo! she saw me standing by her upon the very same rule. And whence came this but because thine ears were applied to the petitions of her heart, O thou Good omnipotent, who so takest care of every one of us as if there were none but he alone, and of us all as if each in particular were alone.

Whence also came it that, when she told me of this vision and I would fain have twisted it to mean that she should not despair, because one day she would prove to be of the same religion as I was, she at once without any hesitation made answer: "No, I was not told, 'where he is thou shalt be,' but 'where thou art he will be.'" I confess unto thee, O Lord, that to the uttermost of my remembrance—and I have often recalled it—I was far more moved by this answer of thine, given to me by my mother, and by the quickness thereof—for she was not at all perplexed by the likely but untrue interpretation which I had made, and saw at a glance what was plain to see, though verily I myself had not observed it before she spake—than by the dream itself, whereby the joy of that holy woman was foretold so long before for her comfort in that then present grief. For nine years almost did follow, all of which time I tumbled and was the more grievously tormented in that dirty pit and darkness of error, the more often I sought to rise from thence. While yet that chaste, devout, and sober widow, such as thou lovest, being now of more cheerful hope but not more slow in shedding tears and heaving sighs, did not fail in all the hours of her prayer to lament before thee still on my behalf. These petitions of hers *did enter into thy sight,* yet thou didst suffer me still to be wrapped and further enwrapped again in that cloud of darkness.

What answer his mother received from a certain bishop about his conversion

IN the meantime also thou didst give another answer which I remember; though I pass over many things and hasten on to that which it imports me more to confess, and many things also I have forgotten. Thou didst therefore give another answer by a priest of thine, a certain bishop bred up in thy Church, and well studied in the learning of thy books. When, therefore, that woman had besought him that he would vouchsafe to confer with me and to refute my errors, to teach me what was good and to unteach me what was otherwise—for this office he was wont to perform when he found such as were likely to benefit thereby—he declined, and that indeed with great discretion, as I came to see afterwards. For he answered that I was as yet unfit for instruction because I was puffed up with the novelty of that heresy and had perplexed many unlearned persons with a world of questions and doubts; as indeed she had herself declared to him. "Let him alone awhile," said he, "only pray unto our Lord for him; he himself, by reading, will find out his errors, and how great is the impiety thereof."

Then withal he told her how he, when he was a little one, had himself been delivered over to the Manichees by his misguided mother, and that he had not merely read over almost all their books but had even written out some of them, but that afterwards, without the labour of any disputation or conference, it had become manifest to him how detestable that sect was, and so he had forsaken it. When therefore he had ended that narration and she would not yet give over, but was rather grown the more earnest in abundantly weeping and entreating him that he would see me and confer with me, he said, being somewhat vexed, "Go thy ways and God bless thee, it is impossible that the son of these tears should perish." Which words she took—as she told me afterwards in our familiar converse—as if they had been sent down from heaven.

BOOK FOUR

How long and in what manner he seduced others

FOR the space of nine years then, from the nineteenth to the twenty-eighth of mine age, I was seduced and did seduce others, being both deceiver and deceived in various fond desires; in public by those arts which men call learned, and in secret by attempting it under the colour and cloak of piety, here proud, there superstitious, everywhere vain. So earnestly did I aspire towards the empty sound of popular fame as even to seek after such plaudits as are given in stage-plays, for prizes of straw garlands, the vanities of the theatre, and the intemperance of lust. Yet desiring to be purged from this filth with the aid of them that were called " elect saints," I carried to them certain provisions of meat, wherefrom in the forge of their fat paunches they might hammer out Angels and Gods after their own fashion, by whom I might be delivered. These things did I follow and these things did I practise together with my friends, who were deceived both by me and with me.

Let such deride me as be arrogant and as yet are not profitably humbled and abased by thee, O my God; but I will confess my shame to thy glory. Suffer me, I beseech thee, and give me grace, that by my memory I may retrace the errors of my life, and *offer unto thee the sacrifice of praise*. For what am I unto myself without thee, but a guide which runneth upon precipices? Or what am I, even at the best, but an infant sucking milk from thee, and enjoying thee who art *the incorruptible food* of our souls? And what kind of thing can any man account himself since he is but a man? Let such as are strong and powerful laugh at me, but let us who are *weak and poor confess to thee*.

*He teacheth rhetoric and despiseth the victory which was
   promised him by a wizard*

I TAUGHT in those years the art of rhetoric, and being myself
overcome by a desire of gain, made sale of loquacity which
might overcome others. Yet I desired rather, O Lord, as
thou knowest, to have honest scholars—as such are
accounted in the world—and without deceit I taught them
how to deceive. Yet not that they should ever plead against
the life of one that was innocent, but sometimes perhaps
for one that was guilty. And thou, O Lord, from afar off
didst see me sliding in that slippery place, and amid a thick
smoke my faith did sparkle a little, which I made manifest
in that function of mine to them *that loved vanity and
sought a lie;* as I also did together with them. In those days
I lived with one not united to me in lawful marriage,
whom the wild ardour of my affection, wholly destitute
of understanding, had found out; yet to her only was
I faithful. And herein did I learn of my own experience
the difference there would be between the knot of a true
marriage, which is made for the generation of children,
and a bargain of lustful love, where children are born sometimes even against our wills, which yet, when they are born,
compel us to love them.

I remember also that, when I was once a competitor for
the prize with a dramatic poem, a certain wizard sent to me
to know what I would give him that I might win. But I
detesting and abhorring those vulgar and filthy mysteries
of iniquity, did answer, that if the garland were to be of
gold and withal immortal, I would not suffer a fly to lose its
life to obtain me a victory. For he would have slain certain
living creatures in his sacrifices and, as it seemed, by doing
such honour to the devils, would have procured their
favour for me. Yet I did not forbear to take part in that sin
of his for true love of thee, O thou God of my heart, for I

had not then learned to love thee, seeing that I could conceive of nothing better than certain shining bodies. Now the soul that lies gasping after such fictions as those, doth it not defile itself in fornication against thee, leaning upon broken staves and *feeding upon the air*? For whilst I would not permit that others should sacrifice to the devils for me, I myself did sacrifice to them by my superstition. And what other thing is it to feed the air, than to feed the devils; that is, by erring, to make ourselves the subject of their pleasure and their scorn?

Being given to astrology, he is reclaimed by one who was both a good physician and a wise man

BUT as for those Planet-mongers, who will be called Astrologers, I did not forbear to consult with them, because they used no sacrifices, nor directed prayers to any spirit which might inform them of things to come. Yet this also true and Christian piety doth reject and condemn. For it is a good thing to confess to thee, O Lord, and to say, "Have mercy upon me and cure my soul, for it hath sinned against thee," and not to abuse thy tender goodness for a liberty of offending thee, but to remember the voice of our Lord, saying, *Behold thou art made whole, sin no more, lest a worse thing happen unto thee.* How much do they endeavour to strike at the root of a man's soul, when they say, "The cause of thy sinning is inevitably ordained from heaven," or "Venus did this, or Saturn, or Mars," so that man, who is but flesh and blood and proud corruption, may be without sin, while the Creator and Moderator of the sky and the stars must bear the blame of it. And who is this but our God, the very sweetness and first source of Justice, *who will render to everyone according to his works, and despiseth not the heart which is contrite and humbled*?

There was at that time a sharp-witted man and one most

skilful and ingenious withal in the art of physic.[1] This man, being Proconsul, did with his own hand put a garland, which I had gained as a prize, upon my head; which truly was disordered enough, though he did not this as a physician. For of that disease of mine it is thou who curedst me, thou who *dost resist the proud and givest grace to the humble*. But yet thou didst not forbear or fail, by the means of that old man, to recover my soul. For indeed I grew to be more familiar with him, and did daily and earnestly hang upon his discourse, which was pleasant and grave through the vivacity of his good sense, though without ornament of words. And as soon as he came to know, by speaking with me, that I was addicted to the books of Nativity-casters, he did benignly and fatherly advise me to throw them away, and not idly to employ my care and pains, which were needed for better things, upon that vanity. He said that, at the outset of his career, he had applied himself to that art with a purpose to earn his living thereby, and that, since he had understood Hippocrates, he was well able to understand those books also; but afterwards he had rejected them and taken to the profession of physic for no other reason than this, because he had found those things to be most false; and he would not descend, being a worthy man, to get his living by deceiving others. "But thou," said he, "hast Rhetoric, whereby thou canst live among men, and this deceitful art thou followest for thine own pleasure, not being urged thereto by the necessity of thy fortunes; wherefore thou art so much the more bound to believe me herein, because I did so laboriously study it as the only thing whereby I meant to live."

When therefore I demanded of him what was the cause that so many things were foretold truly, he answered, as well he might, that the power of chance, which is sprinkled with so great variety upon human affairs, was the reason thereof. For if any man should consult the poets by

---

[1] His name, Vindicianus, is given in Bk VII, chap. 6.

a chance opening of the pages,[1] the verse might happen to be strangely consonant to the present business, though yet the poet both sang and intended something which was very different; so it was not to be wondered at if somewhat did proceed out of the mind of man, by a kind of superior instinct, himself not knowing what was done in himself, and thus—rather by chance than by good cunning— he might deliver somewhat which had reference to the condition and affairs of him that asked the question. And this I learned of that man, or rather thou didst procure it for me by his means, and so didst thou lay the seed in my memory of that doubt which afterwards I might seek out by myself. But at that time neither he nor my dearest Nebridius, a young man both excellently good and very circumspect, deriding all this kind of divination, could persuade me that I should cast these things away. Because the authority of the very authors that wrote hereof did move me more, and I had not then met with any certain reason whereby it might appear to me without ambiguity that those truths, which they told their clients, were delivered by chance and not by the art of Astrology.

The sickness and baptism of his friend, and how bitterly he grieved for his death

ABOUT that time, when I began to teach in the town where I was born, I found a friend freshly growing up with me in the same bud of youth, whom the society of our common studies made extremely dear to me. We had been together even from the state of childhood, together we went both to school and to play. Yet I account not that he was then such a friend as he became afterwards, nor indeed even then were we united according to the law of true friendship, for there is none true but that which thou knittest between such as adhere to thee *through charity, diffused in our hearts by*

[1] See Note 4.

the Holy Ghost which is given us. Howsoever it was very delightful to us, being entertained and as it were ripened by the heat of our common studies. I had already diverted him from the true faith—though he had cordially and from his tenderest youth embraced it—towards those superstitious and paltry fables, which my mother so lamented in me. This man therefore was now in error with me, and my soul could not tell how to live without him.

And behold, thou who followest close upon the heels of such as run away from thee—at once *a God of revenge* and a fountain of mercies, converting us to thee by admirable ways—behold I say, thou tookest that man out of this life, when he was scarce a year old in my friendship, he who was dear to me beyond all the delights of this life. *What man is able to sing those praises* which, even in himself alone, he hath had knowledge of? What was it which thou didst then, O my God, *most unsearchable, in the bottomless depth of thy judgements?* For when he lay sick of a burning fever, continuing so for a long time in a kind of deadly sweat, his recovery was despaired of. And so he was baptized, without knowing of it, myself not caring much though he were so, and presuming that his soul would retain a greater impression of that which I had taught him, than his body could of that whereof himself was wholly ignorant. But it happened far otherwise, for he was restored and recovered to health. As soon therefore as I could speak with him— which was as soon as he could bear it, for I parted not from him, so much did we depend upon each other— I began to scoff at the baptism which he had received when he was senseless, though by that time he knew he had received it, imagining that he would join with me therein. But he looked upon me with extreme aversion of mind, as if I had been an enemy, and with an admirable and sudden liberty he advised me that, if I meant to be a friend of his, I should give over such discourse with him.

Myself, all troubled and even astounded thereat, deferred to manifest my thoughts till, he being perfectly cured, I might proceed with him as I thought fit. But he was taken speedily away from that madness of mine that, to my comfort, he might be preserved with thee. For, within a few days after, he had a relapse of his fever and died whilst I was absent.

With this affliction my whole heart was darkened, and whatsoever I beheld had the face of death. My country became a punishment to me, my father's house an extreme misery, and all that which I was wont to share with him was converted into a vast kind of torment, now that I was without him. In every place mine eyes would look for him but found him not, and I hated all things because they told me no news of him. Neither could they say any more, "Behold, he cometh," as they did when he was absent, being alive. I became unto myself an enigma, and I would ask *my soul why it was sad, and why it afflicted me so vehemently,* yet it could make me no answer. If I said unto it, "Hope in God," it had good reason to obey me not; because that man, that most dear friend whom I had lost, was both truer and better than was that false imagination of mine concerning thee, wherein my soul was bidden to hope. Only tears were delightful to me, and they succeeded to the place which my friend was wont to hold in the dearest parts of my affection.

Of tears which are shed in prayer, for the grief of losing anything which is dear

AND NOW, O Lord, those things are past and the rage of my wound hath been appeased by time. May I then understand from thee, who art Truth itself, and may I apply the ear of my heart to thy mouth, that thou mayest tell me why tears are sweet to such as are in misery? Is it that, although thou art present everywhere, thou hast cast our misery far from thee? Thou remainest in thyself, but we are tossed up and down in certain painful trials; yet if we might not pour forth our complaints into thine ears, we should be wholly deprived of hope.

Whence therefore comes it that to groan and weep, to complain and sigh should be a pleasant fruit, though gathered from the bitter tree of life? Is it sweet to us in respect of this, because we are in hope that thou hearest us? With reason may this be said when men are making prayers to thee out of the desire they have to obtain anything. But could this be so in the grief I had for the loss of my friend? No, I had no hope he could revive, nor was it this I begged for by my tears; but I grieved and wept for this alone, that I was miserable and had lost my joy. Or is it this, that tears are bitterness, and are delightful to us only because we hate the things wherein we once did take contentment, and but for so long as we continue to hate them?

He expresseth the great affection wherewith he loved his friend

But why do I speak of these things? For now is no time to ask questions, but to confess to thee. I was miserable, and so is every man who is bound by the love of things that pass away; he is torn in pieces when he loseth them, and then it is that he feeleth the misery which yet was his before he lost them. So was I at that time, and I wept most bitterly, and I found my only repose in that bitterness of weeping. So was I miserable, yet I loved this miserable life more dearly than I had done that friend. For though I gladly would have changed this life, yet would I not have been glad to lose it rather than him. And I know not whether, even for him, I would have done that which is related—if it be not rather devised—of Orestes and Pylades, who were willing to die for one another, because death to them was more desirable than such a life as was not mutual to them both. But in me there was grown up a strange state of mind, wholly contrary to this, for I had an extreme weariness of living, and withal no less a fear of death. I think that, by how much the more I loved him, so much the more I abhorred and feared death as my fiercest enemy, which had deprived me of him; and I thought it was instantly to take the same course with all others, because it had been able to destroy him. Even thus did I stand affected, I well remember it.

Behold my heart, O my God, behold and see within, for I remember myself well; O thou, my hope, who dost cleanse me from the impurity of such affections, directing *my eyes unto thee and drawing my feet out of the snare*. For I wondered how other men could live now that he was dead, whom I had loved as if he could never die. And I wondered the more that I, who was nothing but his other self, was able still to live when he was dead. Well indeed did he speak of his friend who said, "O thou half of my soul."[1] For I had found both my soul and his to be but one and the same, though in two bodies; and for this was my life a horror to me, because I would not live by halves; and therefore perhaps I feared to die, lest thereby he should come to have wholly died, whom I so extremely loved.

How the impatience of grief made him to change his place of abode

O MADNESS, which knoweth not how to love men, as men should love. O sottish man, who so impatiently suffereth the things which are incident to the condition of all mankind; yet such was I. Therefore did I rage and sigh and weep and was troubled, nor was I capable either of rest or counsel. For I carried my soul as it were

[1] Horace, Odes i, 1, 8.

sliced in sunder, and gored with blood, and impatient even to be carried by me; yet could I find no place wherein to lay it. Not in pleasant groves, not in sports or music, not in fragrant odours, not in exquisite banquets, not in pleasures of the chamber, nor yet in books or songs could it take any rest. All things, even the very light itself, to me were gloom; whatsoever was not that which he was, became both wearisome and odious to me excepting only my sighs and tears, for in these alone I found a little comfort.

But when again I refrained my soul from these, that huge load of misery, which was first to be lightened and afterwards removed by thee, O Lord, lay heavy upon me. I knew it, but I would not or I could not seek the remedy, because, when I thought of thee, it was not anything substantial or firm that came into my mind; nor was it thou, but mine own vain imagination and error, which was indeed my God at that time. If I endeavoured to discharge my burden upon that, to the end my soul might be at ease, it slipped away for lack of ground to rest upon and came rushing back again upon me; and I remained, a wretched dwelling for myself, where I could neither stay nor yet depart thence. For whither was it possible for my heart to fly from my heart? Or whither could I escape from myself? But at least I fled out of my country, for mine eyes did less expect to find him there, where I had not been accustomed to see him. For which reason I betook myself from Tagaste to Carthage.

Time cureth grief

TIME doth not rest, nor rolls it idly round about these senses of ours, but it worketh strange changes in the mind. Behold it came and went, day by day, and by such coming and going it brought into me other hopes and other memories, and by degrees they patched up my mind again with such

delight as formerly had taken me, to which that grief
of mine began then to yield. Yet to that again succeeded
not indeed other grief but the causes of other grief.
For how came grief to pierce me both so easily and to the
very quick, but because I had poured out my soul upon
a bed of sand, by loving a man that was to die as if
he had been immortal? But the solace which I had
in other friends did chiefly restore and recreate me, with
whom I loved that which enslaved me still; and this was a
huge fable and a lie that cannot soon be told, by the
seductive itching whereof, for ever tickling in our ears,
our minds were still corrupted.

But that fable died not in me, though any of my friends
might chance to die, because there were other things in
them which did yet more possess my mind. To talk and be
merry together, to be sweetly obsequious to one another,
together to read vain books, together to jest and again to
keep a kind of civil gravity, to dissent sometimes from one
another even as a man would do from himself, yea and by
those dissentings—which yet did happen very rarely—
to season our usual consent of minds, to teach one another
somewhat or to learn something of one another, to expect
such as were absent with impatience and to embrace such
as returned with joy. And by such signs as these, issuing
out of the hearts of us, who loved and who repaid each
other's love by the countenance, the speech, the eyes,
and by a thousand most delightful motions, did we melt
our minds, which were as several fuels to one fire, and out
of many fashioned only one.

A comparison of human friendship with divine

THIS it is which is beloved in friends, and so beloved that a
man even chargeth his conscience with it, if he love not
again the person who loveth him, demanding nothing else
of him save the mutual demonstration of goodwill. Hence

proceeds that grief, if a friend chance to die, and that darkness of sorrow; the heart being steeped in tears, the sweet being all turned to bitterness. Hence groweth too the death of such as live, by losing out of their lives those who die. Blessed is the man that loves thee, and his friend in thee, and his enemy for thee. For he alone never loseth a dear friend, to whom all men are dear for his sake who is never lost. And who is this but our God, the God who made heaven and earth, who filleth them and, even by filling, maketh them? No man loseth thee but he that forsaketh thee; and he that forsaketh thee, whither goeth he or whither flyeth he, but from thee being pleased, to thee being offended? And where shall such a one find thy law save in his punishment? For *thy law is truth,* and *Truth is nothing else but thou thyself.*

All beauty proceeds from God, who is to be praised in all things

O God of power, convert us unto thee; shew us thy face and we shall be safe. For which way soever the soul of man turneth, unless towards thee, it is affixed to pain; yea though it fasten upon delightful creatures, which are both outside thee and outside itself, which yet would be nothing were they not of thee. These things have their spring and their fall. When they spring they begin to be, and grow towards perfection; and being perfected they grow old and die, or, if all do not grow old, yet do all wither. When therefore they spring and grow, by how much the more speedily they grow to be, by just so much the more do they hasten not to be. Such is their nature and so much hast thou given them, for they are but parts of things, which exist not all together, but, by departing and succeeding, do all constitute one whole, whereof they are the parts. Even in the selfsame manner is our speech delivered by the words that are spoken.

For a whole speech will never be made if one word depart not when his sound is past, so that another may in turn succeed.

From out such things then let my soul praise thee, O God, thou Creator of all things, but let it not be fastened to them with the glue of inordinate affection by the senses of the body. For these creatures go on, whither they were to go, towards a not-being, and so do they cleave the soul apart with pestiferous desires. For the soul desires to be, and would fain repose in those things which it loveth, but in those things it cannot repose, for, instead of remaining, they fly away; and who is he that can follow them with his bodily sense? Yea, or who can overtake them, even when they are near at hand? For the sense of the flesh is slow, because it is the sense of the flesh, and the nature of it is such. It sufficeth for that end whereto it is made, but it arriveth not so far as to hold fast things transient, as they pass from their due beginning unto their appointed end. For in thy word, by which they are created, they receive their mission, "Hence and so far thou art to go."

An admonition to his soul, to be wary in loving creatures

Be not foolish, O my soul, and let not the ear of thy heart grow deaf by the tumultuous noise of vanity. So hearken now; the Word itself calls to thee to return, for in Him is the seat of rest which cannot be disturbed, where love shall never be forsaken, unless it be the first to leave its Love. Behold, here some things pass away that others may succeed them, and this lowest world is formed by the succession of all its parts. "But do I ever depart?" saith the Word of God. There fix thy mansion, O my soul. There lay up whatsoever thou hast thence received. Now, at least, that thou art over-wearied in deceitful ways, commend unto this Truth whatsoever it hath imparted unto thee, thou canst not lose by that bargain. Nay, all the withered parts of thee shall thereby reflourish, *all thy languishing weaknesses shall be cured,* thine instabilities shall be renewed, made strong, and all braced up to thee; nor shall they pluck thee down whither they are descending, but they shall stay with thee and shall stand fast for ever in God's own presence, *who is immutable and eternal.*

To what end dost thou still follow that perverse flesh of thine? Rather let it be converted and follow thee. Whatsoever thou feelest by it, is but in part, and thereby thou growest ignorant of that whole whereof these are but parts, and yet this pleaseth thee. Whereas if the sense of thy flesh were but able to comprehend the whole, and were not, for thy punishment, justly confined to a part of that whole, thou wouldst desire that whatsoever existeth in this present should pass away, to the end that the whole might rather please thee. For even the words that are spoken thou hearest by the sense of thine ears, and thou dost not desire that the several syllables should stand at a stay, but thou wouldst have them to fly on apace, that others may come and so thou mayest possess the whole discourse. Even so is it with all things which make up one whole, for those things whereof that whole is made do not subsist together. All of them together would delight thee more than the several parts thereof, if the pleasure of them all could be felt at once. But incomparably more excellent is he who made them all, and this is our God, who never departs, because there is nothing that can succeed to him.

In all the things which please us it is God who is to be loved

IF bodies please thee, praise thou God in them, and dart back that love upon their Creator, lest otherwise thou displease him in those things which please thee. If it be souls thou lovest, let them be loved in God, because in themselves they are changeable, but in him they remain established; for otherwise they would but pass on and perish. In him therefore let them be loved and, in company with thee, draw thou towards him as many of them as thou canst, and say unto them, "Come, let us love him, let us love him. *He made all these things and he is not far from us.*" For he did not make them and leave them, but they came from him, and in him they have their being. Behold, he is there, where Truth with sweetness is tasted. He is in the very centre of man's heart, and yet that heart hath strayed from him. *Return, O ye sinners, into your own heart,* and be united unto him that made you; stand with him, and you shall stand fast; repose in him, and you shall be truly at rest. Whither go you in those craggy ways, whither go you? The contentment that you seek doth wholly depend upon him. In as much as concerneth him it is both good and pleasant, but to you it is justly an occasion of bitterness, because it is injustice to forsake him, for the love of any thing which hath its being from him. What mean you thus to travail and trudge on through these hard and painful ways? There is no rest where you are seeking it. Seek still that which you seek, but seek it not there where you seek it. You seek for a happy life in the very region of death. Not there is it to be found. For how can a happy life be found there, where there is not so much as any life at all?

Our one true Life descended hither and bore our death, and killed this death by the abundance of his own life; and with a voice of thunder crieth he out to us to return to him, into that secret place whence he proceeded, when first he came into that pure Virgin's womb where created manhood was espoused to him—even our mortal flesh, though not for ever to remain mortal—and from which he went forth *like a bridegroom from his bedchamber, and rejoicing like a giant to run his course.* He tarried not but ran and cried out; by words and deeds, by death and life, by descension and ascension cried he out, bidding us return to him. Then he withdrew himself from our sight, that we might return into our own hearts and find him there. For he departed, and behold he is here. He would not long remain with us, yet did he never leave us. For thither hath he gone whence he was never parted, because *the whole world was made by him, and in this world he was, and into it he came that he might save sinners.* To him my soul maketh these confessions, that he *may cure it, which hath sinned against him.*

O ye sons of men, how long will ye be heavy-hearted? Now that the true Life is come down to fetch you, are you not willing to rise up and live? But how may you ascend when you are *high in your own conceits, and have lifted up your head against heaven?* Descend, that you may ascend, and may ascend to God. For you are fallen away from him, by rising up against him. Tell the souls whom thou lovest such things as these, that they may bewail their sins *in this valley of misery,* and so thou mayest draw them up with thee to God. For by his Spirit it is that thou speakest thus unto them, if thou do it with a heart inflamed by the fire of charity.

Whence love doth grow

THESE things I knew not then, but I loved these inferior fair creatures, and I was going down into the very depths. I said to my friends, "Do we love anything but what is fair? And what is beauty, and in what does the beautiful consist? And what is it that doth entice and win us to those things which we love? For unless there were comeliness and beauty in them they would by no means draw us unto them." And I observed and saw in the bodies themselves, that it was one thing to be a kind of whole, complete and in that respect beautiful, and another for anything to have beauty in it, because it was accommodated aptly to some other things, as a part of the body to the whole, or as the shoe in respect to the foot, and the like. And these considerations did rise up clearly in my mind out of the innermost part of my heart, and I wrote those books " *De pulchro et apto,*" of the Fair and Fit; two or three I think there were. Thou knowest, O God, but as for me, I have forgotten; for I have them not by me, they went astray from me, I know not how.

Of his book " De Pulchro et Apto," of the fair and fit

But what moved me, O Lord my God, that I should address those books to Hierius, an orator of Rome, whom I knew not so much as by his face? But I loved the man for the fame of his learning, which was renowned, and some words of his I had heard, which pleased me, and so much the more because he pleased others. For men did praise him even to admiration, because, being by birth a Syrian and learned at first in the Greek eloquence and afterwards in the Latin, he was grown to be a wonderful speaker, and most skilful in those things which appertain to the study of Philosophy.

Thus is a man praised and loved even when he is absent. Doth then this love enter into the heart of the hearer from the mouth of him that praiseth? It is no such thing, but one man is kindled to love by the love of another. For he who is praised comes to be loved, because we believe in the well-judging heart of him that praiseth, that is to say when one that loveth, praiseth. For in such wise was it that I loved men then, upon the judgment of men and not upon thy judgment, O my God, in whom none is deceived. But why did I not love Hierius in such sort as I might have loved a noble charioteer, or a hunter who is celebrated by vulgar tongues? Yet I loved him far otherwise and more seriously, and even in such a way as I should have been glad to be praised myself. For I had no desire to be praised and beloved as stage-players are, though I would even praise and love them too; but for myself I would rather choose to be concealed than to be known in such wise, and to be hated than so loved. Where are there disposed in one and the same soul these different weights, for weighing loves so diverse and so different? What is it that I am in love with in one man? Or what is it again in another which I hate? For if I did not detest it, I should not drive him away from me, seeing that we both are men. But in the case of a stage-player, who is of the same nature as we ourselves, it is not as it is with a fair horse, which a man loves indeed though he would not himself be a horse, even if he might. Do I therefore love in a man that which I hate to be, when yet I am a man? Man is a great deep, *the very hairs of whose head are numbered* by thee, O Lord, so that not one escapes thee; yet are those hairs more easily to be numbered than are the affections and the motions of his heart.

But this orator, whom I so loved, was a man of such condition that I myself would gladly have been such a one, and I erred through swelling pride, and was *whirled about with every wind,* but yet, most secretly, was I guided by thee. And yet how do I know and how shall I confess to thee with certainty, that I loved this man more for the love of them that praised him, than for the qualities themselves for which they praised him? Because if they should have discommended him instead of praising him, and should have recounted the same things of him to his despite and dispraise, I should not have been kindled and moved to love him. Yet both the man and the things in themselves would be still the same, and only the feelings of them that spake about him would be different. Behold where the weak soul doth lie, which adhereth not yet to the solidity of Truth. For as the breadth of tongues doth blow out of the minds of such as think they know, so it is carried, turned, returned, and tossed about, and the light grows to be overshadowed with a cloud, and Truth is not seen, yet behold it stands before us. But I conceived it to be a matter of much importance to me, if my words and my learning might be published in the ears of that great man, that if he should approve them I might be the more set on fire, while, if he should disesteem them, this vain heart of mine would have been deeply wounded, being empty of thy solidity. And yet that matter of the Fair and Fit—by occasion whereof I had addressed myself to him—I gladly turned over with the lips of my contemplation, and if no one else were by to praise it, I admired it myself.

That, being darkened with corporeal images, his mind could not conceive spiritual things

But as yet I could not discern how all this great matter hinges upon that skill of thine, O thou omnipotent, *who alone doest wondrous things.* And my mind was moving amongst corporeal forms, and I defined and distinguished and, by means of corporeal examples, did enunciate this opinion, that a thing was Fair when it was of itself and independent, but a Fit thing was one which received grace by being accommodated to something else. And I cast my mind to consider the nature of the Mind itself, but the false opinion that I had of spiritual things did not suffer me to see the truth. Yet the very force of Truth was flashing into mine eyes, but I withdrew my weak and panting mind from anything that was incorporeal, fixing it upon lineaments and colours and swelling quantities. And because I could not find these things in my mind, I thought I could not see that mind of mine. And whereas in Virtue I love peace, and in Vice I hated discord, I held unity to be in the former, but division to be in the latter. And in that Unity, as I conceived, there was the rational soul of man, and the nature of truth, and the supreme goodness; while in this Division, of the irrational life, I held there was some kind of substance, of the nature of the worst evil, which was not only substance but was expressly Life, and yet was not of thee, O my God, of whom are all things. And the first indeed I called Monad or Unity, as if it were a mind devoid of sex; and the other I called Dyad or Division into two, as wrath in heinous crimes, and lust in flagitious sins, not knowing what I said. For I knew not, neither had I learned, that no substance at all is evil, or that our mind itself is not the supreme and incommunicable good.

For as they are called heinous crimes, wherein there is a vicious motion of mind in which impetuosity is seen, and which behaves itself with insolency and confusion; and those are flagitious sins, when there is an immoderate affection of the soul whereby carnal pleasures are sucked in; just so do false opinions corrupt this life of ours, when the rational part itself is vicious. So was it in me at that time, who knew not that the mind must be illuminated by another Light, that it might be made partaker of Truth, for of itself it is not the essential truth. But thou wilt give light to my lantern, O Lord my God, *thou wilt lighten my darkness, and of thy fulness have we all received.* For thou art *the true Light which illuminateth every man coming into this world,* because in thee *there is no transmutation nor shadow of change.*

But I was working my way towards thee, and I was driven back from thee, that I might savour of death, because *thou dost resist the proud.* And what could be prouder than for me, with a strange madness, to assert myself to be, of my nature, that which thou art? For whilst I was mutable—and of that I was sure, because even then I desired to be wise, and to grow from worse to better—yet I chose rather to think that thou also wert mutable, than I was not that which thou art. Therefore I was driven back again, and thou didst resist that neck of mine, stiffened with pride. And I imagined to myself certain corporeal forms, and being flesh, I accused flesh; and being *a wandering spirit I returned not* yet to thee. Thus I wandered on and on into things that have no being, neither in thee nor in me, nor in any body; neither were they created for me by thy truth, but were devised by mine own vanity out of the fancies that I had concerning body. And I cried unto the faithful little ones of thy flock, my fellow citizens—from whom unwittingly I did exile myself—I cried to them, prating and foolish, "Why then doth the soul err, if God created it?" And yet I would not endure that any man should ask of me, "Why then doth God err?" For I laboured to maintain that rather thine unchangeable substance was constrained to err, than I would confess that my changeable substance had voluntarily strayed, and that it was now erring as its punishment.

I was perhaps of the age of six or seven and twenty years when I wrote those volumes, turning around within myself these corporeal fictions, which buzzed about my heart and ears, and which I applied, O thou sweet Truth, to that interior harmony of thine; meditating about the Fair and Fit, and standing attentive with desire to hear thee, and to *rejoice with joy at the voice of the Spouse.* Yet I could not do it, for I was carried away by the noise of mine own error, and by the weight of my pride I was pressed down into the depths. For thou didst not give me to hear of joy and gladness, nor did *my bones rejoice, which had* not yet by thee *been humbled.*

How, without a teacher, he yet understood the writings of Aristotle

AND what did it profit me that, being scarce twenty years old, the book of Aristotle, called the *Ten Categories,* fell into my hands, and I read and understood it without a teacher? Yet the very name of that work I used always to breathe forth as if it were something great and almost divine, when my master, the Rhetoric teacher at Carthage, and others too that were accounted learned, would discourse thereon, their cheeks swelling with pride. And when afterwards I conferred about them with others they professed that they had much to do to understand them, though they had been instructed therein by most learned masters, and that not by lectures only but by means of many delineations drawn in the sand; yet could they not, for all that, tell me anything about the matter, which I myself had not learned, by reading them alone. And it seemed plain enough to me, whilst they spoke of Substance, such as man, and of whatsoever things are inherent in Substance, as the figure or shape of man, what kind of thing he is, of what stature, of what kindred, whose brother he is, or where he is placed, or where he was born, whether he sit or stand, whether he be shod or armed, or whether he do or suffer anything, I could understand all, whatsoever comes into these nine classes, whereof for example's sake I have given some instances, or the countless other things in the class of Substance itself.

What did this profit me, I say, when I may rather account that it did me harm? For, in as much as I thought thee, O my God, who art of an admirably unchangeable and simple essence, to be contained like all other things in the ten predicaments, I tried to understand thee as if thou hadst been subject to thine own greatness and beauty, in the same way that these things are in thee, as in a subject like a body; whereas thy greatness and beauty are thy very self, while a body is not great or beautiful because it is a body, for it would still be none the less a body were it less great or less fair. That which I conceived of thee, therefore, was not true but was truly false, for these things were fictions of my misery and not the foundations of thy felicity. For thou hadst commanded, and so it fell out with me, that *the earth should bring forth thorns and brambles* for me, and that *in the sweat of my brow I must come to eat bread*.

What also did it profit me that I, being then a most wicked slave to vile and base affections, did read and understand of myself all the books of those arts that are called liberal, which I could come by to read? I took pleasure therein, but I considered not whence proceeded all that which was true and certain in any of them. For my back was turned towards the light and to those things which might have illumined my face, and by this means that face of mine, whereby I saw those other things illuminated which were placed before it, did still itself remain in darkness. Whatsoever I read concerning the arts, either of Logic or Rhetoric, of Geometry, Music or Arithmetic, I understood without any great difficulty, and without the instruction of any man, as thou knowest, O Lord my God. For swiftness of understanding and sharpness of wit in learning anything is thy gift, but I took not occasion thereby to offer a sacrifice of thanksgiving unto thee. Wherefore all this was rather of much prejudice than of use to me, since I desired to have the liberal portion which thou bestowedst upon me in mine own hands, and I preserved not the strength of my soul for thy service, but I went into a far country remote from thee, that I might waste it upon the satisfying of unclean and profane desires. For how was I the better for having those good parts, since I did not use them well? Nay I did not so much as know that these arts were to be understood only with very great difficulty, even by such as excelled both in wit and in study, until such time as I myself endeavoured to expound the same in the hearing of others. For then I found that he was accounted the most excellent among them, who was able to follow not too slowly whilst I expounded.

But still I say, what was I the better for all this, when I thought that thou, O Lord my God, wert no better than some vast and shining body, and that I myself was but some piece or lump thereof? O extreme perverseness of understanding, yet such was I at that time. Nor will I be ashamed,

O my God, to confess thy mercies unto me, and to call upon thee, I who was not then ashamed to proclaim my blasphemies before men, and to bark in their hearing against thee. What was I the better for having a nimble wit and being able to explicate and unfold, without any master, the most knotty and abstruse knowledge contained in so many books, when all the while I did deformedly and with a shameful kind of sacrilege forsake the doctrine of piety? Or what the worse were many of thy little ones for having a much less capacity, when withall they were not far from thee, that in the nest of thy Church they might securely feather themselves, and nourish the wings of charity by the food of uncorrupted faith? O Lord, our God, *our hope is in the covering of thy wings,* oh protect us and support us. Thou shalt carry us whilst we are but little ones, yea, *even to our last age shalt thou carry us.* When thou art our strength, we have strength indeed, but when we rely upon ourselves, our strength is nothing but weakness. With thee always liveth all our good, and when from thee we are averted, we are perverted. To thee, O Lord, let us now return, that we may not be overturned; because with thee our good liveth clear of all defect, for thou art thyself this Good. And we need not fear that there is no place for us to return to, because we fell headlong from it; for, whatsoever become of us, that house of ours, which is thine eternity, will stand fast for ever.

BOOK FIVE

He stirreth up his mind towards the praising of God

RECEIVE the sacrifice of my confessions from the hand of my tongue, which thou hast framed and stirred up to confess unto thy name. Heal thou all my bones, O Lord, and let them say, *"Who is like unto thee?"* He that confesseth unto thee, doth not teach thee thereby to understand what he doth within himself. For a heart which is shut up doth not exclude thy sight, nor doth the hardness of man resist thy hand; but thou dost open it when thou wilt, either by way of pity or revenge, *nor is there any that can hide himself from thy heat*. But let my soul praise thee that it may love thee, and let it confess thy mercies to thyself, that I may praise thee.

Thy whole creation forbeareth not and ceaseth not to praise thee; the spirit of man by his own lips which are turned towards thee, thy creatures animate and inanimate by the lips of such as consider them. For thus our souls may rise up from weariness, climbing upon those things which thou hast made, and passing on to thee, who didst make them in an admirable manner, in whom there is comfort and true fortitude.

The presence of God cannot be avoided, for he is everywhere

LET the restless and the wicked flee and depart from thee, thou seest them yet, and thine eye pierceth the shadows. And behold, all things that be around them are beautiful, but they themselves are deformed. But how indeed can they hurt thee or where in could they disparage thee, for thy dominion is entire and just, even from the highest heaven to the lowest deep. For whither did they fly, when they fled from thy face, and where can they be, that thou mayest not find them? But they fled, to the end that they might not see thee, whilst yet they were seen by thee, and being thus blinded might fall upon thee, *for thou forsakest none of those things which thou hast made.* The unjust fall upon thee that they may be justly vexed by it; withdrawing themselves from thy mercy, and stumbling upon thy justice, and falling foul of thy severity. And all because they knew not that thou art everywhere, whom no place circumscribes, and who alone art present, even to them that make themselves far from thee.

Let them therefore turn back again and seek thee, for though they have forsaken thee, their Creator, thou hast not forsaken thy creatures. Let them return and seek thee, for behold thou art there, even in their heart; in the very heart of them that confess to thee, that cast themselves upon thee, that pour forth their tears in thy bosom, after they have wearied themselves in those painful ways. And thou, full of mercy, wilt dry their eyes and wipe away their tears, that they may weep yet more and may even rejoice in their weeping. For it is thou, O Lord, not any man of flesh and blood, but thou who madest them, that dost also cherish and comfort them. Where then was I, when yet I sought for thee? Thou wert before me; but I had departed even from myself, neither did I find myself, then how much less could I find thee.

Of Faustus the Manichee, and of astrology

I WILL declare in the sight of God that nine-and-twentieth year of my age. There was then coming to Carthage a certain Manichæan Bishop, called Faustus, a great snare of the devil, whereby many were entangled in the deceitful smoothness of his speech. This I too praised, although I was able to discern between it and the truth of those things which I was greedy to learn. Nor did I care so much in what pretty dish of eloquence that Faustus, who was so famous among them, would serve me, as what food of science he would set before me therein, for me to eat. For fame had been a forerunner of him, and gave out that he was most skilful in all fair and civil kind of learning, and extraordinarily well seen in the liberal sciences.

Now because I had read many of the philosophers, and remembered much of what I read, I began to compare some part thereof with the tedious fables of the Manichees. And those things seemed more probable to me which were taught by the Philosophers, who were able to prevail so far as to make some fair judgment of the created world, *although they never found out the Sovereign Lord thereof. For thou, O Lord, art great and regardest those that are humble, but thou lookest from afar upon the haughty,* and dost not approach but to them that are contrite of heart. Nor art thou found by the proud, though by a curious skill they may number the stars and the sands of the sea, and measure the tract of heaven, and trace out the way of the planets. By their understanding, and by the wit thou hast given them, do they seek out these things, and many have they found out. For they have foretold, many years beforehand, the eclipses of those great lamps, the sun and moon, upon what day, in what hour, and to what extent it would prove, and their account did not fail, but lo, it fell out as they had foretold. And they wrote exact rules, which to this day may be read, and by these is foretold in what year, and upon what month of the year, and upon what day of the month, and what hour of the day, and in how many parts of its light the sun or moon shall be eclipsed, and just so doth it happen. And men who know not this art wonder, and are astonished at these things; and they who know it triumph, and are puffed up by a wicked pride, departing from thy light; for they foretell so long before the sun's eclipse, the which is future, and see not their own, the which is present. For they inquire not religiously whence they have that wit, by virtue whereof they inquire into these things, nor, finding that thou has made them, do they give themselves up to thee, that thou mayest preserve what thou hast made. Nor do they sacrifice to thee such things as they themselves have caused to be, by slaying their vain thoughts like fowls of the air, and their curiosity —whereby they penetrate the secret ways of the deep— like fishes of the sea, and that luxuriousness of theirs as the beasts of the field; that thou, O God, *who art a devouring fire,* mayest consume those dead cares of theirs, and recreate them after an immortal manner.

But they know not the Way, thy Word, by which thou madest all those things which they calculate, and they themselves who number them, and the sense whereby they see that which they number and the faculty of mind wherewith they number; nor do they know that *of thy wisdom there is no number.* But thine only begotten Son *is made unto us wisdom and justification and sanctification,* and was numbered among us, and *paid tribute to Caesar.* These men know not this Way, whereby they may descend from him unto themselves, and by it again may ascend unto him. They know not this Way, and they take themselves to be high and bright like the stars, and behold, they are cast down upon the ground, *and their foolish heart is darkened.* They speak many things truly of the creatures, but the Truth, the artificer of the creature, they do not piously seek, and therefore they do not find him. Or if they do find him and *recognize him to be God, they do not honour him or thank him as God, but they become vain in their cogitations,* and say that they are wise, attributing to themselves those things which indeed are thine. And by these degrees they come also to endeavour, with a more perverse blindness, to impute those things to thee which are their own, casting their lies upon thee, who art Truth itself, and *changing the glory of the incorruptible God into the likeness of a corruptible man, and of birds, and four-footed beasts, and serpents, converting thy truth into a lie, and choosing rather to worship and serve a creature than the Creator.*

Yet I remember many things, which by the philosophers were truly said concerning creatures, and it seemed to me that there was reason in their calculations, in the orderly sequence of times, and in the visible testimonies of the stars. And these things I compared with the sayings of Manichæus, who, most richly doting, had written much of these things; and here I could see no reason, either of the solstices, or the equinoxes, or of eclipses, or of any such things as I had learned in the books of secular wisdom. In his books I was ordered to believe all, yet it did not answer unto those reasons which had been made good and approved, both by my actual calculations and by mine own eyes; but from all this he was quite different.

Of the vanity of human knowledge

TELL me, O Lord God of truth, is a man pleasing unto thee because he is full of such knowledge? No, but unhappy is he who knoweth all things of this kind, if he be ignorant of thee; and happy is he that knoweth thee, though he be ignorant of all these things. But he, that knoweth both thee and them, is not the happier for them, but for thee only is he happy, if knowing thee *he glorify thee and give thanks unto thee, and become not vain in his own cogitations.* For as he that knoweth himself to possess a tree, and giveth thee thanks for the use that he can make of it—though he know not how many cubits high it is, nor how broad it spreads—is better than he who measures it, and counts all the branches it hath, yet neither possesseth it, nor knows nor cares for the Creator thereof; so is it a foolish thing to doubt but that a faithful man, to whom the whole world is subject, and who *having nothing yet possesseth all things,* although he know not the circles of the Great Bear, is, in like manner, much better than another who can weigh out the elements, and number the stars, and measure the skies, if withal he neglect thee, O Lord, who disposest of all things in number, weight, and measure.

Of the rashness of Manichæus, in that he taught he knew not what

But yet who urged Manichæus to write of all these things without knowledge, whereof true piety might yet have been learned? For thou hast said to man, *" Behold, piety is wisdom,"* of which he might have been ignorant, though he had perfect knowledge of those other things; nay rather he must have been ignorant of this, else had he not presumed so impudently to teach that which he did not understand. For it is a kind of vanity to profess a knowledge of these worldly things, but it is piety to confess to thee. But this wanderer from piety spake much of these things that, being confuted therein by such as understood them truly, it might evidently be discerned how little skill he had in other things that were more hidden. For the man would not have himself held at a low value, but he endeavoured to persuade others that the Holy Spirit, the Comforter and Enricher of thy faithful children, was dwelling in him with plenary authority. Therefore, whensoever he was found to speak false things of heaven, and of the stars, and of the motions of the sun and moon—although these things belong not to the doctrine of religion—his sacrilegious presumption was thereby made apparent enough; seeing that he not only delivered himself of things whereof he was ignorant, but which were actually false, and that too with such a mad vanity of pride that he would attribute them to himself as to one of the divine Persons.

For when I hear this or that Christian brother of mine, who is ignorant of these things and who mistaketh one thing for another, I can patiently behold him giving his opinion, nor do I see what hurt it doth him—so that he believe nothing unworthy of thee, O Lord, Creator of all things—though peradventure he be ignorant of the situation or condition of some material creature. But it doth him hurt if he esteem the matter to belong to the very essence of true doctrine, and will yet needs affirm with pertinacity that whereof he is ignorant. But even such an infirmity as this, in the infancy of faith, may be endured by such a mother as Charity is, till such time as this new creature grow up to be a perfect man, *not to be tossed up and down with every wind of doctrine*. But in that Manichæus, who presumed to make himself a doctor, an author, a leader, and a prince of those whom he might persuade, and that in such a fashion that all they who followed him must esteem themselves to be following not a sinful man but thy Holy Spirit, who would not judge that his madness was to be detested and cast off as far as to the world's end, if he were convicted to have spoken falsehood? But as yet indeed I had not clearly found out whether that which I had met withal in other books, concerning the vicissitudes of longer and shorter days and nights, and even of day and night itself, and of the eclipses of the great lights, and other things of this kind, might not be explained in accordance with his opinion. If it might be explained so, although it would still remain uncertain to me whether the things were so or not, I was prepared to submit my faith to his authority, on account of the sanctity which was said to be in him.

Faustus was eloquent by nature, but not by art

By the space of almost those whole nine years, wherein, like a vagabond in mind, I gave ear to the teachings of Manichæus, I did expect the coming of this Faustus with extreme appetite. For the rest of them upon whom I had fallen, who were not able to solve the objections which were made by me, did promise me that, by conference with him on his arrival, both these and even greater difficulties, should I put them, would be most easily and clearly discharged. As soon therefore as he came I made trial of him, and found him to be a man of a very agreeable and sweet language, who did prate over the self same things which the others were wont to deliver, but much more delightfully. But what did it help my extreme thirst, to have a most courtly cupbearer, and a most precious cup? Already mine ears were glutted with such toys, nor did they seem any better to me because they were better said, nor true because they were eloquent; nor did the soul seem wise, because the countenance had a wise look, and the speech was well tuned. But they who had made me such great promises in him were not good judges of things, and therefore to them he seemed both wise and prudent, because he could charm them with his tongue.

Yet sometimes also I have met with people of another kind, who call the truth itself in question and refuse to acknowledge it as such, if it be propounded in a fluent and smooth discourse. But thou hadst already instructed me, O my God, by strange and secret ways, and therefore I believe it was thou that taughtest me, because it is the truth; neither is there any other teacher of truth but only thou, wheresoever and whencesoever it may shine. Now therefore I had learned of thee, that nothing ought to be accounted true because it is eloquently delivered, nor accounted false because the words are rude; nor again true

because it is spoken without polish, nor therefore false
because it is clothed in courtly speech. But that wisdom and
foolishness are like food that is wholesome and unwhole-
some, which may be served in plain or costly dishes, as the
other in words that are choice or homely.

My greediness then, wherewith I had so long expected
that man, was indeed entertained and delighted with the
way and the manner of his discourse, and with his apt
words, which flowed easily on towards the apparelling of
his conceptions. I was, therefore, pleased, and I
commended and praised him among the rest, yea and
more than many of them; but I was nothing well content
that, in the throng of them that listened to him, I might
not be suffered to urge him and to impart to him the burden
of some questions that I had a mind to ask, by familiar
converse and the giving and taking of discussion. But
when I found opportunity to do this and was able to
gain his ear, at such time as it was in no way unfit
for us to enter upon a discussion, I put forward some of
the things which were weighing much upon me. At once I
found him to be a man quite unskilled in all the liberal
sciences, save in grammar only, and even in that he was no
way out of the common. But because he had read some of
Tully's orations, some very few of Seneca's works, divers
of the poets, and any volumes of his own sect that were
written in Latin and were of a good style, and by reason
of the fact that he had also daily exercise in speaking, he
was furnished with an eloquence, which became the
more agreeable and seductive by the application of his
mother wit, together with a certain grace which to him
was natural. Is it not so, as I am now recording, O Lord my
God, thou who art the arbiter of my conscience? Before
thee is my heart and my remembrance, O thou, who then
didst exercise me by the hidden and secret means of thy
providence and *didst place before my face* those shameful
errors of mine, to the end that I might see and hate them.

How he grew to be alienated from the sect of the Manichees

FOR after it had sufficiently appeared to me that Faustus was unskilled in those arts wherein I had thought him to excel, I began to despair that he would be able to open and untie those knots that bred difficulty in me; for these were matters of which a man might be ignorant while still embracing the truth of piety, but only if such a one were not a Manichee. For their books are full of lengthy fables, of the heaven, of the stars, of the sun and moon; and while I greatly desired to discuss with him the reasons of these things, which I had read elsewhere, and to find out if the things delivered about them in the Manichæan books were true or at the least possible, I did not now think that he would be able to explain them with any true knowledge, which yet was the thing I desired. But I confess that, when I brought forth these matters to be considered and discussed by us, he did with true modesty forbear even to undertake that burden, for he knew that he did not know these things, nor was he ashamed to acknowledge as much. For he was not one of those talking fellows, many of whom I had suffered, who would endeavour to teach me these things, when yet they said nothing of any moment. This man had a heart which, though it was not right towards thee, was not dishonest as regards himself. He was not wholly ignorant of his own ignorance, nor would he rashly engage himself to dispute of those things, through which he could make neither a clear path forward, nor yet an easy way of retreat. For this too I liked him the better, for the modesty of a confessing mind is better than those things were that I desired to know; and such I found him to be in all these more difficult and subtle questions.

And so, the pursuit whereby I was bent towards that learning of the Manichees being checked, and I myself yet more in despair of their other doctors, since this man had been so greatly cried up for the clearing of those doubts that had troubled me, I began at his request to pass some time with him in that study after which he thirsted. This was the study of letters, which I, being then Master of Rhetoric at Carthage, did teach my scholars; and I read with him either those books which he himself desired to hear, or else those which I thought most fit for such a kind of wit as his. But all the endeavour whereby I had purposed to proceed in that sect, was absolutely given over by me, now that I had come to know that man. Not because I was yet separated wholly from them, but as not having then found anything better than that course into which I had thrown myself; wherefore I resolved to remain as I was, until somewhat should appear which I might have reason to prefer before it.

Thus did Faustus, who had been to many a very snare of death, without his knowledge and against his will release the snare wherein I was. For thy hands, O my God, in the hidden path of thy providence, did not forsake my soul, and by night and by day a sacrifice was offered unto thee by the tears of my mother in her heart's blood, and thou didst proceed with me by wonderful and secret ways. It was thy doing, O my God, *for the steps of a man are directed by the Lord, and he shall dispose his way.* For by what means shall we procure salvation, but by thy hand repairing that which it hath made?

How he deceived his mother, and set out for Rome

It was thy doing, O Lord, that I should be persuaded to go to Rome and to teach there, rather than at Carthage. Nor will I fail to confess to thee how I was persuaded to this, because hereby thy profound secrets and thy most present mercies may be considered and published. I did not therefore dispose myself to go to Rome because more gain or greater honour was promised me by those friends that inclined me to that journey—though these things also wrought somewhat then upon me—but this was the chief and almost the only cause, that I had heard how there the young men used to study more quietly and were subject to better discipline, not being permitted to rush, in a confused and insolent mob, in upon those schools where their own master did not teach, no, nor even to enter therein at all, unless he should permit thereof. Whereas at Carthage the scholars take a deformed and insolent liberty to break in audaciously, and almost after the fashion of madmen to disturb that order which any master has instituted for the profit of his scholars. They do many things injuriously with a strange kind of stupidity, and even such as are justly punished by law—were it not that they are pardoned out of custom—a custom which shows them to be the more miserable, in that through it they do these things as lawful, which will never be so by thine eternal law. And they think they do it without punishment, whereas indeed they are punished by the blindness to which they are subject in so doing; and thereby do they suffer that which is incomparably worse than the things which they impose upon others. It came about therefore that I, who as a student would not have to do with the manners of these men, when I grew to be a teacher was fain to endure them in others; and so I was desirous to go to some such place as where, by general report, I had learned that no such thing was in use. But thou, *O my hope and my portion in the land of the living,* in order that I might change my earthly dwelling for the saving of my soul, wast driving me forth from Carthage and drawing me on to Rome, by means of certain men who took pleasure in this dying-life—in the one place doing mad things, and promising vain things in the other—and for the reforming of my ways wast secretly using both their perversity and mine own. For both they who disturbed my quiet were blinded by that ugly rage of theirs; and I, who there detested true misery, did aspire to find a false happiness somewhere else.

But indeed, to what end I went thence and thither, thou knewest, O God, though thou didst not then discover the fact to me nor to my mother, who passionately lamented my journey, and who followed me so far as the sea would let her. But I deceived her, though she even held me by force, either to make me stay with her or to take her with me. For I pretended that I had a friend whom I could not leave until he should embark with a fair wind. Thus I lied to my mother, yea, to such a mother, and so escaped from her. Even this sin thou hast mercifully forgiven me, preserving me, though full of execrable uncleanness, from those sea waters, that I might arrive to the water of thy grace in baptism; that thereby my soul might be washed, and those floods which fell from my mother's eyes might be dried up, which for me did daily bedew the ground whereon she prayed. But she refusing to return without me, I hardly persuaded her to remain for that night in a place very near to our embarkation, where stood an oratory in memory of the blessed Cyprian. But that night I secretly departed, and she remained weeping and praying. And what did she beg of thee, O my God, with so many tears, but that thou wouldst hinder my navigation? But thou, profoundly considering and hearkening to that whereon her main desire was set, didst not regard what she then particularly desired, that thou mightest the better accomplish in me what she had begged so long.

In the meantime the wind blew, the sails were filled, and the shore withdrew itself from our sight. But she, the morning after, grown wild with lamentation and grief, with sobs began to fill thine ears, which at the time did heed them not; when, by means of mine own desires, thou didst both hasten me towards the ending of the same desires, and didst punish my mother's carnal affection towards me with the just scourge of sorrow. For she loved my presence, after the manner of mothers, and much more than many mothers, and she knew not what joy thou wouldst impart unto her by occasion of that absence of mine. She knew it not, and therefore did she exclaim and weep, and by those torments was she proved to be one of the children of Eve, with sorrow seeking that which with sorrow she had brought forth. But after she had ended her accusation of my falsehood and my cruelty, betaking herself again to pour out her prayers for me before thee, she returned to her house, and I went on towards Rome.

Of a dangerous sickness that he had

AND behold, there was I visited with the scourge of corporal sickness, and I was then verily going down into hell, bearing all those grievous sins which I had committted against thee and myself and many others, besides the bond of original sin whereby we *all die in Adam*. For as yet thou hadst not forgiven me any of them in Christ, nor had he yet, by his cross, *discharged the account of those enmities* which I had incurred by my sins. For indeed, how should he discharge it by the crucifying of that phantasmal flesh which I then believed to be his? For the death of his body did not seem to me more false, than the death of my soul was then true; and as true as the death of his body was indeed, so false was the life of my soul which believed not his true death. My fever growing upon me, I was even upon the very point of perishing. For whither could I have gone, if I then died, but into such fire and torments as had been worthily allotted unto my sins by thy just decree? My mother knew nothing of this, yet was she praying for me in my absence; and thou, who art everywhere present, didst hearken to her where she was, and hadst mercy on me where I was, so far as to restore my bodily health, though my sacrilegious soul was still sick and mad. Nor did I desire baptism in that so great danger of mine, for I had been better affected when I was but a boy and begged it of my mother's devotion, as I have already recited and confessed.

But now I was grown worse as I was grown older, and, like one who is frantic, I scoffed at that medicine of thine, by which thou wouldst not suffer me, though such as I was, to die a double death; for if my mother's heart should have been pierced through with that wound, it could never have been cured. For I have not words sufficient to express what extreme affection she bore towards me, and with how much more solicitude she brought me forth daily in spirit, than she had done with pain in the flesh. I see not therefore how she could have been cured, if such a death of mine as that had transpierced the bowels of her love towards me. And what should have become of those prayers, so fervent and so frequent, which she made for me at all times and in all places before thee? Or couldst thou, O God of mercies, *despise the contrite and humble heart* of a widow, so chaste and so devout, who was ever giving of alms, in humility serving thy saints, omitting upon no day to be present at the oblation upon thine altar, coming to the church twice daily, morning and evening without intermission, not caring for old wives' tales nor tattling, but desiring that she might hear thee in thine inspirations, and that thou wouldst hear her in her petitions? Couldst thou by whose mercy she was made such, refuse to succour her, and contemn those tears whereby she begged not gold or silver of thee, or any other transitory or frail fortune, but only the salvation of her son's soul? Surely not, Lord, thou couldst not; nay thou wast present and didst hearken unto her, and fulfil what she desired, though in such sort as thou hadst preordained. Let it be far from my heart to think that thou couldst deceive her in those visions and answers which she had of thee—both such as are and such as are not herein recorded by me—which she laid up in her faithful breast, and which in her prayers she would ever be urging upon thee as thine own handwriting. For thou dost vouchsafe, O Lord, *because thy mercy endureth for ever,* to become by thy promises a debtor even to them all whose debts thou dost forgive.

His errors before he came to embrace the evangelical doctrine

THOU didst therefore recover me of that sickness, and didst cure, at that time, the son of thine handmaid in his body, that at another time he might be capable of a more certain and better health, which thou hadst in mind to give. I associated myself, even then at Rome, to those false and deceiving saints, and that not only to those who were their disciples—of which number he also was, in whose house I had been sick and did recover—but withal to them who were called " elect." For as yet it still seemed to me that it was not we who sinned, but that this was done by I know not what other nature that remained in us. And my pride took pleasure to be without fault; and, when I had done any ill, not to confess that I had done it, that so thou mightest heal my soul *because I had sinned against thee.* But I loved to excuse myself, and to accuse some other thing, which was with me and yet was not I. But in truth I was all one whole, and my iniquity had divided me against myself, and my sin was so much the more incurable for that I did not count myself to be a sinner, and most execrable was my iniquity, because I would rather have thee, O God omnipotent, even thee, I say, to thee, I say, to be overcome by me to my destruction, than myself to be overcome by thee to my salvation.

Thou hadst not yet therefore *set a guard before my mouth, nor locked the door of self-control about my lips,* that *my heart might not incline to wicked words, or to the making of excuses which I made for my sins, amongst men who were workers of iniquity.* Therefore did I still live in

society with those " elect " of theirs, though now despairing
that I should profit by that false doctrine. And though I
was resolved to remain quiet in the same, if I should
discover nothing better, yet did I more remissly and more
negligently retain the same.

Then also this thought grew upon me, that those philosophers who are called Academics are wiser than the rest,
because they hold that all things are to be doubted of, and
have defined this opinion, that no truth can be compre-
hended by man; for to me they did seem clearly to
think thus, as indeed is commonly understood, though as
yet I did not understand their true meaning. Nor did I
forbear to dissuade the master of the house wherein I lay
from the too great confidence which I found he had in
those fabulous narrations, whereof the Manichæan books
are full. But yet I still embrace the friendship of such as
held to this heresy more familiarly than I did that of other
men, though I did not any longer defend it with my former
ardour, howsoever my familiarity with these persons—for
Rome did hide a great number of them—made me more
slothful to seek out any other. Especially considering that
I despaired to find in thy Church that truth from which
they had diverted me, O Lord of heaven and earth, Creator
of all things visible and invisible. And it seemed to me a
matter of great turpitude to think that thou hast the figure
of our human flesh, and art limited by the corporal
dimension of our body. And because, when I desired to
think upon my God, I knew not how to think but upon the
bulk of bodies—for that which was not such seemed to me
to be nothing—this was the greatest and almost the only
cause of my inevitable error.

For hence it was that I believed that evil was a kind of
substance, and that it had a kind of bulk belonging to it,
either deformed and gross, which they called earth, or light
and subtle, such as is the body of air; and this wicked substance or mind they imagine to be creeping on the earth.
And because the little inclination to piety which I then had

did yet oblige me to believe that the good God had not created any wicked nature, I fancied to myself two bulks, which I placed one against the other, both of them infinite, but the wicked nature more narrow and the good one more large; and out of this pestiferous principle other sacrileges did follow. For when my mind endeavoured to have recourse to the Catholic faith, I was beaten back again, because that was not the Catholic faith which I thought to be it. And I seemed to myself less irreverent if I should believe thee, O my God, to whom thy mercies do now confess by my lips, to be infinite in all other respects but one—for where I opposed to thee that bulk of evil, I was constrained to confess thee to be finite—than if I should pronounce thee to be determinate by the form of a human body. And I thought it better for me to believe that thou hadst created no evil—because to me, who was ignorant, evil did not only seem to be some kind of substance, but even a corporeal substance, because I knew not how to think of a mind or spirit except as being a subtle kind of body and that diffused through space—than that I should believe such a thing, as I conceived evil to be by its nature, could have come from thee. Our Saviour also himself, thy only begotten son, I so conceived to have been brought forth for our salvation out of the most bright part of thy bulk or substance, since I believed no other thing of him but what I could vainly imagine. Such a nature as that, therefore, I thought could not be born of the Virgin Mary, unless it were incorporated to her flesh, but how it could be incorporated and not thereby defiled I could not see because of the fancies I had framed about it. I feared therefore to believe that he was born in the flesh, lest so I should have been obliged to believe that he was defiled by the flesh. Now will thy spiritual children laugh at me in a gentle and loving manner if they read these confessions of mine, but yet such I was.

How he conferred with the Catholics

BESIDES I thought that those things which the Manichees reprehended in the Scriptures could not be defended; but yet I sometimes desired to examine them one by one with some man most learned in those books, and thereupon to see what he held. For already the speech of a certain Helpidius, speaking and discoursing against the Manichees, had begun to move me, even whilst I was still at Carthage; since he produced passages out of the Scriptures such as could not easily be impugned. And I thought the answer of the others was weak, the which, forsooth, they would not willingly be drawn to deliver in public, but only to us in secret. For they would say that the Scriptures of the New Testament were falsified by I know not whom, that had a mind to engraft the Jewish law upon the faith of Christ; whereas they themselves did yet produce no copies thereof which were uncorrupted. But most of all was I held fast and suffocated by my cogitations as to those " bulks," under which I was struggling for breath, but knew not how to inhale that pure and clear air of thy Truth.

The fraud which the scholars at Rome used against their masters

I DID begin, therefore, seriously to do that for which I came, which was to teach Rhetoric at Rome; and at first to draw some home to my lodging, to whom and by whom I might be made more known. And behold, I found that some disorders were committed at Rome, which I used not to endure in Africa. For of a truth I was told that no " destroyings " were suffered to be made by those wicked youths; " but," said they to me, " to avoid the payment of that stipend which they owe to their masters, it is a common thing for many to conspire and transfer themselves suddenly from one master to another, being betrayers of their faith and such as tread Justice under foot for love of money." My heart also did hate these men, though not *with a perfect hatred;* for perhaps I hated them more because I myself was to suffer from them, than for that they did wickedly to other folks.

Yet certainly such persons are base, and they defile themselves by departing from thee, by taking pleasure in putting upon men certain lewd tricks of the times, and also in their dirty gain which, when it is apprehended, defiles the hand, and by embracing this world which flieth away and contemning thee who art abiding, and who callest back and pardonest the adulterous soul of man, if it will return to thee. Even now I hate such perverse and crooked natures as those, though I would love them if they would mend, by preferring the knowledge of what they learn before their money, and before their learning preferring thee, O God, the Truth and plenty of all assured good and the most chaste peace. But at that time I was rather unwilling to suffer their evil doing in mine own respect, than I was desirous that they should become good for thine.

How, going to Milan to teach rhetoric, he was there received by Saint Ambrose

ACCORDINGLY, when they of Milan had sent to the Prefect of the city of Rome to provide a Master of Rhetoric for their city, and to furnish him for the journey at the public cost, I made application therefor, by means of those very Manichees who were so spiritually drunk, and whose company I went away to avoid, though both of us were ignorant thereof at that time. And I procured that Symmachus, who was then the Prefect, on my making a public oration for the post, should approve and send me thither. Thus I came to Milan and to Ambrose the Bishop, a man known and esteemed throughout the world and a devout worshipper of thee, whose discourse did plentifully dispense abroad the *fatness of thy wheat and the smoothness of thine oil and the sober delights of thy wine, unto thy people*. To him I was led by thee, all unknowing that I was led to him that I might know thee.

That man of God received me after a fatherly manner, and approved my coming as became a true bishop. And I began to love him, not at first as one who was a teacher of true doctrine—which I wholly despaired of finding in thy Church—but as a man who was courteous to me. I willingly heard him preaching to the people, yet not with that intention which I should have brought, but spying, as it were, upon his eloquence, whether it were agreeable to the fame that ran of him, or more or less than was reported. I was careless and despised the matter which he delivered, but I was attentive and delighted with the sweetness of his speech, which—howsoever it were more learned—I found not to be so pleasing and winning as was that of Faustus. But in point of the matter there was indeed no comparison to be made, for Faustus did but wander up and down among the fallacies of the Manichees, whereas Ambrose did most substantially teach salvation. But *salvation is far from sinners,* such as I was then, and yet, by little and little, I grew daily nearer to it, though I knew not how.

How, having heard Saint Ambrose, he by little and little did forsake his errors

THOUGH I troubled not myself much to learn those things which he taught, but only to observe in what manner he expressed them—for since I despaired of ever finding any way to thee, this vain care alone was left to me—yet, together with his words, which I liked, the things themselves, which I neglected, came into my mind, for I knew not how to sever the twain. And whilst I opened my heart to perceive how eloquently he spake, the consideration of the truth of what he said did enter also, though indeed it was by small degrees. For first of all it seemed to me that what he said could be defended, and I thought no longer that the Catholic faith—for which I was wont to think that nothing could be said against the assaults of the Manichees—could not be maintained without absurdity; especially when I heard the hard places of the Old Testament explained one after another, for while I used to read those Scriptures *in the letter, I was slain in the spirit.* And so when many passages of those books had been expounded, I began to cast away that desperate conceit of mine, whereby I thought that the Law and the Prophets could not by any means be upheld against the hatred and scorn of such as were the adversaries thereof.

Yet I did not think myself obliged thereby to hold the Catholic way, although it might have many learned men who answered all objections both copiously and with probability. Nor yet conceived I that opinion to be false which formerly I had professed, because now I thought that both the sides were equal. For although the Catholic cause seemed not to me to be overcome, as yet withal I took it not to be victorious. Now therefore I did earnestly intend my mind to see if it were possible to convince the Manichees of falsehood by any certain argument; and, if I could once have come to conceive of a spiritual substance, all their fancies and devices would have been dissolved and rejected utterly, but this I could not yet do.

Yet forasmuch as concerned the mass or body of the world and all those other natural things which the sense of man could reach unto, the more I observed and compared these men with others, the more I was assured that many of the Philosophers had discoursed with greater probability than they. And therefore, doubting now of all things, and wavering up and down in the midst of them after the manner of the Academics, or as they are supposed to do, I resolved that I must abandon the Manichees, conceiving that, even in this time of my suspense, it was not fit for me to continue in that sect, before which I preferred many of the Philosophers I did not wholly commit the care of my languishing soul, because they had no knowldge at all of the saving name of Christ. I resolved, therefore, to be a catechumen in the Catholic Church, which had been so earnestly recommended to me by my parents, until such time as some certainty of truth should appear, whereby I might direct my course.

BOOK SIX

How Augustine was neither a Manichee nor a Catholic

O Thou, my hope even from my youth, where wast thou,
and whither wert thou gone? Was it not thou who madest
me, and didst distinguish me from the beasts of the earth
and the fowls of the air? Thou madest me wiser than they,
and yet I went walking *through dark and slippery places,*
and I sought thee without myself, and I found not the God
of my heart; but I came on even to the depths of the sea,
and I distrusted and despaired of ever finding out the
Truth. By this time my mother, whom devotion and affection had made adventurous, was come to me; for she
followed me by sea and land, and in all her dangers she
was secure in thee. Yea, even in the storms at sea she
would be cheering up the mariners—by whom the
apprehensive passengers, when they be perplexed, are wont
to be comforted—assuring them that they would arrive
in safety, for so much hadst thou promised her in a vision.

  She found me deeply endangered by a despair of ever
coming to know the truth. But when I had told her that
while as yet I was no Catholic Christian, I was no more a
Manichee, she did not leap for joy—like one who had heard
some very unexpected thing—although thereby she was
made secure as to that half of my misery, wherein she used
to weep for me as one dead yet not past being revived by
thee, and used to offer me upon the bier of her prayers that
thou mightest say to the son of this widow woman, *"Young
man, I say unto thee, arise";* and he might revive and begin
to speak, and thou mightest restore him to his mother. Her
heart, I say, did not beat in any turbulent rejoicing when
she heard that to be already done in great part which, with
daily tears, she desired might be wholly done; and that I

was free from falsehood though not yet given up into the hands of truth. Or rather because she was certain that thou, who hadst promised her the whole, wouldst also vouchsafe to impart the rest, she did most peacefully with a heart full of confidence make answer to me, how she hoped assuredly in Christ that, before she was to depart out of this life, she would see me a faithful Catholic.

This she said unto me. But to thee, O thou fountain of mercies, she despatched more fervent prayers and more frequent tears that thou *wouldst make haste to help me* and to *illuminate my darkness;* and she would run more eagerly to the church and hang upon the lips of Ambrose, *as a fountain of water springing up unto eternal life.* For she loved that man as a very angel of God, because she knew that by his means I had been brought to that wavering state of mind, and she felt assured that I should be carried on from the sickness wherein I was unto perfect health; though perhaps I might first seem to incur some further danger, as it were by a crisis, to speak after the manner of physicians.

Of the offerings of bread and wine, which were wont to be made at the tombs of the martyrs

WHEN, therefore, my mother brought to the shrines of the saints some provision of cakes, bread, and wine, according to the custom in Africa, and was forbidden by the door-keeper to carry them in; as soon as she understood that the Bishop had so ordained, she did piously and obediently submit, so that I myself did wonder to see her brought with such ease to condemn her own ancient custom rather than to question the present prohibition. For no delight in material wine had overtaken her spirit, nor did the love of it make her hate the true wine, which is thy Truth, as happeneth in the case of many men and women, who take no more gust in soberly celebrating thy praises, than drunkards would do to have their wine soundly watered. But she, though she used to bring her little basket with those provisions, whereof she was wont reverently to taste and then give the rest away, would proffer but one small cup of wine, tempered with much water, according to her sober palate, whereof she might taste a little. And if there were many shrines of such as were deceased which seemed worthy of the like honour, she was wont still to carry the same measure, which thus became not only almost all water, but even, by that time, to be lukewarm with long carrying about; and this she would impart to such as were present by small sips only, because she came not thither to seek pleasure but devotion.

As soon, therefore, as she found that this custom was prohibited by that most excellent preacher and holy prelate Ambrose, even to them who yet did use it modestly—both that so no occasion of riot should be given by the sober-minded to such as were given to excess in drinking, and also because that manner of celebrating the memory of the dead did very much resemble the superstition of the gentiles—she did most willingly abstain from the same. And instead of a basket filled with the fruits of the earth, she learned to carry her heart full of more pure desires to the tombs of the martyrs; that she might bestow upon the poor what she was able, and that the communion of the body of our Lord might be rightly celebrated where, in the imitation of his Passion, those martyrs had been sacrificed and crowned.

But yet it seems to me, O Lord, and this is the thought of my heart hereof in thy sight, that my mother would not perhaps have yielded so easily to the putting away of her custom, if she had been prohibited by any other whom she had not loved so well as Ambrose, but him she did extremely affect out of regard for my spiritual good. He also loved her for her most religious conversation, who, full of good works and fervent in devotion, did so frequent the church, that he would often, when he saw me, break out into praises of her, congratulating me in that I had such a mother, whilst he knew not withal what kind of a son she had in me, who made doubt of all these things, and thought that the way of life could not by any means be found.

Of the earnest business and the studies of Saint Ambrose

Nor as yet did I groan in prayer that thou wouldst help me, but my mind was eager to search and earnest for discussion. And I accounted Ambrose to be a happy kind of man according to this world, whom persons of such rank did honour; only his celibacy seemed to me a thing too hard to be borne. But what hopes he carried in his breast, or what difficulties he had in resisting the temptations to which even his very eminence made him subject, what comforts he found in his adversities, what savoury joys he took in feeding upon thy Bread in the hidden mouth of his heart, I had neither tried myself, nor could I conjecture. Nor did he know ought of my secret fever, nor of that pit of danger into which I was fallen. For I could not demand of him what I would, nor in what manner I would, since so many troops of men full of business, to whose infirmities he condescended, were interposing themselves and shutting me out both from his ears and from his tongue. When he was not with them, which yet was very seldom, he would be refreshing his body with the necessary food or his mind with study. For, while he was reading, his eyes would run over the leaves and his heart would search into the sense, but his voice and his tongue were silent.

Often when we were present—for he did not forbid any man to enter, nor was it his custom to be told beforehand of such as came to speak with him—we found him thus reading to himself and never otherwise. And after sitting there a long time in silence—for whom amongst us would venture to interrupt him so intent upon his study?—we were fain to depart. For we conjectured that he would not willingly be distracted from recreating his mind with study in the little time wherein he found himself at rest from the clamour of other men's business. And perhaps he had a fear lest, his auditors being doubtful and unsatisfied if the author whom he had in hand should deliver anything obscurely, he might be forced to explain it, and, by occasion thereof, might fall into the discussion of yet harder questions; and so, his time being spent upon such speech, he should have less leisure than he desired to turn over the volumes that he wished to read. Peradventure also he had a respect to the conserving of his voice, which was weakened very easily if he spoke much, and this might be a more just reason for his reading in silence. But whatsoever was the motive for which he did it, in such a man it was certainly a good one.

Thus it was that I had no opportunity to ask those things which I desired to know from that holy oracle of thine, his breast, save only in such cases as when the answer might be put in few words. For those tumults of my heart would have required to find him full of leisure, that so I might have poured them out before him, but this fortune they never met withal. Only every Sunday I heard him *preaching the word of truth* aright to the people, and I was more and more confirmed in this, that all the knots of crafty calumnies might be dissolved, which those our deceivers had used to bring against those divine books of thine.

But when at length I also found that the words *Man was made by thee after thine own image* were not understood by thy spiritual children, whom of our Catholic mother thou hast regenerated by grace, as if they did believe or so much as conceive thee to be determined by the limits of a human body—although I did not at all apprehend, not even in a confused manner, how there could be any spiritual substance—yet did I blush, though full of joy, to find that for so many years I had been barking not against the Catholic faith but against the fancies and fictions of carnal thoughts. But yet I had been rash and impious in that I had said those things accusingly which I ought to have learned inquiringly. For thou, who art most high, most near, most secret, and most present, who hast not members some greater and some less, nor art in any place but art all everywhere, thou, I say, art assuredly no corporeal thing; yet *thou madest man after thine own image,* and behold from head to foot he is contained in some certain place.

Of the letter and the spirit

SINCE therefore I was ignorant how this image of thine could subsist, I ought studiously to have inquired how it was to be believed by me, and not insolently to have opposed it, as if it were in such wise believed. And the gnawing care as to what I should hold for the truth did feed upon my very heart so much the more sharply, for that —being so long mocked and deluded by the promise of certainty—I had with childish error gone prating of so many uncertain things as if they had been certain. For that they were falsehoods did not appear to me until afterwards, but already I was certain that they were uncertain, though I had held all this while that they were certain, when, with a blind and contentious spirit, I had accused thy Catholic Church; which, though I had not yet found to teach truly, I had already found not to teach those other things whereof I so bitterly accused her. Therefore was I confounded with shame, and I began to be converted, and I rejoiced, O my God, to learn that thy one Church, the mystical body of thine only Son, wherein the name of Christ had been laid upon me while yet an infant, did not relish those childish toys, nor had any such thing in her sound doctrine as that thou, the Creator of all things, wast contracted or thrust into any space or measure of place which, how large and sublime soever it might be, was yet limited and determined by the figure of human limbs.

I was glad also that the ancient writings of the Law and the Prophets were no longer read by me with that eye to which formerly they seemed absurd, when I misliked thy saints as if they taught such and such things, when as indeed they did not do so at all. And I rejoiced when I heard Ambrose in his sermons to the people most diligently recommend unto them as a rule those words, the *letter killeth but the spirit quickeneth;* and when those things which, if understood literally, might seem to induce a man to a perverse belief, were spiritually opened and expounded by him, the mystical veil thereof being removed. Nor spake he anything which offended me, although he said those things concerning truth whereof I was ignorant. For I kept my heart free from giving a firm assent to anything, and fearing the precipice was slain yet more surely by the halter.[1] For I desired to be assured of that which I did not see, as fully as I was certain that seven and three make ten.

For I was not yet so far out of my wits as to think that this last proposition could not be known for certain, but the same certainty which I found in this I desired also to find in other things, whether they were corporeal, though not then present to my senses, or spiritual, whereof I knew not yet how to think but in a corporeal manner. By believing I might have been cured and, the eye of my mind being made clean, it might have been directed in some sort towards thy truth, which is eternal and never failing at any point. But as sometimes it happeneth that he who hath fallen into the hands of an unskilled physician is loth afterwards to commit himself even to a good one, so was it in the state of my soul, which could not be healed but by believing. Yet, for fear of believing false things, it refused to be cured, resisting those hands of thine which had compounded the remedies of faith, and sprinkled them upon the diseases of the world, and recommended them to mankind with so great an authority.

[1] See Note 5.

Of the authority and necessary use of the Holy Scripture

HEREUPON therefore, I now began to prefer the Catholic
doctrine, and to think also that it acted more modestly and
with far less deceit when it required men to believe something which was not demonstrated—whether it could be so
demonstrated, but not to all perhaps, or whether it could
not be demonstrated at all—than did the Manichees,
who first, with their rash promises of scientific knowledge,
brought credulity into derision, and then enjoined men to
believe many most fabulous and absurd things, even because
they could not be demonstrated. Then by little and little,
O Lord, thou didst, with a most sweet and merciful hand,
stroke and compose my heart, causing me to consider what
innumerable other things I believed, which I had never seen
and at the doing whereof I was not present, such as those
numberless things which are recorded in the history of the
several nations, of places and cities which I had not seen, so
many also which are the reports of friends, of physicians
and of many other men; things, too, which we must
believe, else could nothing be done in this life. And lastly
I retained a most unshaken assurance that I knew of what
parents I was born, which yet I could not know but by
giving credit to hearsay. And thus didst thou persuade
me that they were not blameworthy who believed thy
books, which thou hast established by so high an authority
throughout almost all nations of the earth, but that they
indeed were blameable who believed them not; and that
no ear was to be given to any if peradventure they should
say to me, "How dost thou know that these books were
imparted to mankind by the spirit of the One, True, and
most Truthful God?" For that is the very thing which is
most credible, since not all the brawling about captious
questions, whereof I had found so many of the Philosophers
fighting with one another, could ever extort from me that

at any time I should believe thee not to be—though what indeed thou art I might not know—or that the government of human things did not belong to thee.

This of a truth I believed—though sometimes more stiffly and sometimes again more remissly—yet did I ever believe that thou art, and that thou hast a care of us; albeit I was ignorant both of what was to be thought touching thy substance, or what way did lead men unto thee, or bring them back. And seeing therefore that we were thus weak in finding out the truth by the way of evident reason, and that for this cause we had need of the authority of thy holy books, I began to believe that thou wouldst in no case have given so eminent authority to that Scripture throughout the whole world, unless thou hadst been pleased that we should both believe in thee and should seek thee by means thereof. For that in those books which was wont to offend me as if it had been absurd, since now I had heard many of them expounded probably, I began to refer to the height of the mysteries which they contained. And the authority thereof seemed so much the more venerable to me and worthy of our religious credit, because it was both open for all the world to read, and yet it reserved the dignity of the secret which it carried in a more profound sense; exhibiting itself to all in terms most evident and in a manner of speech most humble, and exercising the attention of such as are not light of heart; to the end that it might receive all men into that ample bosom, and through those difficult passages might convey and ferry over some few towards thee. Yet even those few are many more than they would have been, if either it had not obtained so great an eminence of authority, or if it did not draw the multitudes of thy people into the bosom of its holy humility. Such things as these I thought, and thou wast with me; I sighed, and thou didst hear me; I drifted up and down, and thou didst guide me; I walked through the broad way of the world, and thou didst not forsake me.

Of the misery of such as are ambitious, and how he was moved by the example of a beggar

I was gaping after honours, wealth, and marriage, and thou laughedst at me. In these desires I was subject to most bitter difficulties; for thou thyself wast so much the more merciful to me therein as thou wert far from suffering anything to grow delightful unto me which was not thyself. O Lord, behold my heart, thou who art pleased that I should remember and confess unto thee. Now let my soul cleave unto thee, which thou hast freed from that so clinging slough of death. So miserable was it, that it had lost the feeling of that wound it had; and thou didst cleanse it, to the end that, leaving all other things, it might be converted unto thee, who art above all things, and without whom all things are nothing, that it might be converted to thee and so be healed. How miserable therefore was I, and how didst thou proceed with me that I might be able to find my misery, upon that day when I was preparing to make an oration in praise of the Emperor, wherein I was to utter many untruths, and was to be applauded by them who knew that they were so; and my heart was panting with the heat of these cares and did even boil again with the fever of these consuming thoughts. As I was passing through one of the streets of Milan I observed a poor beggar, at that moment half drunk, I believe, for he was jocund and full of sport, whilst I the while was sad of heart. At this I discoursed with my friends who were with me, about the many afflictions to which we were obliged by these mad affections of ours. Because, by all those labours under which we then groaned—dragging after us the burden of our misery, and urged by the spurs of sharp desire which we made worse by dragging thereat—we aspired to nothing else but some secure kind of joy, to which that beggar had already attained, while we perhaps might never come there. For that temporal felicity which he had won by means of a few pence that he had begged, the same was I contriving and compassing by other so intricate and painful ways.

True it is that the joy which he had was not the true joy, but yet I, by my ambition, was seeking after one more false by far. And certainly he was merry while I was melancholy, and he was safe while I was full of fear. If any man should ask me whether I had rather rejoice or fear I should say "rejoice." Again if he should demand whether I had rather be that beggar or myself, I should rather choose to be myself, although I was wearied with cares and fears; yet would not this be against reason, for could it be so in truth? For I ought not to prefer myself before him on the ground that I was more learned than he, for this was not the cause of my rejoicing; but by it I sought only the means of pleasing men, not to instruct them but only to please them. For this cause thou didst even break these bones of mine with the rod of thine instruction.

Away from the soul then with those who say unto her, "The important thing is from what ground a man's joy proceeds; that beggar was glad through being filled with wine, but thou desiredst to be made glad by the purchase of glory." What glory, O Lord? The glory which is not in thee! For as that joy of his was no true joy, so neither was the glory I aspired to any true glory, and it turned my head even more. For he that same night would sleep off his drunkenness, while I had carried mine to bed with me and had risen with it many a time, and might do so yet again for I knew not how long after. Yet still I know that the important thing is from what ground a man's joy proceeds; and that the joy of a true and faithful hope is incomparably to be preferred beyond that vanity. But still between us two there was yet a great difference, for he was happier then than I, not only because he was full of mirth when I was even embowelled with care, but because he had gotten his wine by wishing men good luck, while I was striving by my flattery to swell myself up with pride. Many things did I then say to this purpose to my dear friends, and I often saw in them that which I now found in myself; and I found myself in an evil way. And for this I grieved, and thereby I doubled my grief; and if any prosperity smiled upon me it grieved me to apprehend it, because, almost before I could close my hand upon it, it flew away.

How he delivered Alipius, his dear companion, from the madness of the circus

WE who lived together as friends were jointly afflicted with such thoughts as these, but most familiarly and confidently did I communicate them with Alipius and Nebridius, of whom Alipius was born in the same town as myself, of parents who were the chief persons in that place. He was somewhat younger than I, and had studied under me; first in our town, when I had begun to teach, and afterwards at Carthage. He loved me much, because I seemed to him to be learned and of a good disposition; and I him, for the promise he gave both of virtue and of wit, which appeared to be great, even when his age was not so. Yet the whirlpool of those ill customs that were received at Carthage, where the idler sort of public spectacles was in great request, had engulfed him in the madness of the circus. Whilst he was swallowed up thereby, I had already become a teacher of rhetoric there and kept a public school, but he frequented me not as a master, by reason of some difference that had arisen between his father and me. Therefore, although I found that he was ruinously devoted to the circus, and I was myself much disquieted that he should thus go about to quench the hope that was conceived of him, if indeed he had not already done so, I yet had no means of recalling or restraining him, either by authority as a master, or by the interest of friendship; for I supposed him to be of his father's mind concerning me, although indeed he was not so. But he, laying aside his father's wishes in the matter, began to salute me, coming sometimes to my lecture hall, to hearken awhile and then be gone. In the meantime I had forgotten my design of remonstrating with him, that he should not destroy so good a wit by the blind and furious pursuit of those vain sports.

But thou, O Lord, who sittest at the helm of all those things which thou hast made, didst not forget that he was one day to stand forth among thy children as a chief priest of thy sacrament; and, that his amendment might clearly be seen to be thy doing, thou didst even effect it by my means, who yet knew nothing of it. For one day, while I was sitting in my accustomed place with my scholars before me, in he came, saluted me, sat him down, and attended to what we were saying. I had by chance a passage in hand such that, whilst I was explaining it, a similitude from the circus came in very fitly, whereby that which I expounded was the more pleasantly and more easily to be received, and withal a sharp kind of derision was cast upon such as were subject to that madness. Thou knowest, O thou God of ours, that at the time I had no thought of curing Alipius of that plague. But he took it to himself, and conceived me to have spoken it only in respect of him. And that which another man would have made an occasion of wrath against me, this honest young man made a reason why he should be offended with himself and should love me the more ardently. For long ago thou didst say and write in thine own book: *Reprove a wise man, and he will love thee.*

Yet for my part I had not reproved him, but thou, using all men—as well those who know what they do, as those who know it not—in that order which thyself knowest, the which is just, didst frame and draw out of my heart and tongue certain burning coals, whereby thou mightest sear and heal that promising mind of his, which was pining away. Let such a one conceal thy praises who considereth not thy mercies, which the very marrow of my bones doth confess to thee. For he, after those words, did speedily snatch himself out of that pit so deep, wherein he was wilfully plunged over head and ears and blinded with so strange a delight; and with strong temperance he shook his mind so that all the filth of the circus flew off from him, and returned no more. Nay, after this he overcame his father's unwillingness so far as to make me his master, for the latter gave way and consented. Thus Alipius, being again a scholar of mine, was also wrapped up with myself in that superstition, loving in the Manichees that ostentation of continency which he conceived to be sincere and true. But indeed it was senseless and seducing, and it led into captivity precious souls, such as were not yet able to reach the height of virtue, but were easily deceived with a show of that which indeed was but a kind of shadow and counterpart thereof.

How Alipius was taken with a desire of seeing the fights of Gladiators, which formerly he had abhorred

HE, therefore, since he forsook not that worldly course which his parents had inculcated to him, went before me to Rome that he might study the Law, and there he was carried away with an incredible appetite for the fights of gladiators; is it not incredible? For when at first he was utterly averse to and detesting such spectacles as those, certain friends and fellow-students of his, coming casually upon him one day after dinner, did conduct him, with a kind of friendly violence, to the amphitheatre, at a time when those tragical and deadly pastimes were being presented, he the while protesting thus: "Though you drag my body thither to that place, shall you therefore be able to make me open my eyes and apply my mind to those spectacles? No, but I will be absent, even while I am present, and so will I conquer both them and you."

Whereupon they were not the less slow to lead him on, perhaps out of a kind of curiosity to know whether he could be as good as his word. They arrived therefore, and took what places they could find, just as that whole world was seething with the wildest excitement.

Alipius shut the windows of his eyes and forbade his mind to mingle with those crimes. Would to God he had stopped his ears also! For, by occasion of some turn in the fight, a deafening shout of the people burst forth about him and—being overcome with curiosity, and re-solved, whatsoever it was, to despise it when seen and to overcome it—he opened his eyes. Then was he stricken with a deeper wound in his soul than the other was in his body, and he fell more miserably than the poor wretch whom he desired to behold, and upon whose fall that cry had been made; that cry which entered his ears and unlocked his eyes, that a way might be made for the wound-ing and defeating of his soul, which was bold rather than valiant, and so much the weaker for that he trusted upon himself, who ought to have confided only in thee. For as soon as he beheld that blood he drank down with it a kind of savageness; he did not now turn away but fastened his gaze upon it, and drinking up the cup of fury ere he knew it, he became enamoured with the wickedness of those combats, and drunk with a delight in blood. He was no more the Alipius who had come there, but one of the common herd to which he came, and an entire companion of those that led him. What shall I say more? He gazed, he shouted, he burned with the desire of it, and he carried home from thence such a measure of madness as provoked him to return, not only with them by whom he was formerly debauched, but more earnestly than they even go-ing so far as to seduce others also. Yet even from all this thou drewest him with a most strong and merciful hand, and thou taughtest him to confide no more in himself but in thee only; but that was not till a long time after.

How Alipius was apprehended upon suspicion of theft

But this was laid up in his memory for a medicine hereafter, as also was that which befell him when a student under me at Carthage. For walking once at noonday in the market-place, and repeating to himself something that he was to recite, according to the custom of scholars, thou didst suffer him to be apprehended as a thief by the officers of the place. Nor didst thou, as I think, permit this for any other reason, O my God, but that he, who was afterward to prove so great a man, might early begin to learn that one man was not easily to condemn another, of whose cause he was the judge, out of any too easy credulity. He was walking then alone before the Tribunal, with his tablets and *stilus* in his hand, when behold, a certain young scholar, who was indeed a thief, bringing a hatchet with him secretly, did enter—Alipius not perceiving him— and begin to cut away the leaden gratings which cover the booths of the silversmiths. But the noise of the hatchet being heard, the silversmiths who dwelt beneath began to mutter, and sent forth to apprehend whom they should chance to find. The thief, therefore, so soon as he heard their talk, fled away, leaving the instrument behind him, lest with it and by it he might be taken.

But Alipius, who perceived him not as he came in, heard him as he went out, and saw him depart speedily away; and being desirous to understand the cause, went to the place, and finding the hatchet, he paused awhile and wondered at it. When behold, they that were sent found him alone, with the instrument in his hand by the noise whereof they were stirred up. They lay hold of him, drag him away, and having gathered together the neighbours dwelling in the market-place, they congratulate with themselves for taking a notorious thief, and thence they begin to carry him off to the Justices. But no further than this was his lesson to go.

For instantly, O Lord, thou didst come to the succour of his innocency, whereof thou wert the only witness. For, as he was being led off either to prison or to punishment, there encountered them a certain Architect, who had the care of the public buildings. Glad were they to meet him, because he was accustomed to suspect them of stealing goods which were missing from the market-place; so that now he might come to know by whom offences of such a sort were committed.

But this man had often seen Alipius at the house of a certain Senator, to whom he used to pay court, and instantly knowing him, he took him by the hand and led him apart from that confusion of people. Then, inquiring after the cause of that so great mischance, he understood what had been done. Thereupon he required all them that stood around in rage and tumult to go along with him, and so they went to the house of that young man who had committed the theft. Now there was a slave-boy standing at the door, so young that, being without fear of doing his master any hurt thereby, he might likely enough disclose the whole matter to them, for he had followed his master to the market-place. As soon then as Alipius remembered this, he intimated so much to the Architect, and he, showing the hatchet to the boy, asked of him whose it was. "Ours," answered he instantly, and then, being further examined, confessed the rest. Thus was this crime removed from Alipius unto that house, and the multitude was confounded, which had already begun to triumph over him, who thereafter was to become a dispenser of thy word and an examiner of many causes in thy Church, and who now departed with increase of experience and of wisdom.

Of the manner of life which he held with his friends

THIS Alipius then I found at Rome, and he became bound
to me with the tie of inseparable friendship, wherefore he
went with me to Milan that he might not forsake me, and
withal that he might proceed in the study of the Law, unto
which he had applied himself more by his parents' wish
than his own. And there he had thrice sat as Assessor to the
Magistrates, with a contempt for bribes which was the
wonder of all others; while he in his turn was filled with
wonder at those who preferred gain to honesty. His
character was assaulted likewise, not only by the entice-
ment of gain but by the inducement of fear, when at Rome
he was Assessor to the Prefect of the Italian Bounties.

There was at that time a certain Senator, most potent,
to whose favour and fear many were obsequious, and this
man would needs have some matter passed in his favour, as
his influence ofttimes enabled him to do, although by the
laws it was not permitted. Alipius refused. A bribe was
promised him; with his very heart he despised it. Then
threats were used, but he trod them under foot. All the
world admired that rare courage of his, who neither desired
as a friend nor feared as an enemy a man so great and so
infinitely famed for the means he had either to do good or
to do harm. Even the Judge himself, in whose court Alipius
was then Assessor, although he desired not that the thing
should pass, durst not yet refuse the Senator expressly, but
laid the fault upon Alipius, pretending that he was
hindered by him; for in very truth, if he had complied,
Alipius would have left the court. But one thing there
was that did almost pervert him, namely his love of study,
when he was offered the chance of having books copied
for him at a reduced price. But he took counsel with
Justice, and changed his purpose for the better; esteeming
the strict rule of right, whereby he was forbidden to do

such a thing, a better rule to follow than that of opportunity, whereby the chance was offered. This is, indeed, but a little matter, but *he that is faithful in little is faithful also in much,* nor can that possibly be for nothing which proceeded from the mouth of thy Truth: *If you have not been faithful in the unjust Mammon, who shall entrust you with the true riches; and if ye have not been faithful in that which is another's, who shall give you that which is your own?* Such as I have described, then, was Alipius when he adjoined himself to me, and with me he hesitated in his purpose concerning the manner of life which should be followed.

Nebridius also, who, having left his native place near Carthage, and Carthage itself where he used ordinarily to live, and the estate that he had from his father, which was of great value, and having left also his mother—who yet meant not to follow him as mine had done—was now come to Milan, for no other cause but that he might live with me in the most unwearied search after Truth and Wisdom. Together with me he sighed, and with me he hesitated, being a most ardent seeker after the blessed life, and an indefatigable penetrator of the hardest questions.

Thus were we three before thee as so many beggars, sighing out their wants one to another, and *waiting upon thee that thou mightest give to them their meat in due season.* And in all that bitterness which, through thy mercy, did still accompany our worldly activities, continually we saw darkness before us; and we, full of sadness, would turn from it and say, "How long shall things continue thus?" This we often said, yet we left not those things though we spoke thus, because as yet there appeared no certain course for us to follow when we should have left the things whereto we clung.

He deliberateth about the course of life that he would lead

AND I wondered extremely, whilst I was earnestly considering and searching my memory, how much time had slipped away since that nineteenth year of my age, when I began to be earnest in the search of wisdom, and resolved, upon the finding thereof, to give over the empty shadows and lying madness of vain desires. And behold, I was now thirty years old, but still sticking fast in the same mud of my appetite to enjoy things present, which yet were flitting away and dissipating my soul. I still said, "To-morrow I shall find it out, behold it will appear plainly, and I will embrace it." And again, "Faustus the Manichæan will shortly be here, and he will clear away all my difficulties." Or "O ye great men, ye of the Academics, can there be found, as ye say, no certainty concerning the ordering of man's life?" Or "Nay, let us seek the more diligently and pursue it, and let us never despair thereof. Behold already I know that those things which seemed absurd in the Ecclesiastical books are not indeed absurd, and can be honestly understood in another way. I will plant my feet firmly on those steps whereon, as a child, they were set by my parents, till such time as the clear truth may be found out.

" But yet, where shall it be sought, and when? Ambrose is not at leisure, nor have I myself the time to read. Where too shall I find the books? Whence or where shall I obtain them, or of whom can I borrow them? Let my time be distributed, and certain hours set apart for the salvation of my soul. Already there is a great hope, the Catholic Church does not teach that which I conceived, and whereof I did absurdly accuse it. The learned men of that religion do hold it for a detestable opinion that God should be corporeal, and why do I doubt still to knock, to the end that other truths also may be opened to me? My time in the morning is taken up by my scholars, what do I in the rest? Why do I not this? But then, when am I to visit my great friends, of whose favour I have need? When am I to prepare the lectures that I sell to my scholars? When am I to find refreshment and release my mind from the excess of care? Let all these things perish, away with these vain and silly toys; let me employ myself wholly upon the acquisition of Truth alone. This life is miserable, the hour of death uncertain. If suddenly it come upon me, in what case shall I depart hence, and where shall I learn those things which here I have neglected? Shall I not rather undergo the torments due to such negligence? If it be said that death will make an end both of all care and feeling of such matters, let the truth of this be first inquired into; but God forbid that it should be so. It is no matter of light importance, it is no toy, that which is spread over the face of all the world by a height of authority so eminent as hath the Christian faith. Blessings so many and so great would never have been poured down on us from heaven, if the life of the soul did depart with the death of the body. Why, therefore, do I delay to give over all care of this world, and to employ myself wholly upon the finding of God and of the blessed life?

"Yet stay a while. Even these worldly things are pleasant, and carry no small sweetness with them. I must not so easily divorce my mind from them, for it would be shameful if I should make love to them again. Lo, it will be no hard matter to obtain some position of honour, and what should a man desire more? I have store of noble friends, if nothing else, and, if I press my claims, even a post as Governor may be bestowed upon me. Then perhaps a wife with some money may be had, to ease our charges, and there shall be the limit of my desires. Many great persons, and those most worthy of our imitation, have given themselves to the search for Wisdom in the state of marriage."

Whilst I was speaking thus, and my heart was driven to

and fro with every wind, time still slipped away, and I was slow in being converted to my Lord; from day to day I deferred to live in thee, but I deferred not *to die daily* in myself. While I thus desired a happy life, I yet feared to seek it in its true abode, and I fled from it while yet I sought it. For I thought I should be too miserable if I were deprived of the embraces of a woman; and I considered not the medicine and the power of thy mercy in the cure of that infirmity, for thereof I had taken no experience. For I believed that continency was a matter of our own strength which, for my part, I did not think that I possessed; and withal I was so foolish as not to know that it is written: *none can have chastity, unless thou give it.* Yea and thou wouldst not fail to give it me if, with heartfelt groaning, I had besieged thine ears, and if, with solid faith, I had but cast my cares upon thee.

A conference between Alipius and Augustine, concerning marriage and the single life

ALIPIUS indeed it was that kept me from marrying a wife, alleging that, in such event, we could by no means go on living together in that security of leisure for the search after Wisdom which we had so long desired. For in this matter, he was even then of such chastity that it was a thing most admirable; for in the beginning of his youth he had tried that pleasure but was not engaged thereby, so that, being sorry for it and despising it, he lived afterwards in extreme continency. But for my part I opposed to him the example of them who, being married, were yet great lovers of Wisdom, and who were grateful unto God, and who had found and had faithfully loved their friends; though I indeed was far from them in greatness of spirit. Thus I, fast bound with the diseases of the flesh and with the deadly sweetness thereof, dragged my fetters after me, fearing lest they should be loosed; and, as if my wound had been chafed thereby, I repelled the words of good counsel, as I would the hand of one that sought to free me.

Moreover, the serpent spoke by me to Alipius, and by my tongue he wrought and spread in his way certain sweet snares, whereby his honest and still free feet might be entangled. For when he wondered at me, whom he so much admired, for cleaving so fast to the pitch of that pleasure as to affirm, so often as we had speech thereof, that I could not by any means lead a single life, and to defend myself, when I found him wondering at me, by saying that there was a great deal of difference between the pleasure which he had tried by stealth and by snatches—which he now scarce even remembered, and therefore with some colour might despise—and the delight of my daily custom; and that if to this the honourable name of marriage might be added, he ought not to marvel why I contemned not that kind of life. Upon this, I say, he himself also began to desire marriage, not being overcome by the appetite of that pleasure, but only by curiosity; for, said he, he desired to know what kind of thing that was, without which my life, which to him was one of such contentment, would seem to me not a life but a punishment. For his mind, being then free from that bond, was amazed at my servitude, and through that amazement he went on to the desire of making trial thereof, from which he would have passed to the experiment itself, and thereby perhaps might have fallen into that very slavery whereat he was amazed in me; because he would needs *enter into a covenant with death,* and *he that loveth danger shall fall into it.* For neither of us was moved herein, save perhaps but the slightest, by heed to the honour due to the married state and the begetting of children; but the custom of satisfying an insatiable desire of lust did chiefly and vehemently torment me, who was already enslaved thereby, while he was being led on to servitude by wonder only. In this case we were, O most high God, till thou, *being mindful that we are but dust,* hadst mercy on us who were miserable, and didst succour us by wonderful and unknown ways.

How a marriage was arranged for Augustine

AND now there was much ado to get me a wife. Now was I a suitor for her, now she was promised to me, my mother using all endeavour herein to the end that, when I should be married, I might also be baptized. For she was glad to see me daily more and more disposed thereto, and to observe that her prayers and thy promises were to be fulfilled in me by my embracing the faith. Yet when, both through her own desire and at my entreaty, she craved of thee daily with a loud cry of her heart that thou wouldst by a vision discover to her somewhat concerning my future marriage, thou wouldst never do it. She saw indeed certain vain and fantastical things, such as are conjured up by a human spirit which hath wrought busily about some matter, and to me she declared them, but not with that confidence which she used to have when thou thyself didst reveal any matter to her. For she could, as she said—through I know not what gust or taste, which she was not able to express in words—discern between that which was of thy revealing and that which was of her own conceiving. Yet the matter went forward, and the young maid was demanded. She wanted some two years of being marriageable, but because I liked her otherwise, I was content to stay out that time.

How he and his friends laid a plan to live together apart from the world

Now there were many of us friends who, considering and detesting the extreme vexations of a worldly life, deliberated and had wellnigh resolved to live quietly and be far removed from company. And having determined to make that retreat, we purposed to lay together such means as we could get and to frame one purse for all, that, through the sincerity of our affection, there might not be amongst us " mine " or " thine," but that the whole might belong to all, while yet no more might be accounted to belong to all than to every single man. It seemed to us that we might well be some ten persons in this kind of Academy, amongst whom some of us were very rich, and particularly Romanianus, our near countryman, who, even from childhood, had been a most familiar friend of mine, and whom the urgent nature of his business affairs had brought up to the Court. He much encouraged us in this course, and herein his voice was of great authority, because his fortune was much greater than that of the others. It seemed good to us that every year two of our company might be chosen, like officers of a household, to make the necessary provision of our needs, while the rest were undisturbed. But, as soon as we began to consider whether this would be pleasing to our wives—which some of us had already, while I, for my part, was resolved that I would have one—all that scheme, which had been made so well, fell asunder in our hands, and so, being broken, was cast aside. Thence did we return to sighs and groans, and we continued to walk in the broad and beaten ways of the world. For many were the cogitations of our hearts, but *thy counsel doth remain for ever*. And from out that counsel of thine thou didst laugh at ours, and didst prepare thine own; purposing to *give us meat in due season, and to open thy hand and fill our souls with blessing*.

How he continued in his sensuality

In the meantime my sins were multiplied, and that mistress of mine, who was wont to be my bed-fellow, being torn from my side as an impediment to my marriage, my heart that cleaved to her was broken and wounded until it bled.

To Africa then returned she, vowing to thee that she would never know man more, and leaving with me the son whom I had begotten of her. But I, miserable man, unable to imitate the woman, and being impatient of the two years' delay after which I should receive her whom I desired, and being less a lover of marriage than a slave to lust, did procure yet another—though not a wife—by whom that disease of my soul, as strong or even stronger than before, might be sustained and led onward under the safe-conduct of unbroken custom into the kingdom of marriage. Yet neither was that wound cured which had been made in me by cutting off my former love, but after an extreme of burning sorrow it festered, and pained me no less doggedly, although more numb.

Of the immortality of the soul

To thee be praise, to thee be glory, O thou fountain of Mercies. I grew the more miserable, and thou camest nearer to me. Thy right hand was ready even now to take me out of the mire and cleanse me from it, but I knew it not. Nor did anything recall me from that deep pit of carnal pleasure, save the fear of death and of thy future judgement which, for all the changing of my opinions, never departed from my heart. I used to discourse with my friends Alipius and Nebridius concerning the limits of good and evil, and I said that, to my mind, Epicurus should have won the garland, had I not believed that the life of the soul and the reward of our deeds do continue after death, which Epicurus would not believe. And I asked why, if we were immortal and might live in the continual enjoyment of bodily pleasure without any fear of losing it, we should not be happy; or what more could we desire? I knew not that this was a part of my great misery, that I was so drowned and blinded as not to be able to apprehend the light of virtue, and of that beauty which is to be embraced for its own sake, which the eye of flesh cannot see, but only the inner man. Nor did I, miserable wretch, consider from what vein it flowed that I did so delightfully confer with my friends about these things, shameful as they were. For indeed I could not have been happy without friends, in the opinion that I then was, though all carnal pleasures had been at my command in abundance; since I loved those friends for themselves, and I found that I was beloved by them in like manner.

O crooked ways of mine! Woe be to my audacious soul, which hoped that, had it forsaken thee, it might find something else which was better. Though it turn and toss, upon the back and side and breast, it hath found all things hard; and that thou alone art Rest. And behold, thou art near at hand, thou deliverest us from our wretched errors, thou dost place us in thy right way, and dost comfort us, saying, "Run on, and I will carry you, I will conduct you to the end, and even there will I uphold you."

BOOK SEVEN

Rejecting corporeal images, he began to acknowledge God to be incorporeal

Now was the wicked and profane time of my youth dead, and I went on into the state of manhood; and as I was the more grown in years, so much the more was I defiled with vanity. I could conceive of no substance but such as I could see by these eyes of mine, yet I did not conceive of thee, O God, under the figure of a human body. For, from the time that I had first inclined mine ear unto Philosophy, I had fled that falsehood, and I was glad to have found this truth in the faith of our spiritual mother, thy Catholic Church. Yet what I should conceive thee to be, I knew not. And I, being but a man, and such a man, did yet endeavour to conceive thee to be the supreme and only true Good. And with all the powers of my soul I believed thee to be incorruptible, and inviolable, and unchangeable. Because I plainly saw and was certain—though I know not how or by what means I came to know it—that whatsoever was corruptible was worse than that which was not corruptible; and that which could not be violated I did instantly prefer before that which might be violated; and I resolved that what was subject to no mutation was better than that which might be changed.

My heart did violently cry out against all the former fictions of my brain, and at a clap I endeavoured to drive away that fluttering troop of unclean imaginations from the sight of my mind. And yet, being but scarce removed by the twinkling of an eye, behold it came clouding in again upon me, and rushed upon my sight, and darkened it. So that, although I conceived thee not in the form of a human body, yet was I forced to think thee to be some corporeal substance, taking up mighty spaces of place, either infused into the world, or else diffused through infinite spaces without the world. Yea, even thus did I think of the incorruptible, the inviolable, the unchangeable itself, which I preferred before the corruptible, the violable, and the changeable. Because whatsoever I deprived of those spaces seemed to me to be nothing, yea, even very nothingness, not even so much as an emptiness. For if a body were taken out of a place, and the place should remain void of any body, either earthly, or humid, or airy, or celestial, yet would that place still remain, though empty, as it were a measurable nothing.

So gross then was I in mind—though I could not see my own self—that I did think all that to be wholly nothing which was not spread out over certain spaces, or diffused abroad, or amassed into bulk, or swelled up into breadth, or which had not or was not capable of having some such dimensions. For over such forms as these mine eyes were wont to range, through images such as these my mind was wont to rove; nor did I see that this very action of my mind, whereby I framed those images, was no such corporeal thing, inasmuch as it would never have been able to frame them, unless it had itself been somewhat of greater nobility.

So also did I conceive that thou, O thou Life of my life, being great on every side by infinite spaces of place, didst penetrate this huge bulk of the world, and didst pass also beyond it everywhere, vastly and without limit; so that the earth and the heaven and all things did participate of thee, and that they in thee were determined, but not thou at all by them. But, as the body of this air, which we have upon earth, doth not hinder the light of the sun from transpiercing it with the beam thereof nor from penetrating the same, and that not by cutting or by breaking, but by fulfilling it, so did I think that not only the body of heaven, and of the air, and of the sea, but even also that of the earth was pervious and penetrable by thee, in all the parts thereof whether they were great or small, for the receiving of thy presence;

which, by a secret inspiration, doth internally govern all things which thou hast created.

Thus did I conceive, because I knew not what else to think, but yet this was false. For thus the greater part of the earth was to have a greater part of thee, and the less a lesser. And all things should then have been full of thee, in such sort that the body of an elephant should contain so much more of thee than the body of a sparrow, because the one is greater and doth possess more of space than does the other. And so thou shouldst by gobbets have made the great parts of thyself answer to the great parts of the world, and thy lesser parts to the little. But not in such a fashion as this art thou present, but as yet thou hadst not illuminated my darkness.

The manner wherein Nebridius used to confute the Manichees

I HAD answer enough to serve my turn, O Lord, against those deceivers, who were also themselves deceived, and those dumb babblers, who were dumb because they did not utter thy word; I had answer enough, I say, in that which was wont to be propounded long ago by Nebridius, even at Carthage, by which all we that heard it were puzzled. For what, he used to ask, would that imaginary nation or power of darkness, which the Manichees are wont to set up in opposition to thee, have done against thee, if thou shouldst have refused to fight with it? For if it be answered that it would have done thee some hurt, it would follow therefrom that thou wert violable and corruptible. But if it were said that it could not hurt thee at all, there would then have been no reason for fighting; far less for such a fight in which a part of thee, a member of thee, or any issue flowing out of thy substance, should be mingled with those contrary powers and natures not created by thee, and by them be changed and corrupted so far as to be translated from happiness to misery, so that it could not be delivered and purged without thy help. And this child, they said, is the soul, and thy Word—which is its help in its bondage, in its defilement, in its corruption—must needs Itself be free and pure and uncorrupted. Yet must that Word itself be corruptible, as being of one and the same substance with thee.

If therefore they should say that thou, whatsoever thou art, that is to say thy substance, wert incorruptible, all those other fancies of theirs would prove to be false and execrable. But if they should say that thou wert corruptible, that very thing is evidently false and at the first sight to be abhorred. This argument then, of Nebridius, might have served my turn against those fellows, who were fit only to be cast wholly out of my sick stomach, because they had no means of escape from the guilt of a hideous sacrilege both in heart and tongue, whilst they thought and spake of thee such things as these.

That freewill is the cause of sin

BUT howsoever I did firmly believe and declare that thou wert pure and inviolable and wholly immutable, O thou, my Lord and true God, who didst create not only our souls but our bodies also, and not only our souls and bodies but all men and all things; nevertheless I understood not as yet what was the explicit and clear cause of Evil. But whatsoever it might be, I perceived that it must be sought in such wise that I must not thereby oblige myself to believe that the immutable God was subject to mutability; lest myself should thus become the very thing that I was seeking after. Now therefore did I securely search after the cause of Evil, because I was certain that what was taught by the Manichees, from whom I fled with my whole heart, was not true. For now I perceived that, when they inquired whence Sin proceeded, they were themselves most full of all sin, because they affirmed that thy substance did suffer evil, rather than admit that their own did commit evil.

I did therefore bend myself to understand the truth whereof I had heard, namely that the Freedom of the Will was the cause of our doing ill, and that thy just Judgement was the cause of our suffering ill. But I was not able clearly to see this truth. And so, when I was striving to draw up the eye of my mind out of that deep pit, I fell back into it again, and so often as I strove to escape therefrom, did I fall back. That which raised me up towards thy light was the knowing that I had such a will, whereof I was as sure as that I did live. When therefore I did will anything, or not will it, I was most certain that it was I and no other that willed or did not will it; and I did even observe that the cause and root of my sin lay there. But whatsoever I did unwillingly, I saw that I did suffer rather than do, and I esteemed that not to be a fault but a punishment; and I quickly confessed—when I remembered that thou art just—that I was not punished unjustly.

But yet again I said, " Who made me? Is it not God, who is not only Good, but is even Goodness itself? Whence then come I thus to will that which is evil, and not to will that which is good, by means whereof I may come thus to be justly punished? Who placed this power in me, and who engrafted upon my stock this branch of bitterness, seeing that I was wholly made by my God, most sweet? If the devil be the author thereof, whence is that same devil? And if he himself, by his own perverse will, from a good angel became a devil, whence grew that will to be wicked in him, seeing that he had been made all good angel by that most good Creator?" By these cogitations I was again depressed and even overwhelmed, but I was not laid so low as that hell of error where no man confesseth unto thee, and where thou art thought to suffer evil, rather than man to work it.

That God cannot be violated nor constrained

AFTER this manner did I now endeavour to find out other things, as I had already found out that it was better to be incorruptible than corruptible; and therefore, whatsoever thou wert in thy nature, I confessed thee to be incorruptible. For never yet was any soul able, nor never will any one be able, to conceive anything which is better than thou, who art the sovereign and most excellent Good. But now, since that which is incorruptible is most truly and most certainly to be preferred before that which is corruptible, as I did then prefer it, I should already in my mind have been able to lay hold of something which was better than my God, unless thou wert allowed to be incorruptible. When therefore I saw that the incorruptible was to be preferred before the corruptible, I ought to have sought thee at that point, and by means thereof to have observed whence evil doth proceed, that is to say, from what corruption of itself it doth grow, which nevertheless cannot in any way violate thy substance. For corruption cannot by any means whatsoever violate our God, either by any choice, or necessity, or unlooked for accident, because he himself is God, and what he wills is good, and he himself is that Good; but to be corrupted is not good.

Nor art thou, O God, compelled to do anything against thy will, because thy power and thy will are equal; but one would be greater than the other, if thou thyself wert greater than thyself, for the Will and the Power of God is God himself. And what sudden thing can surprise thee, who knowest all things, and nothing hath any nature, but only because thou knowest it? But why should I affirm by so many words that the substance which is God is not corruptible, since if it were corruptible it would not be God?

He continues his search after the first root of sin

Now I was looking whence Evil did proceed, but I sought it ill; for I saw not the evil which there was in this very inquiry of mine. And I placed before the eye of my mind all things created which I could see, as the earth, the sea, the air, the stars, the trees, and mortal living creatures; yea and whatsoever else I could not see, as the firmament of heaven, all the angels moreover and all the other spiritual inhabitants thereof; but even all these did my imagination yet dispose in order to different places, as if they were bodies. I made indeed the huge mass of all thy creatures, distinguished by several kinds of bodies; whether indeed they were true bodies, or whether they were such as I devised by my fancy instead of spirits. This mass I made very great, not indeed so great as it was, for that I could not know, but so great as I thought convenient, only I made it finite. And thee, O Lord, I conceived to be environing and penetrating it on every side, and every way infinite; as if there were a sea, and nothing but sea, which everywhere and on all sides was infinite, and within it some huge sponge, huge but yet finite. And withal that this sponge should, on all sides and in every part thereof, be full of this immense sea. And thus did I think that the finite creatures were full of thee, who art infinite, and I said, "Behold God, and behold what God hath created, and God is good. Yea, he is most perfectly and incomparably more excellent than his creatures; but as he is good, so are all the things that he hath created good; and behold how he doth environ and doth fill them all."

Where then is Evil, and whence came it, and how crept it in hither? What is the root and what is the seed thereof? Or is it peradventure nothing? Why then do we fear it and shun it, if it is not? For, even if our fear is groundless, yet that fear itself is evil, whereby the heart of man is wounded

and tormented without a cause. Yea, so much the greater
evil is it, if there is nothing which we should fear, for still
we do fear. Therefore, either there is some evil which we
fear, or else the very fearing itself is an evil. Whence is it
therefore, seeing that God, who is good, made all these
things good? True it is that he is the greater and sovereign
good, and that which he created is less good, yet both
Creator and created are good alike. Whence then is evil?
Was it, peradvanture, that he made his work of some evil
matter, which he shaped and disposed of, yet did leave
something therein which he converted not into good? Then
why did he also that? Or was he not able—he that is
omnipotent—to change and convert it all, so that no evil
should remain therein? Lastly, why should he make
anything of such stuff, and not rather, by his omnipotency,
ordain that it should not be at all? Was it able to exist
against his will? Or, if it were eternal, why did he suffer it
to lie idle for such infinite ages as are past, and then be
pleased, after so long a while, to make somewhat of it?

Or if now suddenly he were pleased to act, would not he,
who is omnipotent, rather decree that this stuff should not
be at all, and that he himself should exist alone, that true,
supreme, and infinite Good? Or if it was fit that he, who
was all good, should make and frame somewhat that was
good also, at least, having taken away and annihilated that
evil matter, he might create some good matter, whereof he
might make all things. For he would not be omnipotent if
he could not create any good things, unless he were supplied
with matter which he himself did not create. These things
did I toss up and down in this miserable heart of mine,
which was made heavy through most biting cares, through
the fear of death and of not finding out the truth. Yet did
the belief of the Catholic Church concerning thy Christ,
our Lord and Saviour, stick fast in my heart. In many
things as yet it was unshaped, and it wandered from the
rule of right doctrine; but yet did my mind never forsake it,
nay it was daily drinking more deeply of it.

That the divinations of astrologers are vain

Now also had I rejected those deceitful divinations and impious dotages of Astrologers. Let thine own mercies, O my God, take occasion also from hence to confess to thee, even out of the most inward bowels of my soul. For thou, and thou alone—for who else doth recall us from the death of all errors but thou, the Life which knowest not the taste of death, the Wisdom illuminating our needy minds yet needing for itself no foreign light, whereby the whole world is administered, even to the leaves that flutter on the trees— thou, I say, didst provide a medicine for the obstinacy wherewith I struggled against Vindicianus, that sharp-witted old man, and against Nebridius, that young man of admirable disposition. Against the former, who vehemently affirmed, and the latter who, somewhat doubtfully indeed but yet frequently, used to say that there was no art whereby things future might be foreseen, but that, as the conjectures of men did often obtain credit by some accident that happened, so did the diviners, by saying many things, at times foretell something future; whilst yet they knew not what they were saying, but merely chanced to fall upon the right, by their not saying nothing. Thou didst provide for me then a cure, in the person of a certain friend, who was indeed not negligent in consulting those Astrologers, though not as yet very conversant in their art; but, as I say, he was a curious consultor thereof. But somewhat he knew, which he said his father had taught him, though how much it might serve to overturn the reputation of that art, he knew not.

This man then, who was called Firminus, who had been trained in liberal studies and was skilled in eloquence, consulted me, as a most dear friend, about some affairs of his wherein his hope of preferment was great, and what I conjectured thereof according to his constellations, as he called them. Now I, who by this time had begun to incline towards the opinion of Nebridius in this matter, did not indeed refuse to read the stars for him, and to tell him so much as did occur to my wavering mind. But yet I let him know withal that I was almost persuaded of the vanity and foolishness of these things. He told me, therefore, that his father had been a most diligent student of those books, and that he had a friend who was affected in the same way as much as he. Those two, he said, by their joint study and conference, had so fanned the flame of their affection towards these toys, that they would needs observe the instant of birth of dumb creatures, if any such were littered in their houses, and would note the position of the heavens at the time, whereby they might make experiments in this art.

He therefore said how his father had told him that, when his mother was with child with Firminus himself, a certain slave-girl, who served that friend of his father, was with child also. Which fact was not unknown to her master, who used even with the most exact diligence to observe the birth of his puppies. Now so it fell out that, when these men—the one for his wife and the other for his slave— had counted the day, the hour, and the minute of their being brought to bed, they were both delivered at the same instant; insomuch that they were both constrained to allow the very same horoscope to both the children, one for his son and the other for his slave. For when the women began to be in labour, they mutually reported to one another all that happened in the house of either, and provided messengers whom they might send to each other, that, as soon as the children were born, report might be made to each; of which event they could easily have notice, as being in their own kingdom. And he said that they who were sent from either side met in the way, at such an equal distance from the several houses, as that neither of those, who calculated the positions of the stars or the seconds of the minutes, could observe anything different from what the other had done. And yet Firminus, being honourably born in his parents' house, had his course with ease in the sunnier paths of the world, while the slave—as he that told the history knew well enough himself—continued to serve his master, without ever being eased from the yoke of that mean position wherein he was born.

When I heard and believed these things—for he that related them was a man worthy of all credit—the former reluctance that I had fell clean away. And first I endeavoured to withdraw Firminus himself from that superstition, by telling him that, if I was to pronounce the truth with regard to his constellations, I ought to have seen therein that his parents were persons of importance, that his family was a noble one in his own city, that he was free-born, liberally educated, and estimable in respect of learning. But that, if the slave should have consulted me about the same constellations, which were common to him too, I ought—if I were to speak the truth in that case —to have seen therein his abject lineage, his servile condition, and the rest of his circumstances, which were so far different from the former. Whence therefore it must come to pass that—if I were to speak the truth—I must read divers fortunes from the same constellations, or I must read the same fortunes from them, and so pronounce a falsehood. Whereupon I most certainly inferred that those things, which are said truly upon a view of the constellations, are said by chance and not by cunning, and those which are delivered falsely proceed not from any unskilfulness in the art, but from the deceitfulness of chance.

Having thus gotten an entrance into this matter, and ruminating upon it by myself, I desired instantly to set upon and to confute with scorn the dotards who follow this trade; but I bethought me how they might make answer that Firminus had told me, or that his father had told him that which was false. And hereupon I did earnestly turn my thought upon such as are born twins, who for the most part come into the world so soon after one another that—whatever importance those fellows may pretend to attach to that little moment of time—the difference cannot be estimated by the observation of man, nor is it stamped upon the figure of those constellations which the astrologer must look upon, if he is to declare the truth of things to come. Nor indeed will it be the truth, for so it must have been that he, who looked upon the same figures, must have said the same things both of Esau and of Jacob; whereas the same things did not happen to them both. Such a one therefore must needs lie, or else, if he is to tell the truth, he must foretell different things for them, albeit he looked upon the same constellations; when indeed he might speak truth, but by chance not by art.

For thou, O Lord, most just Ruler of the whole world, whilst both they that consult and they that are consulted know not what they do, dost so work by a hidden instinct that, whensoever one man consulteth another in this kind, he may receive such answer as thou thinkest fit that he should hear, according to the hidden merit of souls and the unfathomable secrets of thy just judgment. Whereunto let no man say, " What is this?" or " Why is this?" Let him not say it, let him not say it, for he is but man.

He is miserably racked by the inquiry which he maketh,
   after the root of evil

Now therefore, O my Helper, thou hadst discharged me out of those fetters, yet I was still seeking for the root of evil, and could find no way out of this difficulty. Yet thou didst not suffer me to be carried away by the waves of those thoughts from that faith whereby I believed both that thou art, and that thou art unchangeable in thy substance. And again that thou hast a care of men and art just in judging of them; and that in Christ thy Son, our Lord, and in the Holy Scriptures, which the authority of thy Catholic Church doth recommend, thou hast placed the way of man's salvation, that leadeth him to that life which succeedeth this mortal life. These things therefore being established peacefully and irremoveably in my mind, I sought with trouble and impatience from what the nature of Evil doth proceed. What torments did my heart endure in that travail, what sighs were those, O my God! Yet even then were thine ears open, and I knew it not; and when in secret I did so vehemently seek after it, the unspoken contrition of my soul appealed loudly to thy mercy.

Thou knowest what I endured, though no mortal man did so, for how little of it could my tongue put into words even for the ears of my most inward friends? Did I express to them that whole tumult of my soul, which neither my time nor my tongue was sufficient to declare? Yet did the whole ascend into thy hearing, which I cried out by the groans of my heart. Before thee did I represent my desires, *and the light of mine eyes was not with me,* for that was in thee and I was without. Or rather that inward light of mine was in no place, to speak properly, but I was fixed upon those things which are contained in space, and therein I found no place for myself to rest in. Neither did those places entertain me, so that I might say, "It is enough, it is well"; nor did they suffer me to return to thee, where I might have been well enough. For I was superior to those things, but inferior to thee, and thou art the true joy of me, thy subject; and those things which thou didst create below me, thou madest subject unto me.

And this was the true mean and middle region of my felicity, that I might remain in conformity to thine image, that, serving thee, my body *might be in subjection* unto me. But when I rose proudly against thee, and did run against my Lord *with the stiff neck of my buckler,* even these weak things overwrought and overweighed me, and nowhere could I find ease or breathing-space. From every side the visible creatures came rushing in upon my sight by troops and heaps as soon as I opened my eyes, and when I tried to think, the images of bodies did waylay me as I tried to turn me back, as if they said, "Whither goest thou, O thou unworthy and sordid creature?" All these had grown out of my wound, for *thou hast humbled the haughty as one that is wounded,* and by my swelling pride I was separated from thee, yea, my cheeks, too swollen, did utterly block up mine eyes.

How he was helped by the divine mercy

But thou, O Lord, abidest for ever, and wilt not be angry with us for ever. For thou hadst compassion on this dust and ashes, and it was pleasing in thy sight to reform my deformities, and with a hidden goad thou didst urge me, that I might be restless until such time as the sight of my mind might discern thee for certain. Thus did the swelling of my heart abate through thy hidden hand, which knew how to cure me, and the troubled and darkened eye of my soul was healed day by day, by the smarting eye-salve of wholesome grief.

Of certain matters that he found in the books of the Platonists, which were agreeable to Christian doctrine

AND thou, being willing first to show me how thou *dost resist the proud, but givest grace to the humble,* and how, with great mercy, the way of humility is traced out to men, in that thy *Word was made flesh and dwelt amongst us,* didst procure for me, by means of a certain man who was puffed up with a most prodigious pride, certain books of the Platonists, translated out of Greek into Latin. And therein I read, not indeed the express words, but the same thing in substance, and supported by many reasons of several kinds, that *in the beginning was the Word, and the Word was with God, and the Word was God, and this same was in the beginning with God. All things were made by Him, and without Him was made nothing of all that was made. In Him is Life, and the life was the light of men; and the light shineth in darkness, and the darkness did not comprehend it.* Further, that the soul of man, though it gave testimony to the light, is not yet the light; but the Word, God himself, is the true light, *which illuminateth every man coming into this world, and the world was made by him, and the world knew him not.* But that *he came unto his own, and his own received him not, and that to whomsoever received him, he gave power to be the sons of God, believing in his name,* this I read not in that book.

But this again I read there, that God, the Word, *was born not of flesh, nor of blood, nor of the will of man, nor of the will of the flesh, but of God;* but I read not that *the Word was made flesh and dwelt amongst us.* I found that in those writings it was said often and in various ways, that *the Son was of the form of the Father,* and that he *thought it not robbery to be equal with God,* because he is by nature the same. But those books have no such matter as that *he emptied himself, taking upon him the form of a servant, being made in the likeness of men; and, being found to be apparelled with the flesh and blood of man, he humbled himself, and became obedient unto death, even the death of the cross; for which cause hath God exalted him from the dead, and hath given him a name which is above all names, that in the name of Jesus every knee might bow, of things celestial and things terrestrial, and such as are under the earth; and that every tongue may confess that our Lord Jesus Christ is in the glory of God the Father.*

Again, that thy only begotten Son, co-eternal with thee, doth remain unchangeable beyond all times, and that from this his fulness all souls do receive that they may be blessed, and that by participation of his wisdom, remaining in men, they are renewed that they may be wise, this is there. But that *in the fulness of time he died for wicked men* and that thou *didst not spare thy only Son but deliveredst him up for us all*, this is not there. For thou *didst hide these things from the wise and prudent, and didst reveal them unto little ones, that, being weak and heavy laden, they might come to him, and he might refresh them, because he is meek and lowly of heart; and he directeth them that are meek in judgement, and he teacheth such as are mild his ways, beholding our humility and our labours, and forgiving all our sins.* But they who are puffed up in the buskin of what they deem a higher knowledge, do not hear him saying unto them: "*Learn of me, for I am meek and humble of heart, and you shall have rest for your souls,*" and if *they know God, they do not glorify him or give thanks to him as God, but they vanish away in their thoughts, and their foolish heart is darkened; and terming themselves wise, they are made fools.*

And therefore, as I read there also, *they changed the glory of thine incorruptible nature into idols and many kinds of images, into the likeness of the image of corruptible man, and of birds, and of four-footed beasts, and of serpents;* and in fine into that flesh of Egypt, for which Esau sold his birthright; for thy first-born people did worship the head of a beast, instead of thee, *turning in their heart back towards Egypt,* and bowing down their soul, which is thy image, *before the likeness of a calf that eateth hay.* These things I found there, but I fed not thereon. For it pleased thee, O Lord, to take away the reproach of inferiority from Jacob, *that the elder might serve the younger,* and thou didst call the Gentiles into thine inheritance.

And I myself came towards thee from among the Gentiles, and I fixed my mind upon that gold, which it was thy will that thy people should carry away out of Egypt, for it was thine wheresoever it was. And thou didst say unto the Athenians by thy Apostle, that in thee *we live and move and have our being,* as some of themselves also affirmed. And these books also came from thence. But I did not addict myself unto those idols of Egypt, to whom they did homage with that gold of thine, *who changed the truth of God into a lie, worshipping and serving the creature rather than the Creator.*

Heavenly things are more plainly discovered unto him

AND being thereupon admonished to return unto myself, I entered into the very inmost part of my soul, thou being my leader, and I was able to do it, because now thou wert become my helper. I entered into myself and with the eye of my soul—such as it was—I discerned, even beyond my soul and mind itself, the unchangeable light of the Lord. Not this common light was it, which all flesh may look upon, nor was it of the same kind but greater, as if this light should shine more and more clearly, and possess the whole world with the greatness thereof. This light, I say, was not that former light but another, and altogether different from all such. Neither was it above my understanding, in such wise as oil swimmeth above water, or as the heaven is raised above the earth; but it was above me because it made me, and I was under it because I was made by it. He that knoweth Truth, knoweth that Light; and he that knoweth that Light, knoweth Eternity. Charity knoweth it.

O eternal Truth, and true Charity, and lovely Eternity. Thou art my God, to thee do I sigh day and night. When first I knew thee, thou didst raise me up, that I might see there was somewhat for me to see, though as yet I was not fit to see it. And thou didst beat back my weak sight, darting thy beams upon me vehemently, and I trembled with love and horror, and I found myself to be afar off in a region of no resemblance unto thee, as if I had heard thy voice from on high saying: "I am the Food of the strong, grow apace, and thou shalt feed on me;

nor shalt thou convert me like common food into thy substance, but thou shalt be converted into me." And I came to know that thou *dost punish man for his iniquity, and hast made my soul to pine away like a spider.* And I said, "Is Truth then nothing at all, seeing it is diffused neither through space finite not infinite?" And thou criedst unto me from afar off, saying, "Yes, Yes; I Am, that Am." And this I heard, as things are heard in the heart, nor was there any possibility for me to doubt thereof. Yea, more easily could I think that I did not live, than that Truth is not, which is clearly seen and understood, by means of the creatures which are made.

In what sort creatures may be said to be, and yet not to be

AND I beheld all other things that are beneath thee, and I saw that they had neither any absolute being, nor that they had absolutely no being at all. They have a being because they are of thee; and they have no being, because they be not that which thou art. For that truly is, which doth unchangeably remain. *It is good then for me to hold fast to God,* because if I remain not in him, I shall not be able to do it in myself. *But he, remaining in himself, reneweth all things.* For *thou art my Lord and my God, nor needest thou anything that is mine.*

How all things that are of God are good

AND it was made manifest unto me that even those things which are corruptible are good. For they could not be corrupted, if they were the Supreme Good, nor yet could they be corrupted if there were not some good in them. Because, if they were the Supreme Good, they would be incorruptible, and if they were not good at all, there would be nothing in them which could be corrupted. For corruption hurteth everything that it works upon; and, if it did not diminish the good thereof, it could not hurt. Therefore corruption either hath in it no hurt at all, which cannot be, or else all things which are corrupted are deprived of some good; and this is a most certain truth. Now if they should be deprived of all good, they would no longer have any being; for if they should continue to be, and yet could no more be corrupted, they would be the better for having been corrupted, since they would now continue incorruptibly. Now what is more absurd than to say that things are made the better by having lost all good? Therefore, if ever they be deprived of all goodness, they shall then be nothing; for, so long as they are, they are good, and so whatsoever things exist are good.

That evil, then, of which I sought whence it was, is not any substance, because, if it were a substance, it would be good. For either it would be an incorruptible substance, that is to say, a chief good; or else it would be a corruptible substance, which, unless it were also good, could not be corrupted. Therefore I saw, and that clearly, that all things which thou madest were good, and there are no substances at all which thou didst not make. And because thou didst not make all things equal, therefore it is that all of them are good together, and each one of them by itself is good, and the sum of them all is very good; *for our God made all things very good.*

All things created give praise to Ood

AND to thee there is no such thing at all as evil, yea, not only to thee but also not in respect of thy creation; because there is nothing beyond it which can break in or pervert the other which thou hast prescribed. But in some parts of thy creation, because some are conceived by men to agree not with others, they are thought to be evil. And yet those same things suit well with certain other things, and are good with them, and in themselves are good. And all these things which have no mutual conveniency with one another do yet well agree with this inferior part of things which we call the earth, which hath such a cloudy and windy region of air hanging over it, as is convenient to it. God forbid, then, that I should now say, " These things have no being at all." Because, although if I should see nothing else but these, I might well desire to see better, still, by occasion even of these, I should have reason to praise thee.

For, that thou art all worthy to be praised on earth, *the dragons do show and all depths, fire, hail, snow, ice, stormy winds that fulfil thy word; mountains and all hills, the fruitful trees and all the cedars; beasts and all cattle, creeping things and feathered fowls; kings of the earth and all people, princes and all the judges of the earth; young men and maidens, old men and children, all praise thy name.* And because they also who are in heaven do praise thee, *let all thine angels praise thee,* our God, *praise thee in the heights. Let all thy hosts, the sun and the moon, all the stars and light, the heaven of heavens and the waters which are above the heavens praise thy name.* Seeing this, I say, I did no longer desire better things, because I now thought of them all together; and with a sounder judgment, I confessed that things above were better than things below, yet that all created things together were better than the things above.

That the sane mind finds nothing to be evil in all that God has created

THERE is no sanity in those to whom any of thy creatures is displeasing; even as there was no sanity in me when many of those things which thou didst make displeased me. And because my soul did not presume to let my God be displeasing unto it, it would not suffer that anything which displeased it should be accounted thine. And so it fell into the notion of two substances, and it took no true rest, but talked idly. And returning from thence, it fancied to itself a kind of God which took up the infinite space of all places; and this it thought to be thee, and this it placed in its own heart, so that it became once more the temple of the idol which it had made, and which to thee was so abominable. But after that thou hadst refreshed my head—I knowing not of it—and after that thou hadst shut mine eyes, *that I might look no more upon vanity,* I was quieted a little in myself, and my former madness was lulled to sleep. And out of it I waked in thee, and I saw thee infinitely otherwise; but this vision did not grow out of the flesh.

How there is truth and falsehood in created things

AND I looked upon other things, and I saw that they owed to thee their being; and that all finite things are in thee, but in a different manner from that which before I thought; for they are not in thee as in a place, but because thou containest all things in the hand of thy truth; and that all things are true in respect of the being which they have, and that falsehood is nothing at all, except that a thing is thought to be, which is not. And I saw that all things did agree, not only with their several places, but with their times also, and that thou, who only art Eternal, didst not begin to work after the lapse of innumerable spaces of time, because all spaces of time, both they which are past and they which are future, may neither go nor come save in thee, who still art working and still abiding.

How all things created are good, though some are not fit for all

AND I found, and that by my own experience, how it was not strange if the same bread, which to a man of sound palate was pleasant, was a kind of punishment to him that was sick; and that the light, which to sore eyes was odious, was lovely to eyes that were sound. And that thy Justice was offensive to the wicked, as are the viper and the vermin, which thou didst yet create good and fitting in the inferior part of thy creation; to which also the wicked themselves are more fit, by how much they are the more unlike to thee though they grow more fitted to the higher parts thereof, by how much the more they come to resemble thee. And still I sought what this Iniquity might be, and I found it not to be a substance, but only that it was a perversion of swerving away from thee, O God, who art the supreme substance, a deflection of the will towards lower things, *casting away its inward parts* and putting itself up as an outlaw.

What things they are that keep a man from the knowledge of things divine

AND I marvelled that now I was come to love thee, and not any fantastical imagination in thy stead. Yet I could not stand still to enjoy my God, for, though I was drawn to thee by thy beauty, by and by I was plucked from thee again by my own weight, and with sorrow I fell back upon inferior things, and this weight was the custom of my flesh. Yet still I had a kind of memory of thee, neither did I doubt in any way who it was to whom I should adhere, but as yet I was not such a one as might adhere thereto; because the body, which is corruptible, doth overweigh the soul, and this earthly tabernacle doth depress the mind which hath many things to think on. And I was most assured that thy invisible things may be seen through those things that are made, even thine eternal power and thy divinity.

For when I was seeking by what reason I might estimate the beauty of corporeal things, whether terrestrial or celestial, or what means I had at hand to judge and pronounce with certainty concerning any of these mutable things, and say, "This ought to be thus, and that ought to be otherwise"; when, I say, I was seeking how I might judge, seeing that I did form judgments herein, I found that there was an unchangeable certainty of truth, superior to this changeable mind of mine. And so, passing by degrees from bodies to the soul, which perceives by means of the bodily senses, and thence to its inner faculty, unto which the senses of the body make report of things exterior, and considering how far the beasts also were able to reach herein, I passed on to the reasoning faculties, to whose judgement is referred whatsoever is received from the bodily senses.

And when this power also found itself to be mutable in me, it raised itself up to its own intelligence, and withdrew its thought from the rut of habit, abstracting itself from those troops of sensuous images which cross and thwart one another, that it might find out what the light was wherewith it was infused, when it cried out, without any hesitation, that the unchangeable was to be preferred before the changeable; for unless in some way it had notice hereof it could by no means have preferred it so certainly to the changeable. And thus, in the flash of a trembling glance, it arrived at THAT WHICH IS. Then indeed I came to have a sight of *thy invisible things, which are understood by the things that are made;* but I could not fix my gaze upon them. For my weakness being beaten back, I was restored to my wonted objects; and I carried along with me no more than a loving memory of those others, and, as it

were, a longing for the odour of those things whereof
as yet I was not able to eat.

Christ Jesus, our Lord, is the only way to salvation

AND I began to search how I might get me the strength
sufficient and fit for the enjoyment of thee. But I could meet
with none, until I embraced *the Mediator between God and
man, the man Christ Jesus, who is above all, God blessed for
ever.* Who calleth us and saith, *I am the Way, and the
Truth, and the Life,* and who mingleth himself with flesh,
and is the food which I was as yet unable to receive. For *the
Word was made flesh,* that thy Wisdom, by which
thou didst create all things, might become milk for us
babes. For I, not being humble as yet, did not apprehend
my God, Jesus the humble, nor yet did I understand
what he meant us to learn by that weakness of his. For thy
Word, which is the eternal Truth, being highly exalted
above the highest of thy creatures, doth raise up unto
himself them that are subject, having built for himself
a lowly house of our clay, so that he might cast down
from themselves and might draw unto himself those that
were to be made subject, curing the tumour of their pride
and nourishing their love; to the end that they might not go
on in their self-confidence, but rather might find their own
infirmity, when they should see the divinity itself lying at
their feet, enfeebled by taking upon him our *coats of skins.*
And so, being weary, they might cast themselves upon him,
that he, in his rising, might raise them up also.

What he thought of the incarnation of Christ

BUT as for me, I had other thoughts, and I conceived of
Christ, my Lord, only as a man of excellent wisdom, to
whom no other man might be equalled. Especially for this

that he was miraculously born of a Virgin—giving us an example of contemning all temporal things, that so we might obtain immortality—he seemed to me, by his divine care of us, to have deserved supreme authority as a master. But what mystery this might contain in it, that *the Word was made flesh,* I could not so much as imagine. So much only I knew as the Scripture hath recorded concerning him that he did eat and drink, did sleep and walk, rejoiced and was saddened, and that he preached; as also that the flesh did not cleave to that Word without a human soul and mind. Every man knoweth this, who knoweth the immutability of thy Word, which I already knew according to my capacity, neither did I doubt thereof at all. For at one time to move the parts of the body by the will, and then not to move them, now to be stirred by some affection, and then to be unmoved; now to express wise thoughts in words, and at another time to be silent; all these are properties of the soul and the mind which are mutable. The which, if they should be falsely said of him in Scripture, all the rest would run hazard of being accounted a lie, nor would there be left in those books any security of faith for mankind.

Because therefore all that which is there written is true, I acknowledged even then that Christ was a whole and perfect man. Not that in him was the body only of a man, or a sensitive soul in the body without a mind, but as I said a whole man. And though I conceived not that he was Truth in Person, yet—he being endued with a rare kind of excellency in his human nature, and a more perfect participation of wisdom—I held that he was to be preferred before all others. But Alipius conceived the Catholics to believe that God was so clothed in flesh that, besides God and the flesh, there was not any soul or mind of man in Christ. And because he was verily persuaded that those things which are recorded of him could not be performed but by a creature that was both vital and rational, for this reason he went more slowly on towards the Christian faith.

But afterwards understanding that this was the error of the Apollinarians, he was glad and well disposed to embrace the Catholic faith. But as for me, I confess that I came not until later to learn how the Catholic truth was distinguished from the false doctrine of Plotinus, in respect of the phrase *the Word was made flesh*. For the refutation of heretics makes that more eminent which thy Church doth hold, and giveth occasion to show what sound doctrine she teacheth. *For there must also be heresies, that they who are approved may be made manifest,* among the weak.

Of the philosophers that followed the school of Plato

By reading these Platonist books then, after that I was admonished thereby to seek for some incorporeal truth, I discerned those *invisible things of thine by means of the things which are made;* and, being put back again, I felt that which the darkness of my soul did not permit me to gaze upon; for I was sure that thou art, and that thou art infinite, and yet are not diffused and scattered through space either finite or infinite. And that thou truly art, because thou art always the same, and art not ever different or otherwise either in any part or in any motion; and that all other things have their being from thee, which thing is demonstrated most firmly, by the very fact that they are. Of these things I was certain, but yet withal I was too weak to enjoy thee. I began to prate like one who had experience, but unless I had sought the Way in Christ our Saviour I should not have had experience of thee, but should have perished without thee. I had then a good will to seem wise, being yet full of that which was my punishment, and I did not lament myself, yea, I was the more puffed up with the knowledge that I had.

For where was that Charity, that buildeth upon the foundation of Humility, which is Christ Jesus? Or when would those books have taught me that? Yet upon those books, I think, thou didst permit me to fall, before I had taken thy Scriptures into any consideration, that so I might remember how I was affected thereby; and that when, afterwards, I should be tamed by those other books of thine, and my wounds should be dressed by thy fingers that cured them, I might discern and distinguish that difference between presumption and confession; between such as saw whither they were to go but knew not the path, and that other way which leadeth not only towards the discovering but also to the inhabiting of that country where alone is true blessedness. For if I had been first instructed in thy holy Scripture, and in the familiar use thereof thou hadst grown sweet to me, and afterwards I had fallen upon those philosophical books, perhaps they would have estranged me from the solid ground of piety; or, if I had continued in the wholesome and devout thoughts which I had first conceived, I might peradventure have thought that these could be attained by means of those Platonic books alone, if a man should study them and nothing more.

What he found in Holy Scripture, which he found not in the Platonists

MOST greedily therefore did I betake myself to the venerable writings of thy Holy Spirit, and above all others to thy Apostle Paul. And those questions vanished whereby he seemed to contradict himself, as also this objection, that the drift of his discourse agreed not with the testimonies of the Law and the Prophets. So there appeared to me but one face in all that pure speech of thine, and I learned to *rejoice with trembling*. So I began, and I found all the truth I had read in the older books to be reaffirmed by him with the commendation of thy grace. For he that seeth may not glory, *as if he had not received, for what hath he which he hath not received?* truly neither the thing which he seeth nor yet the means whereby he seeth. And so is he admonished, not only that he may see thee, who art ever the same, but also that he may be healed and made strong to hold thee fast; and that he who, from afar off, cannot see the Way, may yet walk on in that way, whereby he may at length arrive, and see, and comprehend.

For although a man delight in the law of God, according to the inner man, what will he do with that other law in his members rejecting the law of his mind, and *leading him captive to the law of sin which is in his members? For thou art just, O Lord, but we have sinned, we have done wickedly, we have behaved ourselves impiously, and thy hand is grown heavy upon us.* And justly are we delivered over to that aged sinner, the prince of death, because he persuaded our will to become like unto his will, whereby he abode not in thy truth. What then shall miserable man do? *Who shall deliver him from the body of this death,* but thy grace through Christ Jesus our Lord, whom thou hast begotten, co-eternal with thyself, *whom thou didst create in the beginning of thy ways, in whom the prince of this world found nothing worthy of death;* yet did he slay him, and so *the handwriting which was contrary to us was blotted out.*

The books of the Platonists tell nothing of these matters. Those pages show not the countenance of this piety, the tears of confession, and that *sacrifice of thine which is a troubled spirit, a broken and a contrite heart,* the salvation of thy people, the Spouse, the City, the pledge of thy Holy Spirit, the cup of our Redemption. In them no man singeth, " *Shall not my soul wait upon God, for of him cometh my salvation? For he is my God and my Saviour, he is my Protector, I shall never more be moved.*" In them doth no man hear One calling, " *Come unto me, all ye that labour.*" They disdain to learn of *him that is meek and humble of heart; for thou hast hidden these things from the wise and prudent, and hast revealed them unto babes.* For it is one thing from some wooded mountain top to see the land of peace, without being able to find the way thither, and to strive towards it in vain through certain impenetrable ways, beset round about with those fugitive spirits, deserters of their God, lying in ambush with their prince, *the lion and the dragon;* and another to keep on the way that leadeth thither, secure in the care of that heavenly leader, where there are none that have deserted from the heavenly army lying in wait to rob, for they shun that way no less than their very torment. These thoughts, by wondrous ways, did sink into my very heart, whilst I was reading that *least of thine Apostles,* and I considered thy works, and with terror was I amazed thereat.

BOOK EIGHT

Being inflamed with the love of heavenly things, he goeth to Simplicianus

O MY God, let me remember with thanksgiving and confess thy mercies towards me. Let my bones be filled with thy love and say, *O Lord, who is like unto thee? Thou hast broken my bonds asunder, I will offer unto thee the sacrifice of thanksgiving.* I will declare in what manner thou didst break them, and all men who adore thee, when they hear these things, shall say, "Blessed be the Lord in heaven and on earth, great and wonderful is his name." Thy words did cleave even to the very roots of my heart, and I *was entrenched by thee on every side.* Of the Eternity of thy life I was now become certain enough, though I saw *it but through a glass in a dark manner.* All the doubts which I was wont to have were now taken away, both concerning an incorruptible substance, and how all other substance had its dependence thereon; and I desired not to be made more certain concerning thee, but only to be more established in thee. But, as touching my temporal life, all things were still unresolved, and my heart was yet to be delivered more fully from the old leaven. The Way, the Saviour of the world, did please me well, but I could not find it in my heart to follow it through the strait gate.

And thou didst put it into my mind, and in mine eyes it seemed good, to go unto Simplicianus, who appeared unto me a good servant of thine. For in him thy grace did shine, and I understood besides that, from his very youth, he had led a most devout life. He was then become an old man, and, by reason of the many years which he had spent in thy service, he seemed to my thinking to have learned much by his long experience, and indeed this was true. Whereupon I desired that, out of that skill of his, he would afford me some guidance—upon the account which I made him of my great difficulties—how a man, so affected as he found me, should walk in thy way; for I saw that thy Church was full, and that one went this way and another that. But the life which I was leading in the world was to me displeasing and very burdensome; since my appetite for honour and for profit did no longer spur me on, as it had been wont, towards the bearing of so weighty a yoke, nor did such things now delight me in comparison with thy sweetness, and *the beauty of thy house, which I loved.* But as yet I was tightly bound by the love of a woman, nor did the Apostle forbid me to marry, though he exhorted me to do better, most earnestly *desiring that all men should be like unto himself.*

But I, being weak, chose the softer place, and for this only reason I found myself weak and wallowish in all the rest; yea, I pined away sadly with cares, because, in divers things which I was loath to endure, I was obliged to accommodate myself to a married life, to the which I was so much affected. I had understood from the mouth of Truth that *there are eunuchs, who have made themselves eunuchs for the kingdom of heaven,* but, saith he, *let such as can, embrace his counsel.* Verily *all men are vain, in whom the knowledge of God is wanting, and who cannot, by those things which seem good, find out him who is Good indeed.* But I was no longer in this vanity, for I had overpassed it, and by the testimony of all thy creatures I had found thee, our Creator, and thy Word, God together with thee, and with thee and the Holy Ghost one God, by Whom thou didst create all things.

But there is another kind of wicked men who, *knowing God, have not glorified him as God, nor given thanks, as unto God.* Into this lot also had I fallen, and thy right hand, O God, took me up, and thou, removing my soul from thence, didst place it where it might recover health.

For thou hast said to man, *" Behold, the fear of the Lord is wisdom,"* and *" Be not careful to seem wise,* for *they that affirmed themselves to be wise, became fools."* And now I *had found the pearl of great price,* which I ought to have bought, though I *sold all that I had;* but even yet I doubted what to do.

Of Victorinus, the famous orator, and how he was converted

I BETOOK myself therefore to Simplicianus, the spiritual father of Ambrose, then Bishop, whom indeed he loved as a father. To him I related the winding courses of my error. But when I told him that I had read certain books, which Victorinus, sometime Rhetoric Master at Rome—who, I understood, had died a Christian—had translated into Latin, he congratulated with me that I had not fallen upon the books of other philosophers, which are full of deceits and tricks, *according to the principles of this world,* whereas in these, as he said, God and his Word are insinuated in many ways. Afterwards, that he might exhort me to the humility of Christ, which is *hidden from the wise and revealed unto little ones,* he told me the story of Victorinus, whom he had known most familiarly when he was at Rome, and what he related I will not here conceal.

For indeed it affords matters of much praise and glory to thee, which ought to be acknowledged, when we consider how that most learned old man, most skilful in all the liberal sciences, who had read and criticized so many works of the philosophers, who had been the tutor of so many noble senators, who, for his great services in a high office, had deserved and obtained to have his statue set up in the Roman forum—a thing which citizens of this world do much esteem—who even to his old age had been a worshipper of idols and a partaker in profane rites, wherewith at that time almost the whole nobility of Rome was bewitched, so that they were a-whispering of portents

> Of barking Anubis, and monstrous gods
> Of every shape, who once their strength did pit
> 'Gainst Neptune, Venus, and Minerva sage,[1]

whom Rome had once conquered but now adored, and whose honour this same old man, Victorinus, for many years had championed with his thunderous eloquence; that aged man, I say, blushed not to become a child of thy Christ, an infant at thy font, submitting his neck to the yoke of humility, and subduing his forehead to the ignominy of the Cross.

O Lord, Lord, thou who *dost bow the heavens and come down, who dost touch the mountains and make them to smoke,* by what means didst thou insinuate thyself into the heart of that man? He read, so Simplicianus told me, thy Holy Scriptures, and most laboriously did seek out and travail in the Christian authors. And to Simplicianus he was wont to say—not publicly but in the confidence of privacy—"You must know that I am already a Christian." Whereto the other made answer, "I will never believe it, nor will I repute you for a Christian, until I see you in the Church of Christ." But he indeed laughed thereat, saying, "It is the walls then, which make men Christians?" And often he would repeat that he was a Christian, and as often Simplicianus answered him in the like words, and he, in turn, repeated his jest about the walls. For he feared to offend his friends, those proud worshippers of devils, from the throne of whose Babylonian power, as from the cedars of Libanus which the Lord had not yet broken, he feared lest bitter enmities might rush down upon him.

But afterwards, when by reading and by praying he had gathered strength, and did fear lest he might be denied by

[1] Virgil, *Æneid*, viii, 698, 699.

Christ *before his holy Angels, if he were afraid to confess him before men,* and esteeming himself guilty of a grievous crime, if he should be ashamed of the sacraments of the Humility of thy Word, whereas he had not been ashamed to participate in the sacrilegious rites of those proud devils —whereof he himself had proudly partaken—he did unblush and show a bold face against error, and blushing now to think that he had been so long an enemy to the Truth, he said on a sudden and without warning to Simplicianus, "Come, let us go to the church, I am resolved to become a Christian"; and he, as he told me, unable to contain himself for joy, went thither with him. Soon after he was instructed in the first mysteries of religion, and then shortly gave in his name that he might be regenerated by Baptism, to the wonder of Rome and the delight of the Church. The proud saw it and *were enraged, they gnashed with their teeth, and pined away* with envy at it; but the Lord, our God, was the hope of his servant, who *looked not back upon vanity and lying madness*.

In fine, when the time was come that he was to make profession of his faith, which at Rome was wont to be done in a certain form of words learned by heart, and pronounced by them who were to receive thy grace from some prominent place in the sight of thy faithful people, an offer —so he told me—was made by the priests to Victorinus, that he might make his profession privately, as they sometimes did permit, when the parties were in likelihood of being either afraid or ashamed; but he chose rather to profess his faith in the presence of the holy assembly. For that which he had taught in rhetoric was not matter of salvation, and yet he had publicly professed it; how much less then was he to fear thy meek and humble flock, whilst he was pronouncing thy word, when, in speaking words of his own, he had not feared whole troops of madmen? So that, as soon as he went up to declare himself, all those of his auditors who knew him—and who

was there who did not know him?—did whisper his name
to one another, with a voice of congratulation; and
"Victorinus, Victorinus," ran, with a hushed murmur,
through the lips of them all rejoicing. On a sudden did
they speak for joy, when they beheld him, and as suddenly
were they hushed again, through the desire they had to hear
him. He declared his true faith with an excellent confidence, and all of them would have been glad with speed
to take and lodge him in their very hearts. Yea, greedily
did they take him in thither by loving him and rejoicing
over him, embracing him by their affection instead of by
their hands.

That God and his angels do rejoice in the conversion of sinners

O GOOD God, what is that which is wrought in man, that
more joy is found in the delivery out of great danger of a
soul which had almost been despaired of, than if there had
always been good hope thereof, or the danger had been less?
Yea, even thou also, O merciful Father, *dost rejoice more
over one sinner that repenteth, than over ninety-and-nine
just persons, that need no repentance*. And we also do
hearken with great joy, so often as we hear, how *the lost
sheep is carried home upon the shoulders of the shepherd,
rejoicing;* and when the groat is restored into thy treasury,
her neighbours rejoicing with the poor woman that found
it. And the joy of the solemnity of thy house doth bring
the tears from our eyes, when, in thy house, there is read
how that *younger son was dead, yet is alive again, was lost,
but is found*. For thou dost rejoice both in us and in
thine Angels, who are holy in holy charity. For thou art
ever the same, who ever knowest all things after the
same manner, which yet in themselves are not ever the
same, nor after the same manner.

What then is wrought in the soul when one is more

delighted to find or to regain the thing which it loved, than if the thing had never been lost? For other things also do testify to this, and the world is full of witnesses, which cry out that so it is. The general triumpheth when he is a conqueror, yet he had not overcome, unless first he had fought; and how much the more danger there was in the battle, so much the more joy is there in the triumph. The tempest at sea doth toss the passengers, it threateneth shipwreck, and all do wax pale with the apprehension of death at hand. But what? The sky groweth clear, the sea is stilled, and their joy is great exceedingly, because their fear was no less. A man's dear friend is sick, his pulse reveals the danger, and all they who wish him well are sick with him in mind. But it goeth well with him, he walks, though not with his old strength, and instantly there is more joy for this than when of old he walked sound and strong.

Yea, the pleasures of life do men acquire by means of the pain that preceded them; and not only by that pain which cometh upon us unawares, but sometimes by that which we do seek after and procure. There is no delight in eating and drinking, unless the trouble of hunger and thirst do precede. And such as are hard drinkers do willingly eat salt meats, that they may put their mouths into a kind of heat, in the quenching of which they find delight. It is the custom too that the spouse already affianced may not instantly be put into the power of her husband, lest he should esteem her the less, seeing that he hath less sighed and longed for her. This is seen in that joy which is vicious and to be abhorred, it is seen in that which is lawful and permitted, it is seen in the most sincere and virtuous friendship, it was seen in him who *was dead, and is alive again, was lost, and is found*. There is ever the greater joy, where the greater fear did go before.

What meaneth this, O Lord, my God, since thou art eternal joy unto thyself, and there are ever about thee some of thy creatures that rejoice in thee? What is the reason, I say, that this part of thy creation doth consist, as it were, of rising and falling, of displeasures and reconciliations? Is the nature of things such, and is this the proportion which thou hast allotted to them, that from the highest part of the heavens to the lowest of the earth, from the beginning of this world unto the latter end, from the Angel to the worm, from the first movement to the last, thou didst fix all kinds of blessings and all thy just works in their several places, to be accomplished by thee in their due time? Alas for me, how sublime art thou in the highest and how profound in the lowest! For never dost thou depart from us, yet can we hardly persuade ourselves to return to thee.

Why more joy is found in the conversion of a famous man than in another

Go on, O Lord, make an end, raise us up and call us back, kindle us and draw us to thee, charm us with thy fragrance; let us love thee and run to thee. Do not many return to thee out of a deeper pit of darkness than Victorinus was in, do they not draw near to thee and are they not illuminated, receiving light, which—to whomsoever it is given—*giveth them power to become the sons of God?* But if they be little known, even those few that know them rejoice little over them. For when many men rejoice together, the several joy of each one is more plentiful, and therein they mutually kindle and enflame one another. Besides, they who are known to many, give many an example to follow them, and are authors of salvation to many, and those too who did precede them rejoice greatly for such, because they rejoice not for them alone. Far be it from us to think that, in the tabernacle of thy Church, the persons of rich men should be preferred before the poor, or the noble before the ignoble; since rather thou *didst choose the weak things of the world to confound the strong, and the base things of this world and things that are contemptible, and things that have no being,* as if they had a being, *that thou mayest bring to nought the things that are.*

And yet even that least of thine Apostles, by whose tongue thou hast delivered this truth—when Paulus, the Proconsul, had his pride abated by the other's prowess, and was set to draw in the easy yoke of thy Christ, being made a subject of the great King—even he, instead of Saul, chose to be called Paul, in testimony of so great a victory. For the enemy is the more overcome when one is taken from him of whom he held himself assured, and by means of whom he held many others. He holdeth such as are proud more fast than the rest, by reason of their rank, and through them he hath hold of more by means of their authority. So much the more therefore was the heart of Victorinus esteemed, which the devil had inhabited as an impregnable house of his, and his tongue also, with which as a strong, sharp weapon he had slain the souls of many; and so much the more abundantly did it become thy children to rejoice, because our King *had bound the strong man,* and because they saw those vessels, which the devil had provided for his own service, taken from him and *cleansed and made profitable to the Lord for every good work.*

What it was that hindered his conversion

But when that servant of thine, Simplicianus, had related to me these things, I was inflamed towards an imitation thereof, and for that purpose it was that he spake of them. But afterwards he also added how, in the time of the Emperor Julian, when there was a law made that Christians should not be suffered to teach rhetoric or literature, and Victorinus, having submitted himself thereto, chose rather to forsake the wrangling schools than thy Word, by which *thou makest the tongues of infants eloquent;* he seemed unto me to be no more resolute than fortunate, seeing he found so fit an opportunity of devoting his time to thee alone. For this it was whereunto I did aspire, though I was bound as yet, albeit not with a chain of iron but only with the iron chain of mine own untoward will. Mine enemy made fast this will of mine, and thereof did he forge the chain which bound me. For through the perverseness of our affection groweth lust, and by yielding often to that lust we make a custom, and by not opposing this custom we grow subject to a kind of necessity. By these links fastened one within the other—for the which reason I have called it a chain—did bitter servitude hold me bound. But the new will which I now began to have to serve thee for thyself and to enjoy thee, O God, who art our only certain joy, was not able as yet to master that other, which had been established by so long continuance. Thus did my two wills, one old and another new, one carnal and the other spiritual, fight one against the other, and by their discord did they drag my soul asunder.

Thus came I to understand, by proper experience, that which I had read; *how the flesh lusteth against the spirit, and the spirit against the flesh*. I had, I say, experience in them both, but now there was more of me in that which I approved, than in that which I misliked in myself. For in the latter it was not now so much I that was concerned, because in great part I did now suffer that unwillingly, which before indeed I had done willingly. But custom had grown more peremptory and importunate against me by mine own fault, because of my own will I had come to be that, which afterwards I wished I had never become. And who can with justice complain of this, since punishment doth rightly follow sin? Nor had I any longer that excuse, whereby I was wont to pretend unto myself that I could not contemn the world in order to serve thee, which was that the knowledge of the Truth was uncertain to me, for now I was sure enough thereof. Yet, being still in service to the earth, I refused to fight under thy banner; and I feared as much to be freed from all my cumbersome baggage, as I ought to have feared the being hindered by it.

Thus with the burden of worldly pleasures was I sweetly oppressed, as happens sometimes in a dream; and the thoughts whereby I aspired to thee were like the struggles of such as would awake, when yet—being overcome with the appetite to repose—they fall asleep again. And, just as there is no man who would wish to sleep for ever, seeing that, in the judgement of all discreet persons, it is a nobler estate to be awake, yet a man doth oftentimes defer to put sleep away, when he finds his body greatly subject to it, and—albeit angry with himself therefor—he gladly steals another nap, although his time for rising is arrived; so, in like manner, I held for certain that it was better for me to commit myself to thy Charity, than to submit myself to mine own sensuality. But notwithstanding that former course did satisfy and convince my mind, the latter did yet content and bind my sensual part. For now I had nothing left which might answer to that call of thine, *" Awake, thou that sleepest, and rise up from the dead, and Christ shall give thee light."* On all sides thou didst show me that what thou saidst was true, and I, being convinced of that truth, had nothing to answer thereto but certain slow and sleepy words, as " Shortly, behold, I will do it shortly; have patience with me, yet a little while." But my " Shortly, shortly," grew into great length; and my " Little while," stretched out a long while. In vain was it for me to be *delighted with thy law interiorly,* when there was *another law in my flesh, fighting against the law of my mind, and leading me captive to the law of sin, which is in my members.* For the violence of custom is a kind of law of sin, whereby the mind of man is drawn and holden, even against its will, and that justly, since at the first it slipped into it willingly. *Wretched man that I was, who could deliver me from the body of this death, but thy grace only, through Christ Jesus, our Lord?*

Pontitianus tells him of the life of Antony, the Egyptian hermit

Now will I declare and confess to thy name, *O Lord, my Helper and my Redeemer,* in what manner thou didst free me from the chain of sensual desires, which so straitly bound me, and from the slavery of wordly affairs. I loved after my accustomed manner, but with increase of anxiety, daily sending up my sighs unto thee. I frequented thy Church as often as those employments, whereby I lay oppressed, would give me leave. Alipius was with me, at leisure then in a vacation from his legal labours, after a third term of office as Assessor, waiting for other clients, to whom he might sell his counsel; as I used to sell skill in rhetoric, so far as that can be acquired from teaching. Nebridius also had so far yielded to our importunity as to take the post of sub-lecturer under Verecundus, a Milanese grammarian, and a most familiar friend of us all, who did demand by the right of friendship such assistance from us, whereof he stood much in need. For Nebridius was not led to do this by any desire of gain—for he might have done better in the way of literature, if he had cast his eye upon gain—but being a most sweet and gentle friend, he knew not how to deny the suit which we made to him, out of his courtesy and good will. But he bore himself herein most discreetly, shunning to become known to such persons as this world considers great, and avoiding thereby all unsettlement of mind, which he thus procured to have as free as might be, for seeking, reading or hearing somewhat concerning wisdom.

Now upon a certain day—Nebridius being absent upon some occasion, I do not now remember what it was—there came to Alipius and myself at our house a certain Pontitianus. He was an African, as we also were, and held an honourable position in the household. I do not remember now what the business was which he wanted with us, but we sat down, and fell into discourse with one another. It chanced that, on the playing table before us, he found and opened the book of St. Paul's epistles, a thing quite unexpected by him, for he thought it had been some other book, one of those in the teaching of which I used to wear myself out. But then, looking on me in a smiling and gratulatory manner, he wondered not a little that he had so unexpectedly found that book and only that one lying before me; for he was both a Christian and a faithful servant of thine, and did often prostrate himself before thee, our God, in long and frequent prayers. When, therefore, I had declared to him that I bestowed myself much in the reading of those Scriptures, he took occasion, in the course of his speech, to discourse unto us of Antony, the Egyptian monk, whose name was excellently famous amongst thy servants, but as for us we had never heard of him until that hour. But he, so soon as he perceived this, insisted the longer in speaking of him, insinuating the knowledge of so great a man to us, who were wholly ignorant, and wondering withal at that same ignorance of ours. We, on the other hand, were amazed to hear that so lately, and almost in our own days, such wonderful things had been wrought by thee, in the true faith and the Catholic Church; so that all of us wondered, we at the hearing of things so strange, and he, that we had never heard of them before.

From this he went on to speak of the teeming monasteries, and of them who are a sweet savour unto thee, and of the fruitful bosom of the barren desert, whereof also we had heard nothing. Nay more, there was a monastery at Milan, full of holy brethren, close without the walls of the city, under the fostering care of Ambrose, and yet we knew nothing of it. So did he proceed in his discourse, and we held our peace, listening intently. Whereupon he went on to tell us further how once, at Trèves, he himself, with three companions, while the Emperor was detained at the afternoon games in the circus, went out to walk in some gardens near the city walls; thus it chanced that they became separated into two parties, one of the three keeping with him and the other two walking together. These latter two, as they wandered up and down, came at length upon a poor cottage, inhabited by divers servants of thine, *poor in spirit, of whom is the Kingdom of Heaven,* and there they found a book, wherein was written the life of Antony.

One of them began to read the same, to wonder at it, and to be inflamed by it, and even whilst he was reading to resolve upon leading such a life as that, leaving the service of the world to become wholly thine. And these men were of the number of those styled Agents in the Public Affairs. Then suddenly, being filled with a holy zeal and a sober kind of shame, as if angry with himself, he cast his eyes upon his friend and said, "Tell me, I beseech thee, whither is it that we aspire by all these our labours, what is it that we aim at? In the hope of what do we thus earnestly employ ourselves? Can we have a higher ambition at court than to be, perhaps, the Emperor's friends? And even in that fortune, what is there which is not top full of danger? And by how many dangers do we proceed towards some danger still greater than the rest? And how long shall we sweat in this pursuit? But to be the friend of God himself; if I will, behold, I am made so at this moment."

He spake thus and, travailing in the pangs of a new birth, he turned his eyes again upon the book; and read on and was inwardly changed, where thou alone couldst look upon him, and his mind was wholly weaned from the world, as immediately afterwards appeared. For, whilst he was reading and rolling up and down those waves of his heart, he would sometimes deeply groan, and then pause a while, and at length resolved on a better course. Thus, at length being wholly thine, he said unto his friend, "I have broken now with those hopes of ours, and am firmly resolved to be the servant of God alone, and upon this course will I set forth, in this place and at this instant. As for thee, if thou art not content to follow me, at least dissuade me not." But the other made answer that he would gladly join himself as a companion in a service so honourable, with so ample a pay. Thus both of them, becoming now thine, did *build up a tower at their own cost, by leaving all things to follow thee.* Then Pontitianus and his companion, who had been walking in other parts of the garden, having sought them long and found them in that same place, advised them to return, because by that time it was grown late. But they, declaring their resolution and in what manner the same had grown and how it was confirmed in them, desired them not to take it ill if they refused to return with them. Then Pontitianus and his friend, though not changed from their former course of life, did yet—as he told me—fall into tears, and piously congratulating the others' happy estate, commended themselves to their prayers, and, dragging their hearts along the ground, returned to the palace. But the other two, their hearts rooted in heaven, remained in the cottage. Now both of them, as it chanced, were espoused, but their wives that should have been, so soon as they heard what had happened, did also dedicate their virginity unto thee.

How the story of Pontitianus pierced Augustine to the heart

SUCH were the things related to us by Pontitianus. But thou, O Lord, whilst he was speaking, didst turn me inward upon myself, taking my soul from behind my back, where I had placed it that so I might see it not, and setting it before my face that I might see myself, how deformed I was, how sordid, how full of spots and sores. I saw, and withal I abhorred myself, nor was there any place whither I might fly from that odious spectacle. And if I strove to turn mine eye from off myself, he yet proceeded in his discourse; and thus again didst thou confront me with myself, forcing myself on mine unwilling eyes, that I might discover and hate my own iniquity. Yet rather I had already known it, but I dissembled and connived, and so procured again to forget it. But now, the more ardently I loved those two, of whose excellent resolution I had heard, in that they had given themselves up to thee to be cured, so much the more detestably did I hate myself, being compared with them. For so many of my years—some twelve perhaps—had flowed down stream, since, in the nineteenth year of my age, I was stirred up to the desire of Wisdom, by reading the *Hortensius* of Cicero; yet was I still delaying to contemn earthly happiness, and to search out that, of which not the finding only but the very seeking was to be preferred before all the treasures and kingdoms of the world, and before all pleasures of the body, though they should be mine at a nod. But I, wretched as I was in my young manhood, and yet more wretched at the outset of my youth, had begged for chastity at thy hands, and thus I said, " Give me Chastity and Continence, but do not give it yet." For I was afraid lest thou wouldst hear me too soon, and deliver me instantly from the disease of concupiscence, which I desired might be glutted rather than quenched. And I went along the crooked ways of sacrilegious superstition, not indeed as one assured of the truth thereof, but preferring it before other things, which I did rather oppose with the mind of an enemy, than inquire after piously.

And I had supposed that I deferred from day to day to contemn the world and to follow thee alone, because I thought I was not sure enough by which way I should direct my course. But now the time was come wherein I was set naked before myself, and my conscience did thus reproach me, " Where is that tongue of thine, which said that thou wert not to cast away the certain pleasure of vanity, for the obtaining of an uncertain truth? Lo, now is the truth certain, and yet that burden of thine still oppresseth thee.

Others have gotten wings to fly nimbly from under it, who were neither so overwrought with curious inquiries, nor took they more than ten years of time to think upon it." Thus with a horrible shame was I gnawed within and put vehemently to confusion, whilst Pontitianus related to me the things aforesaid. But, that discourse being ended, with the cause for which he came, he went his way, and I—left to myself—what did I not then say within myself? With what scourges of condemning reason did I not lash my soul, that it might follow me, then striving to go after thee? But still it drew back and refused, though it knew not how to excuse itself. For now its arguments were all confuted and destroyed, and there remained only a kind of speechless trembling; and it feared, as if it were death itself, to be healed from that running sore of evil custom, by which it daily grew more near to death.

Of that which befell him in the garden

So, in that great disturbance of my spiritual house, which I had stiffly raised up against mine own soul in the secret chamber of my heart, being troubled exceedingly in face and mind alike, I turned upon Alipius and exclaimed: "Must we bear this? What is it? What didst thou hear? The unlearned start up and carry heaven by storm, and we, with all our learning, see how we wallow still in flesh and blood! Are we ashamed to follow, because they have gone before, or shall we not be much more ashamed, if we do not so much as follow after them?" Such things as these—I know not what—I said, as the fire of my passion snatched me from him, while he gazed upon me, dumb with amazement. For my words were uttered in no ordinary manner; my forehead, cheeks, eyes, colour, tone of voice cried out, more clearly than the words I spake.

There was a garden to our lodging, of which, as of the whole house, we had the use; for the master of it, our host,

lived not there. Thither the tumult of my heart now
hurried me, where no man might hinder the fiery action
which I had entered against myself, till it should issue
in such sort as thou, O Lord, foresaw, though I did
not. Only, for a while, I was most sanely mad, I was dying
unto life, well knowing the misery that I was, but knowing
not the good I soon should be. Into this garden then I fled,
and Alipius after me, foot by foot. For naught of mine
was too secret to include him, and how could he forsake
me in so great distress? We sat as far from the house
as possible, and I, raging with most tempestuous
indignation, did groan in spirit with myself, to see how I
made no more haste to enter into thy Will and Covenant,
O my God. Yet all my bones cried out that this was the
way, extolling it unto the very skies; for in this way we
travel not in ships, nor in four-horsed chariots, nor yet
on foot, nay, not even for so small a part thereof as from the
house unto the place where we were sitting. For in that
way there is no more required of us—not only for our
setting out, but even to attain our journey's end—than this,
that we have a will to go therein; but indeed we must
will it with an entire and strong will, not with a will half-
wounded, that staggereth and tumbleth hither and thither,
wherein the part that riseth must struggle with that other
part which inclineth to fall.

In those extremities of my delay, I performed with my
body many things which men sometimes would do but cannot; either because they have lost the limbs to do them
with, or because they are bound in fetters; or be weakened
with much sickness, or in some other way be hindered. If I
tore at my hair, if I struck myself upon the forehead, if,
wreathing my fingers in one another, I clasped my knee, I
did these things because I had a will to do them. But I
might have willed and yet not done them, if the movements
of my body had not been obedient to my willing. So
many things, therefore, I now did, wherein the will to act
and the power to act are distinct, yet, on the other hand, I

did not do that which should have contented me incomparably more. Yet in a little while, if I willed, I should be able to do it; because in a little while I should will to will it. For here, the faculty or power of doing is one and the same thing with the will to do it; and to will the thing is to do it; and yet the thing was not done. For my body did more easily obey the least inclination of the mind, in moving of its limbs at her beck, than my mind did obey itself in carrying out this, its great resolve, for which was needed but the resolution of the mind alone.

Why the mind is slow in respect of goodness

FROM whence comes this monstrous thing, and why is it so? Let thy mercy enlighten me that I may ask this question, if perhaps I may find an answer in the obscurity that is wrought in man's mind by sin, and in those most dark miseries of the sons of Adam. Whence comes this monstrous thing, and why is it so? The mind commandeth the body, and immediately it is obeyed; the mind commandeth itself and it is resisted. The mind commandeth the hand to move, and it is done so promptly that the order given is hardly discerned from the execution. Yet the mind is mind, and the hand is but a part of the body. The mind commandeth the mind to do this or that, it is one and the same, and yet the thing is not done. Whence comes this monstrous thing, and why is it so? The mind, I say, commands itself to will a thing, which it would not command, except it would have it to be done; and yet that which is commanded is not done. But the truth is that it doth not will entirely, and therefore it doth not command absolutely. For it commandeth but so far only as it willeth, and that which is commanded is executed only so far as the thing itself is willed. For the will commands that there should be a will, and not another will but itself. Clearly then the will doth not command fully, and for this cause that which is commanded is not done. For if the willing were full and perfect, it would command that the thing should be done, because it would be done already by the very act of willing. It is therefore no monstrous thing to will a thing in part and not to will it in part, but a plain infirmity of mind; because, being overladen by evil custom, the mind cannot rise wholly even though it be supported by truth. Therefore in such a mind there are two wills, neither of which is entire or perfect; and that which one of them hath, the other wanteth.

Of the divers kinds of wills that there are in man

Let them perish from before thy face, O God, as they perish *that seduce the minds of men and that speak vain things,* who, because they observe two wills in men whilst they are deliberating, do affirm that there are two kinds of minds, of two different natures, one good and the other evil. But those men are wicked whilst they believe these wicked things, and the same men shall be good if they will believe true things and consent unto the true, that thine Apostle may say unto them, " *Ye were sometime darkness, but now are ye light in our Lord.*" For they would be light indeed, but in themselves not in our Lord, conceiving the nature of the soul to be the same that God is. Thus do they grow to be thicker darkness, because with hideous arrogancy they have gone further from thee, who art *the true light that enlighteneth every man that cometh into the world.* Consider what you say and blush; *approach unto him and be illuminated, and your faces shall not be ashamed.* Was it not I that willed, was it not I that could not will, when I was deliberating if I should serve the Lord, my God, as I had long designed to do? Truly it was I; yet I could not fully will, or fully not will. Therefore did I strive with myself, and by myself was I dissipated, and this very dissipation of me did happen to me against my will.

Yet this did not show forth the nature of a second mind, but the punishment of my own mind. I therefore was not so much the cause thereof as that sin which dwelt in me, as a punishment of that freer sin of Adam, whose son I was. For if there be as many contrary natures as there are wills opposing one another, there must be not two wills but many more.

If one of the Manichees deliberate within himself whether he shall go to their conventicle or to the theatre, these fellows cry out, " Behold here are two natures, the good one draws him to us, the evil one drags him away. How else is there this hesitation between the two wills, each thwarting the other?" But I make answer that both the two are bad, that one which taketh him to them, no less than that one which draggeth him to the theatre. But they do not believe that will to be aught but good, which leadeth men to them. What then if any one of us should doubt and waver within himself, through the disputing of two wills, whether he should go to church or to the theatre; will not they also waver what they shall answer? For either they must confess —which they will never grant—that the will is good whereby we go to our church, as theirs is in those that go to their church, are partakers of their sacraments, and are retained in that obedience, or else they must conceive that two evil natures and two evil minds do combat together in one man —in which case that will not be true, which they are wont to affirm, that there is one good and one evil will—or else they must be converted to the truth and no more deny that, when any man deliberates, there is but one mind only distracted between two opposing wills.

Let them not say therefore, when they find two wills that are at variance in the same man, that there are two contrary minds, or two contrary substances, and that they proceed from two contrary principles, the one good and the other evil. For thou, O God of truth, dost reprove, and check, and convince them, for both wills may be bad; as when a man deliberateth with himself whether he shall kill a man by poison or by the sword? Whether he shall seize upon the possession of this man or of that one, whereas he cannot do both? Whether he shall purchase pleasure by lust, or hoard up his money through covetousness? Whether he shall go to the circus or to the theatre, if there are spectacles at both on the same day? I add also a third possibility, whether he shall steal something from another man's house, if opportunity be offered him; and yet a fourth also, whether he shall commit adultery as well, if fit occasion for it be found? If it be supposed that all these things concur at the same point of time, the which cannot all at one time be enacted, they do verily tear the mind in pieces for four different wills, which are in contradiction to one another, or by more than four if there be so great a store of things that may be desired; yet they are not wont to affirm that there is so great a multitude of different substances as this.

Even so it is also in the case of wills that are good. For I ask them whether it be a good thing to be delighted with reading of the Apostle, and whether it be good to be delighted with some sober Psalm, and whether it be good to discourse upon the Gospel? They will answer to every one of these things, that it is good. What then if I be equally delighted with all these things and at the selfsame time? Do not these divers wills put the mind upon a kind of rack, when it deliberateth of what chiefly we are to take hold? Yet all these wills are good, and they strive together until such time as some one thing is chosen, whereby the whole will is set at rest, which before was divided among many things. So also, when the thought of eternity delighteth the superior part of the soul, and the pleasure of some temporal good holdeth fast the inferior part thereof, it is but one and the same mind that willeth, though it will neither this nor that with an entire will. Therefore is it torn with grievous trouble to itself, whilst it preferreth this, being urged by truth; yet forsaketh not that, being hindered by habit.

How there was a combat in him between the flesh and the spirit

THUS sick in mind and tormented was I, accusing myself bitterly beyond all custom, and turning and winding myself in my chain, until such time as it might be wholly broken; for though but little, it yet held me. And thou, O Lord, wast urgent even in my most secret parts, redoubling upon me, with a severe mercy, those scourges of fear and shame, lest I should again give over, and lest that little tie which retained me should still remain, yea and grow stronger to bind me faster. For I kept saying within myself, " Behold, let it be done now, let it be done now "; and, as I spake the word, I did almost resolve to do it. I almost began to do it, and yet I did it not. Neither yet did I slide back into my former customs, but stood close by and drew another breath. And once again I endeavoured, and I was even arrived almost near enough to touch and to lay hold of it, yet I was not there, neither did I attain to embrace it, but I was suspended between dying to death and living to life. And my ancient evil custom was of more power with me than the purpose I had towards that which I had not experienced. Yea the very instant of time, wherein I was to be made different, did strike terror into me the more by how much the nearer I drew to it. But it did not drive me back nor yet divert me, but only kept me in suspense.

Very toys of toys and vanities of vanities they were, those ancient favourites of mine which detained me; they caught at the fleshy garment of my soul and softly whispered, " Dost thou cast us off?" and "Can it be that henceforth we shall not be with thee for ever?" and "From this moment shall this or that be forbidden thee for ever?" But those things which they suggested by their "this or that," what was it they suggested, O my God? Oh may thy mercy guard the soul of me thy servant, from all the filthiness and shame they meant! I heard them indeed, though now far less than half their former size, nor daring to withstand me to my face; but softly muttering behind my back, and plucking slyly at me as I went from them, as if in hope of making me look round. And in this sort they did indeed withhold me, who delayed to free myself by shaking them off, and hastening forwards whither I was called; whilst force of habit dinned into mine ears, "Dost think that thou canst ever live without them?"

But by this time it spake even this but very faintly. For in that quarter to which the face of my soul was turned, and whither I yet trembled to advance, the chaste dignity of Continence discovered herself. Cheerful she was, not dissolutely enticing, but sweetly inducing me to advance and to fear nothing; yea, stretching forth to receive and to embrace me those dear hands of hers, that were full of good examples. Many they were both young men and maidens, yea and of all ages, grave widows and aged virgins, and Continence herself in every one of them, not barren but *a fruitful mother of children,* of joys begotten by thee, O Lord, her husband. And she smiled upon me with a mirthful encouragement, as if she said, "Canst thou not do what all of these have done? Or can these men and maidens perform so much by their own strength, and not rather by that of the Lord, their God, that Lord and God, who gave them unto me? Thou standest upon thyself, and therefore it is that thou standest not. Cast thyself upon him and fear not, he will not withdraw himself and let thee fall. Cast thyself upon him securely, he will receive thee and will heal thee." And I blushed the more, for I yet continued to hear the whisperings of those vanities, as I remained still hanging in suspense. But yet again she seemed to speak, saying, "Stop thine ears against those unclean members of thine, that they may be mortified. They tell thee of I know not what delights, but not according to the law of the Lord, thy God." This last debate did pass only in my heart, between me and myself. But Alipius, who sat close by me, did expect in silence the issue of my unwonted perturbation.

How by a voice and by the words of the Apostle, he was miraculously converted

So soon then as deep consideration had drawn up out of the secret depths of my heart the whole heap of my misery, and had piled it up before the sight of my mind, there rose a tempestuous storm which brought with it a huge shower of tears. And that I might pour them forth with cries unheard, I rose from Alipius—for solitude seemed to me more fit for such a business of weeping—and I withdrew so far off that his presence might not be a restraint to me. Thus was it with me at that moment and he perceived it; though I think I had said somewhat, whereby my voice betrayed my load of tears, and how gladly I would be delivered of them. In this sort I rose, and he remained where we had sat together, lost in amazement. I cast myself down, I know not how, under a certain fig-tree, and gave full liberty to my tears, which brake like rivers from mine eyes, *an acceptable sacrifice unto thee, O Lord.* And I cried out at large to thee, not perhaps in these very words, but to this effect, *" And thou, O Lord, how long? How long, O Lord? Wilt thou be angry with me for ever? Remember not my iniquities of old times."* For I felt myself to be still enthralled by them, and therefore did I cast forth these lamentable exclamations, " How long, how long? To-morrow and to-morrow? Why not even now? Why not, even at this instant, make an end of my uncleanness?" Thus did I say, and I wept in the most bitter sorrow of my heart.

And lo, I heard a voice, as if it had been some boy or girl from a house not far off, uttering and often repeating in a sing-song manner, " Take up and read. Take up and read."

And instantly, with changed countenance, I began to consider intently, whether children in some game of theirs were used to sing any such words; yet could I not find that I had ever heard the like. Then, stemming the course of my tears, I rose up, conceiving that I was required from heaven to read that chapter which the first opening of the book should lead me to. For I heard how Antony, by reading of the Gospel—to the hearing of which he came once by accident—had held himself to be admonished, as if the passage read had been particularly meant for him: *"Go, sell all that thou hast, and give it to the poor, and thou shalt have treasure in heaven; and come thou, and follow me"*; by which oracle he was instantly converted unto thee.

Hastily therefore I went back thither, to where Alipius was sitting, for there I had laid the book of the Apostle, when I had risen from thence. I took it quickly into my hand, I opened it, and I read in silence from that chapter, on which first mine eyes were cast: *"Not in rioting and drunkenness, not in chambering and wantonness, not in strife and envying; but put ye on the Lord Christ, and make no provision for the flesh and its concupiscences."* No further would I read, nor was there cause why I should; for instantly with the end of this sentence, as by a clear and constant light infused into my heart, the darkness of all former doubts was driven away. Then shutting the book, and putting my finger or some other mark between the leaves, I declared unto Alipius all that had happened, with a quiet countenance. And he also, in like manner, revealed unto me that which had passed in his own heart, whereof I knew nothing. He then asked to see what I had read. I showed it, and he read on further than I had done, for I was ignorant of what followed, which yet was this, *"Now him that is weak in the faith take with you"*, the which he applied unto himself, for so he told me. And by this admonition he was much strengthened and, without any troublesome delay, he united himself with me in that good purpose and resolution, the which was most agreeable to his disposition, wherein he did ever differ from me greatly, and greatly to the better.

From thence we went in unto my mother, we told her, and she rejoiced. Then did we declare to her in order in what manner the whole was done, whereon she did exult and triumph, and bless thee, O Lord, who *art able to do above that which we can either ask or think;* for now she saw that thou hadst given her more in my regard than she was wont to beg of thee in all her sad and tearful lamentations. For thou didst so convert me to thyself, as that I did no more desire a wife nor any other ambition of this world; setting my feet upon that Rule of Faith, whereon thou hadst revealed unto her, so many years before, that I should stand. Thus *didst thou turn her mourning into joy,* more plentiful than she had dared to wish for, and far more clear and purer than she could have found in the offspring of my flesh.

BOOK NINE

He admireth the riches of God's goodness

O Lord, I am thy servant; I am thy servant and the son of thy handmaid. Thou hast broken my bonds in sunder, to thee will I offer a sacrifice of praise. Let my heart and my tongue praise thee, and *let all my bones say, O Lord, who is like unto thee?* Let them speak, and do thou answer and *say unto my soul, "I am thy salvation."* Who am I, and what kind of thing? What evil is there that I have not wrought by my deeds, or if not by my deeds at least by my words, or if not by my words at least by my will? But thou, O Lord, art gracious and merciful, and thy right hand had respect unto the profoundness of my death, and from the bottom of my heart it drew forth that huge bulk of corruption. And this deliverance, what was it, but that I willed not any more that which I was wont to will, and began to will that which thou willedst.

But where had that freewill of mine remained for so long a time, and from what deep and hidden corner was it called forth, in that moment when I did submit my neck to thy *easy yoke* and my shoulders to thy *light burden,* O Christ Jesus, *my helper and my redeemer?* How delightful did it instantly grow to me to lack the delights of those vain things; yea it was now a joy to me to be deprived of those joys, which formerly I had feared to lose. For thou, O Lord, didst cast them out from me, thou true and supreme delight, thou didst cast them forth, and in their place didst enter in thyself, more sweet than all earthly pleasure, though not to flesh and blood; clearer than any light, yet more hidden than any secret; higher than the highest honour, but not to such as are high in their own conceits.

Now was my mind free from the biting cares both of honour and of riches, as also from weltering in filth, and scratching the itch of lust; and I prattled childlike unto thee, my light, my wealth, my salvation, my Lord and my God.

He forsaketh the profession of rhetoric

AND I thought it fit in thy sight to withdraw the service of my tongue from the mart where talking may be sold—yet gently withal and in no tumultuous manner—that so the pupils, who studied not thy law nor thy peace, but lying madness and a legal warfare, might no longer purchase at my mouth the weapons of their frenzy. And it fell out very fitly that a few days only were to run before the vacation of the vintage time; so I resolved to endure them, that I might make a more formal departure, and, being once bought by thee, might return no more to put myself on sale. Our purpose therefore was known to thee only, and to no other men but such as were of our company. And we had agreed among ourselves that it should not be published abroad to any; although thou hadst already given to us—ascending now from the valley of tears and singing the song of Degrees—certain sharp arrows and hot burning coals, against any such deceiving tongue as might cross our course under the colour of giving us counsel, or might devour us as food under the pretence of love.

Thou hadst shot through our hearts by the arrows of thy charity, and thy winged words were sticking in our flesh, and the examples of thy servants, whom from black thou hadst made to shine and from the dead to live, cast themselves together in the bosom of our thoughts, burning and consuming our weight of sloth, that we might no more be drawn by it unto the depths. And they kindled in us so great a fire, that no breath of contradiction proceeding from any wicked tongue might extinguish us, but rather inflame us the more. But yet, seeing that, for thy name's sake which thou hast sanctified upon earth, our religious desire and purpose would assuredly find such as would commend it, I feared it might look like a kind of ostentation if I waited not the vacation, which was now so near at hand, but should depart from my public profession whilst all the world was looking on; so that, the eyes of all observers being turned towards this action of mine, whereby I should retire before the time of vintage, now so nearly approaching, they would be saying many things, as that I desired herein to be thought a great man. And what would it have served me that they should be thinking and talking of my intentions, that so my good should be evil spoken of?

Besides this, my lungs did begin to give way this summer through my over laborious toil, so that they breathed with difficulty, and by the pain of my breast did prove themselves ill-affected, refusing to let me speak at any length with an audible voice; for the which I was at first somewhat troubled, because I was in a manner constrained by necessity to lay down that burden of teaching, or at least to intermit it, if I would endeavour to cure myself and grow strong again. But so soon as I grew to have a full and confirmed will to *attend and see that thou art God,* thou knowest, O Lord, how I began to rejoice that this excuse, no untruth, was at hand, which might temper the disgust of such men as, for the sake of their children, would needs have kept me ever their slave.

Being full therefore of such joy as this, I had patience till the time which was interposed might fly away. It was, perhaps, about twenty days, but yet it needed courage to endure them; for now the desire of gain, which was wont to bear a part of the business with me, was fled away, and I should have been oppressed, if patience had not succeeded in place thereof. Some of thy servants, my brethren, may say that I committed a sin, when, with my heart filled by the resolution of fighting under thy colours, I suffered myself still to sit in that chair of lying, though it were but for the space of an hour. And for my part I do not defend myself herein. But thou, O most merciful Lord, hast thou not remitted and pardoned this, with the rest of my hideous and deadly sins, in the holy water of baptism?

Verecundus lendeth his country house

BUT Verecundus was even wasted with anxiety upon occasion of this good fortune of ours, since—by reason of his chains whereby he was so fast tied—he saw that he must break company with us. Though not as yet a Christian himself, his wife was of the faith, yet was she the heaviest clog of all to his leg, whereby he was stayed from the journey that we were undertaking; for, as he said, he would not be a Christian in any other manner, save in that which as yet he could not be. Most kindly, however, did he offer unto us that we should have the use of his country house, for so long as we might be there. To him, O Lord, thou *wilt make recompense in the resurrection of the just,* because thou hast already called him to the lot of the just. For although he fell sick in body during our absence—we being then in Rome—yet in that sickness was he made a Christian and one of the faithful, before he departed out of this life. Thus didst thou show mercy, not only unto him but to us also, for otherwise—remembering that great courtesy of our friend—we should have been tormented with intolerable grief, if we were unable to number him among the sheep of thy flock.

Thanks be unto thee, O Lord our God; we are all thine, as thine inspirations and consolations make known unto us. Thou, O faithful performer of thy promises, thou shalt repay to Verecundus, for that country house of his at Cassiciacum where we found rest in thee from the burning heat of the world, the pleasure of thy paradise, for ever green, because thou hast forgiven him his sins upon earth, in thy mountain, *the fruitful mountain, the mountain of fatness*. Verecundus therefore was much troubled at this time, but Nebridius did rejoice with us. For although he himself was not as yet a Christian—seeing he had fallen into that most pernicious pit of error, which believed the flesh of the Truth, thy Son, to be fantastical—yet now was he rising out from thence; and, though not yet washed with any of the sacraments of thy Church, he still continued to be a most ardent seeker after the truth. And not long after our conversion and regeneration by thy baptism, after thou hadst first made him also a faithful Catholic, serving thee with perfect chastity and continence, with all they of his household in Africa whom he had brought to the Christian faith, thou didst take him away from this flesh; and now he liveth in Abraham's bosom.

For whatsoever it be that is understood by this bosom, there doth Nebridius live, that dear friend of mine, and thine adopted son, O Lord, once a slave, indeed, but afterwards freed by thee. There he liveth, for what other place can be fit for such a soul? In that place he liveth, whereof he was wont to ask me, poor inexperienced man, so many questions. No longer now doth he lay his ear to my mouth, but to thy spring he applieth the lips of his spirit, and drinketh wisdom to the full of his powers and of his thirst, being happy for all eternity. Nor do I think that he is so inebriated therewith as that he doth forget me, when thou, O Lord, of whom he drinketh, art mindful of us. Thus was it with us. We comforted Verecundus in his sorrow, with no breach in our friendship notwithstanding our conversion, exhorting him to be faithful according to his state, which was that of a married life. But Nebridius we awaited, expecting the time when he should follow us, which he might shortly do, being so near; and lo, at length those days of waiting were expired. For indeed they seemed long and many, through the longing we had for that easeful liberty wherein we might sing with all our souls,

"To thee my heart hath said, I have sought thy countenance; thy countenance, O Lord, will I seek."

Of the books and the letters that he wrote at Cassiciacum, of his joy in the Psalms, and of the pain he had in his teeth

Now was the day come wherein I was actually released from the profession of rhetoric, from which I was already freed in desire. At last it was done, and thou didst deliver my tongue, as thou hadst already done my heart, and I rejoiced and blessed thee, I and all mine, as we went to the country house. What I did there by way of writing, such skill as I had therein being placed at thy service—though yet, at times, it savoured still of the school of pride, as if panting after a round—my books bear witness; both those Disputations, which I had with them that were present with me, and such as I composed by myself alone, before thy face, and in my Epistles to Nebridius while he was yet away. And when shall I have time enough to make rehearsal of all the great benefits which thou then didst bestow upon us, I who am making haste to speak of matters greater yet? For my remembrance calls upon me, and it is matter of much delight, O Lord, for me to confess unto thee by what secret and sharp goads thou didst tame me outright; and how thou didst abate and humble those mountains and hills of my vain thoughts, *making my crooked ways straight and my rough places smooth,* and how too thou didst subdue that brother of my heart, Alipius, to the name of thy only begotten Son, our Lord and Saviour Jesus Christ, which at the first he thought it not fit to see in our writings. For he desired rather that they should savour of *the cedars* of the Schools, *which the Lord hath broken,* than of those wholesome herbs of thy Church, which have power against the venom of serpents.

What cries, O my God, did I utter unto thee, when I

read the Psalms of David, those faithful songs, whose words
of piety do banish the swelling spirit of pride, whilst I kept
holiday in that country house; though as yet I was but a
kind of rude stranger to thy true love, being but a Catechumen, as Alipius also was. My mother also remained inseparably with us, in habit a woman, in faith a man; hers
were the resignation of age, the tenderness of a mother,
the devotion of a true Christian. What words did I utter
unto thee in those Psalms! How was I inflamed by them
towards thee, and enkindled to recite them—had I been
able—in the ear of the whole world, to the confusion of the
pride of mankind! Yet are they sung already over the
whole world, *nor is there any that can hide himself from
thy heat*. With what vehement and bitter grief was I
offended against the Manichees, while yet I pitied them,
for that they knew not thy sacraments, those true medica-
ments, and that they did run mad against that sovereign
remedy, whereby they might have been recovered. I wished
that they had been somewhere near me, without my
knowing that thy were there, for then they could have seen
my face and heard my words, when I read the fourth Psalm
in that time of my retreat, and might have learned what
that Psalm wrought in me.

*When I called upon thee, thou heardest me, O God of my
justice; thou didst enlarge me, when I was in tribulation.
Have mercy upon me, O Lord, and hearken unto my
prayer*. I would they had heard me without my knowing
thereof, lest otherwise they might have thought that I had
spoken so in regard of them, because I should neither have
said the same words nor in the same manner, if I had
thought they either saw or heard me; nor yet, if I had done
so, would they have understood how I spake with myself,
and to myself before thee, out of the innermost feeling
of my soul. For I quaked with fear, and again I boiled high
with hope and with vehement joy in thy mercy, O Father.
And all these feelings sallied forth by mine eyes and by
my words, when thy Holy Spirit, being turned towards

us, said, *"O ye sons of men, how long will ye be heavy-hearted? How long will ye love vanity, and seek after a lie?"* For I myself had loved vanity and sought after a lie. And thou, O Lord, hadst already *magnified thy Holy One, raising him from the dead and placing him at thy right hand,* whence he would send from on high *the Comforter, the Spirit of Truth.* Nay, he had sent him already, but I knew it not.

Already had he sent him, for now was he magnified by rising from the dead and ascending up to heaven. But before, the Spirit was not given, because Jesus was not yet glorified. And the prophet crieth out, *"How long will ye be heavy-hearted, love vanity, and seek after a lie? Know ye this, that our Lord hath magnified his Holy One."* He crieth out, *"How long?"* he crieth out, *"Know ye this,"* and yet for all so long had I been ignorant, loved vanity, and sought after a lie! Therefore did I hear and tremble, because it is said unto such as I remembered myself to have been. For in those fancies and fictions, which once I had embraced instead of thee, there was both vanity and lying. And many things did I cry aloud both mightily and grievously, which I would that they had heard, who yet *love vanity and seek after a lie.* For perhaps they would have been troubled, and might have cast forth that poison, and thou mightest have heard them when they cried unto thee. Because he died for us with a true death in the flesh, who now maketh intercession for us with thee.

I read on, *"Be angry and sin not"*; and how was I moved, O my God—I who had now learned to be angry with myself in the past, that I might not sin in the time to come. And justly was I angry with myself, for it was not another nature of the kingdom of darkness which sinned by me, as they do say, who, being not angry with themselves, *do treasure up to themselves wrath, against the day of wrath and of the just judgement of God.* Nor was the good that I sought for any longer in external things, nor did I seek them with the eyes of flesh and blood in this visible world. For they who seek their delight in such visible things, do easily vanish away like the smoke, and are poured out upon those *things which are seen and are temporal,* and in the starvation of their thoughts they do lick the very shadows thereof. Oh that they might grow wearied for very hunger, and say, "*Who will show unto us good things?*" Then might they hear us, when we say, "*The light of thy countenance, O Lord, hath shined upon us*"; for we ourselves are not *the light which illuminateth every man that cometh into the world,* but we are illuminated by thee, that we, *who were heretofore darkness, may be light in thee.*

Oh that they might see that inner light, whereby, because I had once tasted of it, I was made angry; because I knew not how to show it to them, unless they should bring me their heart in their eyes, that wander abroad from thee, and should ask me, "*Who will show unto us good things?*" But there, where I was angry with myself—in that inner chamber where I was contrite, where I had offered my sacrifice, slaying my old man and hoping in thee, with the part-formed purpose of a renewing of myself—even there didst thou begin to grow sweet to me, and thou gavest joy to my heart. And I cried out, reading these things in the letter, and finding them to be verified in the spirit. Nor would I any more be increased with worldly goods, wasting my time and being wasted by temporal things, when I had, in thy eternal Simplicity, another kind of corn and wine and oil.

And in the verse following I exclaimed from the depth of my heart, "*O, in peace; O, in the Selfsame,*" what is it he hath said? "*I will lay me down to sleep and take my rest.*" For who can resist us, when the saying is brought to pass which is written, "*Death is swallowed up in victory?*" And thou, O Lord, art admirably *the Selfsame,* who art *subject to no change,* and in thee is rest, forgetting all kind of labour; since there is no other beside thee, nor are we to labour after attaining of other things, which are not thou, *but it is thou, O Lord, thou only that makest me to dwell in hope.* I read, and I was all on fire, yet I could not find what I might do for those deaf and dead ones, of whom once myself had been a pestilent member, a blind and snarling barker against thy scriptures, which are all behonied with the very honey of heaven, and made bright with thine own light; and I did even consume away with zeal against the enemies thereof.

When shall I remember all the things that passed in those days of our retirement? But neither have I forgotten, nor will I keep in silence, the sharpness of thy scourge, and the admirable swiftness of thy mercy. Thou didst then torment me with the toothache, and when it was grown to such height of violence that it made me speechless, it came into my heart to desire all my friends there present that they would pray unto thee, who art the God of all kind of health. This I wrote on my waxen tablets, and gave it to be read by them. Immediately, so soon as with humble devotion we had bowed our knees, the pain fled away. But what kind of pain was that, or how went it from me? I was much afraid, I confess, O Lord my God, for in all my life I had never felt the like. And thus in the depth was thy secret will insinuated to me, and rejoicing in the faith I praised thy name. But that faith would not suffer me to be secure in the remembrance of my former sins, which as yet were not forgiven unto me in baptism.

He consults with Ambrose what books he were best to read

At the end of the vintage I gave warning to the citizens of Milan, that they might provide for their scholars another man to sell them words, both because I had resolved to serve thee, and because I could not longer attend to that profession, through my difficulty of respiration, and the pain of my breast, to which I was subject. And by letter I acquainted thy Prelate, the holy man Ambrose, with my ancient errors and my then present purpose, that he might advise me which of thy books I were best to read to the end that I might grow readier and fitter for the receiving of so great a grace. He willed me to read the prophet Isaias, I believe, because among the prophets he is the most clear foreteller of the Gospel and the vocation of the Gentiles. But I, not understanding that which first I read, and conceiving all the rest to be like thereunto, laid it by, with the intention to resume it when I should be more exercise in the word of the Lord.

How he was baptized at Milan, with Alipius and Adeodatus

WHEN the time was come wherein I was to give in my name for baptism, we left the country and went back to Milan. And with me Alipius also resolved to be reborn in thee, having now put on humility, the fit ground for thy sacraments to work upon, and having become so valiant a conqueror of his body that he would tread the frozen Italian soil with bare feet, an act of unwonted daring. We did also join unto us the boy, Adeodatus, who was carnally begotten of my body, the fruit of my sin. Thy part in him, O Lord, was well made; for although he had but fifteen years of age, in wit he excelled many grave and learned men. I confess unto thee thine own gifts, O Lord my God, who art the Creator of all things, and abundantly able to reform all our defects; for myself I had nothing in this child, but the sin wherewith he was begotten, for that we had care to bring him up in thy fear, it was thou and none other who didst inspire us thereunto. I do, therefore, but confess thy gifts. There is a book of ours, which is entitled " Of the Master," wherein he and I speak together in the form of a dialogue. Thou knowest, O Lord, that all those conceptions are his own, which are delivered therein under the person of him that speaketh with me; and that too when he had but sixteen years of age. Many other things yet more admirable have I discovered in him, and his wit did cause a kind of awe in me, and who but thou can be the worker of such miracles?

Soon didst thou take his life from off this earth; and I remember him so much the more securely, because I fear nothing for his childhood or his youth, nor indeed do I fear anything at all in him. We associated him with us, who was as old as ourselves in the account of thy grace, to be instructed according to thy discipline. Thus were we baptized together, and instantly all solicitude for our former life fled away from us. Nor was there any end in those days to the unspeakable delight wherewith I considered the depth of thy counsels concerning the salvation of mankind. How plentifully did I weep in those hymns and psalms, being touched to the very quick by the notes of thy Church so sweetly singing. Those words did flow into mine ears, and the Truth which was contained therein distilled melting into my heart, and from thence the affection of piety did overflow, so that my tears ran streaming down, and happy did I find myself therein.

Persecution of the Church miraculously diverted

Not long before this the Church of Milan had begun to celebrate that manner of consolation and exhortation, to the great delight of the brethren, who sang together with both hearts and voices. For it might be about a year or not much more, since the time when Justina, the mother of the young Emperor Valentinian, was persecuting thy servant Ambrose, by reason of her heresy, to which she was seduced by the Arians. Then did the devout people begin to watch both day and night in the church, being ready to die with their Bishop, thy servant. There my mother, thy handmaid, being among the foremost in those watches and cares, did employ herself wholly in praying; yea and we also, though at that time unthawed by the heat of thy

Spirit, were yet stirred up by the example of the whole city, which was so amazed and troubled. Then was it first introduced that hymns and psalms should be sung, according to the custom of the Eastern Churches, lest the people should faint through the tediousness of grief; and this custom, which is retained even to this day, is imitated by many, yea by almost all thy congregations throughout the rest of the world.

Thou didst then declare by a vision unto thy Bishop aforesaid, in what place the bodies of thy martyrs Gervasius and Protasius did lie hid, which thou hadst preserved uncorrupt for the space of so many years in thy secret treasure-house, that afterwards thou mightest bring them to light, and repress thereby the rage of that persecutor, a woman indeed but withal the mother of an Emperor. For when these bodies, being discovered and taken up, were translated with due honour to the church of Ambrose, not only they who were vexed by unclean spirits—the devils themselves confessing thereto—were cured; but a certain inhabitant of the city, well known to have been blind for many years, on his asking and being told the reason why the people was in such a tumultuous kind of joy, leaped forward and desired his guide to lead him thither. And being conducted thither, he obtained liberty to touch with his handkerchief the bier of *thy saints, whose death is precious in thy sight*. As soon as he had done this and applied the handkerchief to his eyes, immediately they were opened. Hereupon was the fame spread, hereupon thy praises were published and proclaimed to the world, and hereupon the mind of that enemy, though it could not be brought to the health of the faith, was yet stayed from the fury of persecution. I thank thee, O my God; whither and from whence hast thou brought me to the remembrance of this matter, that I might also confess it unto thee, this great matter which I had forgotten and passed over? Yet even then, albeit the odours of thy precious ointments were so fragrant, we ran not after thee; and for this cause did I weep so much the more abundantly at the singing of thy hymns. Long had I aspired after thee, and now at last was I breathing in thee, so far as one breathes the air in this house of straw.

The conversion of Evodius; a discourse concerning his mother

THOU *who makest men to be of one mind in a house,* didst associate unto us Evodius, a young man of mine own town, an Agent in Public Affairs, who was converted unto thee and baptized before us, and having left the service of the world, had girded himself for thine. We kept together still, intending still to dwell together according to our holy purpose; and, seeking some place where most conveniently we might continue to serve thee, together we began our journey back to Africa. But when we were come to Ostia, at the mouth of the Tiber, my mother departed out of this life. Many things herein do I omit, because I hasten much. Receive, O God, my confessions and thanksgivings for innumerable things whereof I am silent. But I will not omit whatsoever my soul can bring forth concerning her, that handmaid of thine who brought me forth, both in her flesh, thereby to be born to this temporal light, and in her heart, that I might be born again to the light eternal. They are not her gifts that I speak of, but thine in her. For neither did she give birth nor education unto herself, it is thou who didst create her; nor did her father or mother know what kind of creature was to be by their means.

The rod of Christ, the discipline of thy only Son, instructed her in thy fear, in a faithful household, a living member of thy Church. Yet she was not wont to speak so much of her mother's diligence in her education as of that of a certain decrepit maidservant of hers, who had even borne her father in her arms and upon her back, as strong maids are wont to carry little children. For this reason, as also for her great age and her excellent disposition, she was much esteemed in that Christian household by her master and mistress, and she did vigilantly discharge the care of her mistress's daughters, who were committed to her; being earnest in restraining them, with a kind of holy severity, when need required, and at other times using great discretion and prudence in teaching them. For except at those hours when they were most temperately fed at their parents' table, she would not suffer them—how thirsty soever they might be—to drink so much as a draught of water; preventing thereby an ill custom, and accompanying the refusal with this profitable saying, " Now you would be content to drink water, because you are not suffered to have wine; but when you shall come to be married, and be made mistresses of houses and all the provisions thereof, water will be despised by you, but the custom of drinking will prevail upon you."

By this way of directing them, and by her authority in commanding, she abated the edge of their tender years and she brought the thirst of the girls to so modest a term, that they would not now so much as wish for that which was not expedient. Yet in spite of all this, as thy handmaid hath related to me her son, there stole upon her an inclination to the love of wine. For when she, being a sober young maid, was required sometimes by her parents—as the manner was—to draw wine from the cask, she, holding the cup under the tap, before she poured the wine into the flagon, would wet her lips at the mouth thereof with a little sip; for misliking the taste she would not more than this. Nor did she this out of any appetite for drink, but through that overflowing of impulse to which youth is subject, which boileth up into the gamesomeness of that age; which in those years is wont to be stayed by the authority of elders. But she, daily adding a little more to that little which she began to take, since whosoever neglecteth small things will by little and little fall to great ones, she grew at last to such a custom as that she would greedily drink off her little cups of wine almost full.

Where was then that vigilant old woman, with all her earnest prohibitions? Was anything sufficient for the cure of this secret sickness, if thy physic, O Lord, did not watch over us? Her father, mother, nurses, all were absent, but thou wert present, thou who didst create and dost call us, who by the ministry of our superiors art ever doing us some good towards the salvation of our souls; how didst thou carry thyself in this present case, O my God? How didst thou cure her? How didst thou heal her? Didst thou not draw a scornful and sharp reproach out of another's soul, as it were a surgeon's knife out of thy secret store, whereby at a blow thou mightest cut off in her that which was putrefied? For the maid who used to go with her to the cellar, falling to words with her young mistress hand to hand, as sometimes happens, upbraided her fault in a most bitter and insulting manner, calling her "wine-bibber." But she was no sooner struck with this dart than she reflected upon the deformity of her custom, yea and instantly she condemned and forsook it. As friends who flatter do corrupt, so enemies who quarrel with us do many times reform us. Yet dost thou not reward them according to what thou doest by them, but according to that which they intended to do. For that maidservant, being in choler, had a mind to wound her young mistress, not to cure her. Therefore she did it secretly, either because the circumstances of time and place found them alone, or peradventure for fear lest, if she had been known to know it and not to speak of it any sooner, she might herself have been prejudiced thereby. But thou, O Lord, who art the Governor of all things both in heaven and earth, dost wrest to thy use the depths of the running streams, and drawest into order the confused succession of times and things. So by the madness of one soul didst thou cure another. Let no man therefore, when he considereth this, ascribe it to any virtue of his own if another should chance to be reformed by any word of his, whereby he meant not to reform him.

Of his mother's excellent conversation

SHE was modestly and soberly brought up, and made subject by thee unto her parents, rather than by her parents unto thee. When she became of marriageable age, she was bestowed upon a husband, to whom she was obedient as to her lord; endeavouring earnestly to win him to thee, preaching thee unto him by her virtuous character, whereby thou madest her beautiful in his eyes, and both reverently amiable and admirable unto him. She so endured her husband's dishonouring of her bed, that she never had any dispute with him upon that reason. For she expected thy mercy towards him, that by believing in thee he might be made chaste. He was moreover of an excellent good nature, but of a choleric temper. She learned therefore not to resist her angry husband, not in deed only but not so much as in a word; only afterwards, when she perceived that the opportunity was fitter through his being appeased and quiet, she would render account of her actions, if she found that he had been offended without reason.

In a word, while many matrons, who had milder husbands, did sometimes bear in their bruised faces the mark of blows, and in conversation with others would complain of their husbands' lives, she would reprove their tongues, admonishing them seriously—though as if in jest—that, from the time when they heard their contracts of marriage read, they should esteem them as indentures, whereby themselves were declared servants to their husbands, and that therefore they should be mindful of their condition, and not quarrel with their lords. And when they would wonder, knowing what a choleric husband she had, that they could never hear or otherwise perceive that Patricius had ever struck his wife, or that they had ever spent one day asunder by occasion of any strife, and would familiarly ask the reason of it, she taught them the rule which I have already mentioned. And such of them as observed it had cause to give her thanks by their own experience; such again as observed it not continued in subjection to be daily vexed.

Her mother-in-law also, whom the whisperings of ill servants had at the first incensed against her, she did overcome by her attentions and by her continuance in meekness and patience; in such sort that the mother did of her own accord discover unto her son the ill offices which were performed by those servants, desiring him to punish them as disturbers of the domestical peace between her daughter-in-law and herself. And so afterwards he, both obeying his mother in this point, and taking care for the peace and discipline of his family, did rebuke the servants with blows, according to the pleasure of her that brought the fault to light. And she, in her turn, promised that no other recompense should be made to such as would offer to pick a thank by speaking unduly of her daughter. Which none daring any more to do, they lived ever after in a most memorable sweetness of goodwill.

Yet further, O God my Mercy, thou gavest this great gift to that good servant of thine, in whose womb thou didst frame me, that she would carry herself with so much sweetness, according to the opportunity that she had, between such persons as were in greatest enmity with one another, that when she heard them severally to utter many most bitter things—such as are wont to be expressed by swelling and indigested choler, when one speaks to a present friend of an absent enemy, the fierceness of hatred being exhaled herein—she would never disclose more of the one party to the other than might help to reconcile them together.

This virtue might seem a small one if—to my grief—I found not by experience that innumerable persons—I know not by what pestilence of sin, infesting far and near—do not only discover the speeches of angry enemies to one another, but do even add thereto somewhat that was not said. Whereas, on the contrary, it ought to be thought little for a man not to increase and exasperate enmities by ill offices, unless withal he procure to quench them by good ones, as this thy servant did under thee, who wert the inward Master in that school of her heart. At length also she gained her husband to thee, towards the end of his life; nor had she cause to lament those defects in him, being a Christian, which before, he not being so, she had supported in him.

She was also the servant of thy servants, and whosoever knew her did give much praise unto her, and love and honour unto thee; because he found thy presence in her soul, the fruits of her holy conversation bearing witness thereunto. For she was the wife of one husband, she complied with her duty to her parents, she governed her house with all piety, her actions had the testimony of a good conscience, she brought up her children, travailing in labour for them often, so many times as she found them, to be forsaking thee. And lastly, O Lord, of us all who before her death lived together in thy fear, having the grace of baptism, she did so take care, as if she had been the mother of us all; and yet she did so serve us, as if she had been the daughter of us all.

Of the conference he had with his mother concerning heavenly things

BUT the day approaching, when she was to depart out of this life—which day thou knewest, though we knew it not—it happened, as I believe through thy procurement by thy secret ways, that she and I alone were standing, leaning in a certain window, which had a prospect upon the garden of the house where we then lay, at Ostia upon the Tiber; where, being sequestered from company after the labour of

a long journey, we were preparing ourselves to pass over by
the sea into Africa. There did we confer alone, with much
dear tenderness, and, *forgetting those things which are
behind, we reached forth unto those things which are
before,* we did inquire between ourselves of thee, who art
the ever present Truth, of what kind should be that eternal
life of the saints in heaven, which *the eye hath not seen,
nor the ear heard, nor hath it entered into the heart of man.*
With the mouth of our heart we did earnestly aspire
towards the heavenly things of thy fountain, the fountain of
life which is with thee, to the end that, being refreshed by it
according to our capacities, we might in some sort consider
of so high a mystery.

And when our discourse was drawn to such a point, as
that the greatest delight of flesh and blood, in the brightest
of material light, did seem not only unworthy to be compared but even so much as to be remembered in respect of
the sweetness of that life eternal, we, raising ourselves towards that Selfsame with the most ardent affections of our
mind, made a kind of progress by degrees over all things
corporeal, and this vault of heaven itself, from whence the
sun and moon and stars do shine upon the earth. And
higher yet we ascended, by more interiorly conceiving and
discoursing of thee, and admiring thy works. And then we
struck inward upon the consideration of our own souls, and
did even transcend and pass beyond them also, that
we might touch upon the confines of that region of
plenty which never faileth, where thou feedest Israel for all
eternity with the food of Truth, and where Life is that
very Wisdom of thine, by which all these things both are,
and were, and shall be made. And this Wisdom is not
made, but it Is, so as it was and shall ever be. Or rather to
have been in times past, and to be hereafter, is not in it,
but only to be now, because it is eternal; for to have been,
and to be hereafter, is not eternal. And whilst we thus
spake and panted towards it, we grew able to take a little
taste thereof with the whole force of our hearts. And we

sighed, and left there confined *the first fruits of the spirit,* and we returned again to the noise of language, where every word is begun and ended. How little like to thy Word, our Lord, who remaineth in himself without length of days, and yet renewing all things!

We said therefore : If to any man the tumult of the flesh be silent, if phantasies of earth and air and sea be silent also, if the poles of heaven be silent, and the very soul of man be silent to itself, and by not-thinking pass beyond itself, if all dreams be silent and all such things as be revealed by the imagination, if every tongue and every sign and everything that hath its existence by passing-on be silent wholly unto any man—since all these things proclaim to him *that hath an ear to hear,* "We made not ourselves, but he made us who remains for ever"—if then, having uttered this, they too be silent, as fastening their attention upon him that made them; if then HE ONLY speak, not by them but by himself, that we may hear his Word, not by tongue of flesh, nor voice of angel nor by the sound of a cloud that is broken by thunder, nor by the dark riddle of a similitude, and we may hear him, whom in these things we love, himself apart from them—like as we two did now stretch ourselves up, and in swift thought lay hold a little upon the eternal wisdom, that abideth above all things—if this were to continue and all other visions, in order far inferior, might be withdrawn, and this alone might so transport and swallow up and wrap him who beheld it in those intrinsical joys, so that his life might be for all eternity such as was this moment of understanding, which we did so ardently sigh after; would not this be that whereof is written, *"Enter thou into the joy of thy Lord"*? But when shall this be? Shall it be when *we shall all rise, but shall not all be changed*?

Such discourse as this we held; and, if not just in this manner and in these very words, yet thou knowest, O Lord, that in that day when we uttered such things as these, this world with all the delights thereof grew contemptible, even as we spake of it. Then said my mother, "My son, for as much as concerns me there is nothing now in this life wherein I take delight. What I have yet to do here, or why I am yet here I know not, now that the hopes I had in this world are wholly at an end. One thing only there was, for which I desired to stay in this life a little while; namely, that I might see thee a Catholic Christian before I died. And behold, my God hath vouchsafed this to me in a manner more abundant, for now I see thee, with contempt of all earthly happiness, to be his servant. What then do I here any longer?"

Of his mother's sickness, ecstasy, and death

What I answered her to these things I do not well remember. But in the meantime, scarce five days after, or not much more, she grew sick of a fever; and in that sickness, one day, she fell into a fainting, and was withdrawn a little while from her senses. We ran to her and she was soon restored to herself again; and looking upon my brother[1] and myself standing by her, she said to us in the manner of a question, "Where was I?" Then, fixing her eyes upon us speechless with grief, she said, "Here shall you lay your mother." I myself was silent and repressed my tears, but my brother said somewhat whereby he insinuated the hope he had, that she should be more happy than to die in any country but her own. And as soon as she had heard this, having checked him with an anxious countenance, for his being yet so imperfect, she said thus, turning herself towards me, "Behold, what he saith!" And soon after to us both, "Lay this body where you will, let not any care thereof disquiet you; this only I entreat, that you will remember me at the altar of the Lord, wheresoever you be." And when she had expressed this her purpose in words, as best she could, she

[1] See Note 6.

held her peace, being in agony by reason of her sickness, which grew fast upon her.

But I considering thy gifts, O thou God invisible, which thou conveyest into the hearts of thy servants, from whence so admirable fruits do grow, did rejoice and give thanks unto thee, calling to mind how much, as I knew, my mother had formerly troubled herself about her sepulture; which she had provided and prepared close by the body of her husband. For because they two had grown to live in great conjunction of mind, she desired—since human nature is little able to divine the plan of God—that to her other happiness this also might be added and celebrated by men, how it was granted unto her that—after a long peregrination beyond the sea—the same earth might give burial to the earth of both their bodies. But when this vain conceit began to be no longer in her heart by the fulness of thy grace, I knew not; yet was I glad, even to admiration, that so it was. Though indeed, even in that very speech which before she used to me at the window, when she said "What do I here any longer?" she discovered not any desire of dying in her own country. Afterwards I was also told how that while we were at Ostia, she had been familiarly discoursing one day with a matronly confidence to certain friends of mine, myself not being present, of the contempt of this life and the excellence of death, when they—being amazed at the courage of that woman, which thou gavest unto her—and asking her if she would not fear to leave her body so far off from the place where she was born, she answered thus, "Nothing is far off from God, neither is there any cause to fear that, at the day of judgement, he will not know well enough from what place he is to raise me up again." So in the ninth day of her sickness, in the six and fiftieth year of her age, and the three and thirtieth of mine, that religious and pious soul was discharged from the prison of her body.

His excessive grief at his mother's death

I CLOSED her eyes, and there surged into my heart an un-speakable sorrow, which overflowed in tears; and mine eyes, being subject to the imperious dominion of my mind, did even drink their fountain dry, and in that conflict I was sore oppressed. At the instant of her giving up the ghost, the boy Adeodatus brake forth into a loud lamentation, but we all employed ourselves to quiet him, and he held his peace. Nay, there did slip from myself also some shew of childishness in that way, but I repressed it with a man's voice, the voice of my heart, and was silent. Nor did we think fit to celebrate that funeral with weeping and loud-voiced cries, because with such demonstrations of sorrow men are wont to lament who think on death as a misery or even as utter destruction. But she died not miserably, nor indeed did she die utterly, as we were well assured by her true faith, her exemplary life, and by other reasons as certain.

What then was the cause why this green wound did so extremely grieve my heart? What but the sudden breaking off of that custom, which I had, to live in her most sweet and most dear conversation? For I was much joyed by that testimony which she gave me in her last sickness, when —mingling her endearments with my acts of dutiful respect towards her—she vouchsafed to call me her " good son "; and she related with great dearness of affection how she had never heard any harsh or unkind word to be darted out of my mouth against her. But yet, O thou my God, who didst make us both, what comparison was there between the honour I could do unto her, and the painful care which she had of me? Because therefore I was deprived of so great a comfort, my soul was wounded, and my life, as it were, torn in pieces, which till then had been composed of hers and mine.

The boy being restrained from weeping, Evodius opened the psalter and began to sing this psalm: *" I will sing unto thee, O Lord, mercy and judgement,"* to which all the house made answer. And when the people heard what had happened, many brethren and religious women came thither to us, and whilst they, to whose office it belonged, took order for the burial, I myself, in another part of the house, did address to those, who thought it not fit to forsake me, such words as I held to be not unfitting for that time. And by this fomentation of truth I assuaged my torment, which to thee was known, but not to them who hearkened attentively to what I said, and conceived me to be without much sense of sorrow. But in thy ears, when none of them was present, I blamed the effeminateness of my mind, and stayed the course of my sadness, which for that little time began to decrease, though soon after it returned impetuously upon me. Yet not so far as to make me shed tears, or so much as to change my countenance, but well I knew what I kept down in my heart. And because it very much offended me that this human respect had such power over me—which yet cannot choose but happen sometimes, through the common course and condition of our nature—I did grieve with another grief for my own grieving, and so was afflicted with a double sorrow.

And behold, when the corpse was carried forth, we both went and returned without tears. For neither in those prayers which we poured forth unto thee, when the sacrifice of our Redemption was offered for her, the body being placed near the sepulchre before it was buried, according to the custom of the place, not even in those prayers did I weep at all. Yet all that day was I grievously sad in secret, and with a troubled mind I begged of thee, as well as I could, that thou wouldst cure the wound of my grief. Which yet thou didst not, because, as I conceive, thou wouldst make me to know by this one experiment all the enchaining force of custom, even to a soul that feeds no longer on deceiving words. And I thought it would do me some good to go bathe myself, as having heard that the Greeks called the bath βαλανεῖον, because it was good to expel grief from the mind. Behold, I confess even this to thy mercy, O thou Father of orphans, for that, after my bathing, I was the same man I had been before. For the bitterness of the sorrow of my heart did not spend itself by the pores of my skin; but soon after I slept, and when I waked I found it in great part assuaged. And as I lay alone in my bed, this true verse of thy servant Ambrose came into my mind:

> Thou God, Creator of us all,
> Guiding the Orbs celestial,
> Dost clothe the day with clearest light,
> Appointing sleep to come by night,
> Which may our weaken'd limbs restore
> To strength of labour, as before,
> And ease our overchargèd minds
> Of that sad care which there it finds.

And then again, by little and little, I called back thy handmaid to the place in my memory which from the first she held; considering that conversation of hers, so pious and religious towards thee, and towards us so obsequious and so sweet, whereof I was suddenly deprived. Then took I pleasure to weep in thy sight concerning her and for her, concerning myself and for myself. And those tears, which formerly I had repressed, I then gave liberty to run their fill, planting them for a pillow neath my heart, which found rest in them; for thine ears only it was that heard me, not the ears of any man who, in his pride, might have scorned me for weeping. And now in writing I confess it unto thee, O Lord; let him read it who will, and interpret it as pleaseth him. And if he count it for a sin in me, to have bewailed my mother for so short a time as is a portion of one hour—that mother I say, who was dead and departed from

mine eyes, who for so many years had wept for me that
before thine eyes I might live—let him not deride me; but
rather if he be a man of any charity, let him weep for my
sins to thee, who art the Father of all the brethren of thy
Christ, our Lord.

He prayeth ardently for her soul

BUT now, my heart being recovered from that wound, for
which it might be blamed as for a carnal kind of affection, I
pour out unto thee, our God, in behalf of that servant of
thine, a kind of tears far different, such as flow from a spirit
that is shaken by consideration of the danger of *every soul
that dieth in Adam*. And notwithstanding that she was so
quickened and renewed in Christ, while yet she remained
in the flesh, that there is cause to praise thy name both in
her faith and in her life, yet dare I not affirm that, after thou
hadst regenerated her in baptism, there issued no word out
of her mouth against thy commandment. And it is said by
thy Son, who is Truth itself, "*Whosoever shall say unto
his brother, 'Thou fool,' shall be in danger of hell fire.*"
And woe be it even unto men whose life is commend-
able, if, laying aside thy mercy, thou shouldst winnow
them with rigour. But because in examination of our sins
thou art not too rigorous, we confidently hope to find some
place of pardon with thee. But whosoever recounts to thee
his merits, what doth he recount but thy gifts? O that all
men would know themselves to be but men, and that *such
as glory, would glory in the Lord*.

I therefore, O my Praise and my Life, thou God of my
heart, laying aside for a while her good deeds, for which I
joyfully give thee thanks, do now pray unto thee for the sins
of my mother. Hearken unto me, I beseech thee, for his
sake, who is the true medicine of our wounds, who hung
upon the cross, and *now, sitting at thy right hand, maketh
intercession for us*. I know that she hath dealt mercifully,

and from her heart forgiven such as offended her. Forgive thou also her sins, if she committed any in so many years after she was cleansed by the water of salvation. Forgive her, O Lord, forgive her, I beseech thee, enter not into judgement with her. Let thy mercy overtop thy justice, because thy sayings are true, and thou hast promised mercy to such as are merciful; which yet they could not be without thy gift, who *hast mercy on whom thou wilt have mercy,* and wilt shew deeds of mercy to whom thou hast been mercifully inclined. And verily I believe that thou hast already done what I desire of thee, but yet accept, O Lord, this prayer which so willingly I make. For she, when the day of her death drew near, did not crave that her body might be sumptuously adorned, or embalmed with spices, nor desired she any choice monument, nor cared she to be conveyed for sepulture into her native land. Not these things did she recommend to us, but she desired only to be remembered at thy altar whereat she used to assist without intermission of one day, and from whence she knew that holy sacrifice to be dispensed, whereby *the handwriting which was against us is blotted out;* whereby is trodden under foot the enemy who numbereth our sins and seeketh what he may lay to our charge, yet found nothing in Him, in whom we are conquerors. Who shall restore unto him his innocent blood? Who shall repay unto him the price wherewith he bought us, and so be able to take us out of his hand?

To this sacrament of our redemption thy handmaid had tied her soul fast by the bond of faith. Let none sever her from thy protection; let not the lion or the dragon, by force or fraud, interpose himself between thee and her. For she will not answer that she oweth nothing, lest she be disproved and taken by that crafty accuser; but she will answer that her sins are forgiven by him, to whom no creature can repay that which he laid out for us, whilst himself owed nothing. Let her therefore rest in peace together with her husband, before whom and after whom she had no other, and whom she served, *bringing forth fruit to thee with patience,* that she might also gain him unto thee.

And inspire, O Lord my God, inspire thy servants, my brethren thy children, my masters whom with heart and tongue and pen I serve, that whosoever readeth these confessions may at thy altar remember thy servant Monica, with Patricius her husband, through whose flesh thou broughtest me into this world, though in what sort I know not. Let them with pious affection remember those who were my parents in this transitory life, who are my brethren under thee, our Father, in our mother the Church Catholic, and are to be also my fellow-citizens in the eternal Jerusalem whereunto the pilgrimage of thy people doth aspire from their birth unto their return thither; that so what she desired of me in her extremity may be performed unto her in the prayers of many, more abundantly through these my confessions than through my prayers.

NOTES

Note 1, p. 11, l. 25 (Book I)

" They may say, the mothers and nurses, that they expiate these offences, but I know not by what remedies."

It would seem that these exhibitions of temper, etc., on the infant's part were held to be unlucky, and the mother or nurse endeavoured to avert the evil by the use of some traditional charm; much as to-day a person who upsets the salt, will throw some of it over the shoulder. The verb *expiare*, used by St. Augustine here, is found in the same sense in Persius, when describing the charm against the evil eye in Sat. ii 31.

> *Ecce avia, aut metuens divum matertera, cunis*
> *Exemit puerum, frontemque atque uda labella*
> *Infami digito et lustralibus ante salivis*
> *Expiat, unrentes oculos inhibere perita.*

Note 2, p. 17, l. 24 (Book I)

". . . the guilt of my future sins would be both greater and more dangerous after baptism."

Augustine had been initiated as a catechumen at his birth, as appears from the words at the beginning of this chapter, " I was signed with the sign of the cross and seasoned with his salt, as soon as I came forth from the womb of my mother "; which refer to the ceremony of initiation, and to the custom, which prevailed in the African Church, of giving salt to catechumens throughout the year, and not only, as at Rome, to the *competentes* during the Lent preceding their baptism. In postponing his baptism, however, Monica acted in accordance with the custom which prevailed so widely in the fourth century. It is a very difficult matter for a modern churchman to arrive at the precise point of view which obtained herein. On the one hand, the teaching of the Church that Baptism was necessary to salvation and an indispensable preliminary to receiving any of the other Sacraments, was clear and was universally accepted; on the other hand, her discipline with regard to the Sacrament of Penance was much more severe than it is to-day. The faithful therefore found themselves in a dilemma, since the common view appears to have been that to commit grievous sin *after* Baptism was in the nature of a profanation of the Sacrament; while, at the same time, sins of the flesh were regarded as almost unavoidable, at any rate in the case of men during the early years of adult life. If however a subject was only baptized at an age when the danger of grievous sin was comparatively remote, he would have the satisfaction of knowing that his past offences were now washed away, and also that the risk of his profaning the Sacrament by grievous sin was comparatively small. In consequence the custom grew up of delaying to receive Baptism, which was often postponed until the subject was almost at death's door; the risk of his dying unbaptized being held, apparently, to be provided for by the Church's teaching as to the sufficiency of baptism of desire, which would cover any cases where sudden or unexpected death occurred before baptism. It was largely owing to the influence of St Augustine himself, who with other Fathers condemned it, that the custom of deferring baptism died out in the course of the next century or so.

Note 3, p. 60, l. 18 (Book III)

". . . the five elements variously transformed through the five dens of darkness . . ."

In the dualist system taught by the Manichees, the Realm of Darkness—the Evil Principle—was divided into five regions or dens, which were designated as the abodes of Darkness, Smoke, Evil Wind, Evil Fire, Evil Water; in opposition to the five members or attributes of the Light King, or Good Principle, which were the Light, the Air, the Wind, the Fire, and the Water. The "First Man," who fought as champion of the Light King, was armed with the five good elements, and he possessed the power to "transform" these in various ways, in order to deceive his foes. Augustine treats of the matter in *Contra Faustum*, ii 3, 4.

Note 4, p. 79, l. 8 (Book IV)

". . . if any man should consult the poets by a chance opening of the pages. . ."

This method of divination—a favourite one from very ancient times—consisted in opening a book at random and laying a finger upon the page, the passage touched being taken as an oracular response to the question in the mind of the seeker after enlightenment. The Greeks used the works of Homer in this way, the Latins Virgil, from which the name *Sortes Virgilianæ* has come to be used for the custom, although among Christians the Bible or book of the Gospels usually took the place of Virgil. In *Confessions,* viii 12 occurs the famous description of the way in which Augustine was led to open the book of St Paul's Epistles, by hearing the voice of a child singing repeatedly the words *tolle, lege, " take up and read,"* and so hit upon the passage (Romans xiii 13, 14) which put an end to his doubts.

Although Augustine here condemns the practice, there can no doubt that he took the passage of St Paul as a divinely sent message to himself, just as St Antony did the passage from St Matthew (xix 21), which Augustine quotes in *Confessions,* viii 12; and as, at a later date, St Francis of Assisi and Bernard of Quintavalle took their three openings of the book of the Gospels *(St Francis of Assisi,* by Fr Cuthbert, O.S.F.C., p. 64). Indeed, Augustine's famous experience doubtless helped to increase the already great popularity of the custom among Christians, which led to repeated condemnations of it by bishops and councils—*inter alia* the Synods of Vannes (Can. xvi) in 461, of Agde (Can. cxlii) in 506, and of Orléans (Can. xxvxi) in 511. In spite of these condemnations the practice continued to be used, even by Catholic bishops assembled in Synod (Acta Conciliorum, Paris 1714, ii 965), and still continues.

The passage in *Confessions,* iv 3, here referred to, is also a good example of the corrupt text which Sir T. Matthew had to work from. The words of the original, *"si enim de paginis poetæ cuiuspiam . . . cum forte quis consulit . . ."* are translated by Matthew, "For if any man should, by chance consult some one of the *Poets,* amongst the *Pagans . . ."* thus showing that his text read *de paganis* instead of *de paginis.* Similar cases where his text can be reconstructed by means of the errors in his translation are numerous.

Note 5, p. 137, *last line (Book VI)*

"I kept my heart free from giving a firm assent to anything, and fearing the precipice was slain yet more surely by the halter."

This passage is an example of the elaborate play upon

words in which St Augustine often indulges, the point
of which often disappears completely in a translation, as it
can seldom be reproduced in another language. The
Latin text reads, *Tenebam cor meum ab omni adsensione
timens praecipitium, et suspendio magis necabar.* There
is first, an allusion to the suspense of judgement, which was
advocated by the Academic philosophers, secondly, the
words *timens praecipitium* suggest that the word *adsensio*
(assent), is a play upon the word *adscensio* (ascent), just as
suspendium (halter) is upon *suspensio* (suspense of judgement). The word-play might be indicated somewhat
clumsily by paraphrasing the passage thus: "I would
not allow my heart to $\begin{Bmatrix}\text{ascend}\\\text{assent}\end{Bmatrix}$ and, fearing to fall over the
precipice was killed by $\begin{Bmatrix}\text{suspension}\\\text{suspense}\end{Bmatrix}$." The point of the
word "ascend" lies in the fact that St Augustine is
referring to the allegorical method of interpreting the
Scriptures, the usual word for which among the Greek
Fathers was ἀναγωγή, i.e., a lifting up of the soul
to heavenly things, and so a mystical interpretation.

Note 6, p. 252, l. 6 (Book IX)

". . . looking upon my brother."

This abrupt and unexpected introduction of his brother,
with no mention of his name or anything else about him, is
a very strange thing in the work of such a literary artist
as St Augustine, but there is nothing to suggest that anything has dropped out of the text. Of the children of
Monica, other than Augustine, the only other mention in
the *Confessions* is the passage, *nutrierat filios,* "she
had brought up her sons," or possibly "children," in ix 9.

The brother here spoken of was named Navigius. He is
mentioned by Augustine in *de Beata Vita* (chap. 14), one
of the books written at Cassiciacum, as taking part in a

philosophical discussion on the Ides of November, Augustine's birthday, but his contribution thereto tells us nothing of any value about him. He appears to have suffered from weak health—*Navigius splene vitioso*—and presumably had travelled to Italy with Monica, when she came to join Augustine at Milan. Possidius, in his *Life of Augustine* (chap. 26), mentions the *fratris filiæ* or nieces of the Saint; these were probably daughters of Navigius.

THE END

Other Fontana Religious Books

MERE CHRISTIANITY

C. S. Lewis. Here at a popular price is a revised and amplified edition of C. S. Lewis's three famous books, *Broadcast Talks*, *Christian Behaviour*, and *Beyond Personality*, brilliantly presenting the author's modern revaluations of Christian apologetics, ethics and theology.

THE SCREWTAPE LETTERS

C. S. Lewis. This witty and profound analysis of Christian strength and weaknesses outlined in the letters of the elderly devil Screwtape to his young nephew, is a classic of religious exposition.

THE PROBLEM OF PAIN

C. S. Lewis. The author gives his view as a layman on the Christian doctrine relating to all aspects of the problem of pain and explains the existence of pain in a Christian world. "It is really a pleasure to be able to praise a book unreservedly and that is just what I can do with this book."
Manchester Guardian

THE DIVINE PITY

Gerald Vann, O.P. Doubters as well as professing Christians who look for a strong simple statement of the abiding truths of Christianity will find inspiration from this work.

THE PLAIN MAN LOOKS AT THE BIBLE

William Neil. This book is meant for the plain man who would like to know what to think about the Bible to-day. It deals with the relevance of the Bible and restates its message for the Twentieth Century.

THE GOSPELS IN MODERN ENGLISH

J. B. Phillips. "It is all to the good that we should be given a translation in straightforward English, and Mr. Phillips has a flair for doing this that none of his predecessors in the task seem to have had."
Times Literary Supplement

Fontana Books make available, in attractive, readable yet inexpensive editions, the best books, both fiction and non-fiction, of famous contemporary authors. These include books up to 832 pages, complete and unabridged.

If you would like to be kept informed of new and forthcoming titles please apply to your local bookseller or write to:

WILLIAM COLLINS SONS AND CO. LTD.,
144 Cathedral Street, Glasgow, C.4.

Other Fontana Religious Books

THE CONFESSIONS OF ST. AUGUSTINE

The struggles of a young man later to become a great Bishop and saint. His problems are radically those which confront men and women to-day. What is sin ? What is Evil ? The answers in this book have to many brought hope and faith.

A SHORT BIBLE

~~...ed~~ *by Austin Farrer.* "I ~~...~~ Shorter Bible as a ~~...~~ levance of God's Word to our world."
Fr. Trevor Huddleston, O.R.

CHRISTIAN DOCTRINE

J. S. Whale. The author describes and meets the difficulties which the great Christian doctrines raise for us to-day, and shows how the Christian faith understands human history and death.

ON THE EDGE OF THE PRIMEVAL FOREST

Albert Schweitzer. After renouncing his academic future in Europe to qualify as a doctor, the author whose personality is so vividly reflected in his writing, describes the building and growth of his hospital at the edge of the damp, disease-ridden Equatorial forest of the Belgian Congo.

THE SCROLLS FROM THE DEAD SEA

Edmund Wilson. Writing with first hand knowledge the author's account of the discovery, unearthing and ultimate recognition of the Scrolls as priceless Biblical treasures is thrilling reading. Absorbing too are his own ideas on their value and his inquiry into the conflicting views of the experts still studying these remarkable documents.

MAKING MEN WHOLE

J. B. Phillips. Undoubtably one of the author's finest books— a vigorous and searching appraisal of the place of both Christian and non-Christian in the modern world and of their part in God's purpose.

THE DIARY OF A COUNTRY PRIEST

Georges Bernanos. "It is a strange and sad, yet a beautiful and triumphant story. And it is a work of deep, subtle and singularly encompassing art."
The New York Times

CHRISTIANITY AND HISTORY

H. Butterfield. With force and profundity the author states his belief that history testifies to Christianity and Christianity interprets history.

Other Fontana Religious Books

SEX, LOVE AND MARRIAGE

Roland H. Bainton. "Dr. Bainton lays before us the Christian attitude, past and present, to this important subject. He shows us how, amongst others, St. Augustine faced these problems and how it was as real to them as it is to us today. This is a book which no one can afford not to read."

MORE FROM THE PRIMEVAL FOREST

Albert Schweitzer. An unadorned and poignant account of almost incredible difficulties and achievements, this book is based on reports sent home by Dr. Albert Schweitzer during his second period in Africa from 1924-27.

NAUGHT FOR YOUR COMFORT

Trevor Huddleston. The author describes his twelve years ministry in Sophiatown, the coloured quarter outside Johannesburg from 1944-56. Father Huddleston has become world-famous for his championship of the rights and dignity of the non-European races in South Africa.

THE MEANING OF PAUL FOR TO-DAY

C. H. Dodd. Professor Dodd suggests the place of Paul in the history of religion, he has sought to bring out the permanent significance of the apostle's thought, in modern terms, and in relation to the general interests and problems which occupy the mind of the present generation.

SCIENCE AND CHRISTIAN BELIEF

C. A. Coulson. The author sets out to show that ~~...~~ ce is essentially a religious activity, playing its part in the unfolding of the nature and purpose of God.

THE SONG OF BERNADETTE

Franz Werfel. The author tells in this simple and moving book the story of the Apparitions and of the little girl who returned day after day to the grotto to honour silently the Lady who appeared to her there—the Lady whose presence it never occurred to her to call a miracle.

LETTERS TO YOUNG CHURCHES

J. B. Phillips. The author's most famous book, this is more than a mere translation of the Epistles. It has already become a contemporary classic of Biblical interpretation, a valuable guide for all those who in their groping towards a maturer Christian faith, encounter and are perplexed by the vital but difficult Pauline doctrines which constitute the foundation of Christian Theology.